THE GUV'NOR

A BIOGRAPHY OF
SIR NOEL MURLESS

TIM FITZGEORGE-PARKER

THE GUV'NOR

A BIOGRAPHY OF
SIR NOEL MURLESS

❉

COLLINS
St James's Place, London
1980

William Collins Sons and Co Ltd
London · Glasgow · Sydney · Auckland
Toronto · Johannesburg

First published 1980
© Tim Fitzgeorge-Parker 1980
ISBN 0 00 216296 2
Set in 11pt V-I-P Bembo
by W & J Mackay Limited, Chatham
Made and printed in Great Britain
by William Collins Sons and Co Ltd, Glasgow

For Katie and Noel

Contents

Illustrations

Preface

Sir Noel Murless is emphatic. 'I have had four greats in my life,' he says, 'Abernant, Crepello, Petite Etoile – and Gordon.'

He has always felt immense admiration for Sir Gordon Richards, not because Gordon suggested him as Fred Darling's successor, but because it is an ingredient of the wonderful trainer–jockey partnership and friendship which they developed over the years.

Sir Noel had the physical courage to jump his horses over big fences. He has a moral courage too, which has supported him through the most difficult decisions. And he has a loyalty to every animal in his care, to his family, friends, owners, staff and to himself and his ideals.

Courage, integrity and loyalty are man's finest virtues. They are the qualities that characterize the greatest racehorse trainer of our time.

1

Mary Jane: 1910–1930

❀

A little Welsh pony called Mary Jane started it all during the First World War. Although it may seem a far cry from a pony to the mighty Crepello and all the other great thoroughbreds that have been in his care, Sir Noel Murless says today: 'I think I learned more about horses from Mary Jane than from anybody else in my whole life.'

Noel was born on 24 March 1910 at Duckington Grange, between Chester and Whitchurch, where his father farmed that gloriously rich land and enjoyed the excellent local hunting and point-to-pointing. The coming of the war meant that, in common with many other country children, Noel spent a great deal of time alone, with only the farm animals for company.

'My brother, Stuart, was born in 1917,' says Noel. 'My mother began the war nursing with the V.A.D. (Voluntary Aid Detachment) four or five days a week and then she was getting ready to have Stu. My father was away in the army, only returning for short leaves. So I was left on my own. I had nobody but that wonderful little pony. Mary Jane was my constant companion.'

So the relationship between boy and pony kindled in Noel the most extraordinary understanding of horses that I have ever known in any man.

By the time he was eight Noel had already decided on his career; he would be a trainer of racehorses. 'There was no racing blood in the family,' he says, 'just the hunting and point-to-pointing. But I never had any other thoughts or ambition. I knew I had to be a trainer.'

Inspiration was not hard to find. Major and Mrs Hugh Peel, friends and neighbours of the Murless family, owned the greatest steeplechaser of the time: Poethlyn, winner of the Grand National the year before. In the true Aintree tradition, Poethlyn's racing career had had a humble start. He was sold for £7 to a hotelier in Shrewsbury, and then bought for 50 guineas and by Hugh Peel, who gave him to his wife. At the end of 1915 the Aintree course near Liverpool was taken over by the War Office and closed to racing. The Grand National was transferred to Gatwick and there, in 1918, Poethlyn won the third and last substitute National.

In April 1919, five months after the end of the war, the country was still celebrating the armistice and huge crowds flocked to Aintree, wanting to cheer their favourite, Poethlyn, to a second National victory. The field included past winners Sunloch, Vermouth and Ally Sloper and future winners Sergeant Murphy and Shaun Spadah.

That year, Mrs Peel's brave nine-year-old bay was carrying 12 stone 7 pounds. Only Cloister, Jerry M. and Manifesto had carried that weight to victory in the National. Although Poethlyn was sometimes an erratic jumper and needed all his strength to cover those four and a half miles, he had become the course's hero. The crowds backed him down to 11–4, and Poethlyn did not let them down. His jockey, Ernie Piggott, who had won on him at Gatwick the previous year, rode a wonderful race and won confidently from the Irish horse Ballyboggan.

A crystal ball that day might have revealed two remarkable coincidences. Ballyboggan was ridden by Willie Head, father of Alec, who became France's finest trainer and a great friend of Noel. And forty years later, when Noel was Britain's champion trainer, his jockey was Ernie's brilliant grandson. Lester Piggott is immensely proud of his champion grandfather, three times a winner of the Grand National. 'I think it's harder to do that than to win the Derby three times,' says the man who has now won the Epsom classic eight times.

Mrs Hugh Peel became the first woman to own a successive Grand National winner. Poethlyn's victory was one of the greatest sporting triumphs of the century and its impact on a nine-year-old boy was immense. Noel's eyes sparkle as he recalls, 'It was the first time that I was ever taken to any race course. My family took me because the Peels were such friends. The crowds were unbelievable.' Beside that winner's enclosure, that has witnessed so much drama and pathos but remains unchanged today, the little boy was lifted shoulder high by his father to see the great horse. 'It was a tremendous thrill,' he says. 'An unforgettable experience.'

On his long rides through the Cheshire fields he imagined himself as Ernie Piggott and Mary Jane as Poethlyn, and he talked to the pony about the famous flat trainers of the day – Dick Dawson of Whatcombe, Alec Taylor of Manton and Atty Persse of Stockbridge, who in 1913 had set the racing world alight with his 'Spotted Wonder', The Tetrarch. By the time he was six Noel was hunting and as soon as was permitted, riding in point-to-points. By the time he had reached his teens he was impatient to become involved in the *real* racing game, and perhaps because he was so determined things worked out for him in an almost uncanny way. The golden opportunity awaited him just around the corner as Noel remembers.

'First of all I went to ride out for old Max Barthrop at Ternhill, near Market Drayton. Ternhill had been an aerodrome in the First World War and had then been bought by Mr C. F. Kenyon who had made a wonderful training ground on the place. There were about eighty boxes in one hangar – really lovely boxes. There were peat moss and tan gallops. A fellow called Davies trained flat horses there and they enjoyed considerable success. Then Kenyon died and the place was left empty for a while. Now, when Max had married Margery, the daughter of the famous sportsman Dyke Dennis, a tremendous enthusiast for racing and coursing, they were training in Cholmondley Park, but there were no proper gallops there and so they bought Ternhill where they were very successful.' Here, in 1949, George Owen was to train Russian Hero to win the Grand National.

Noel was now sixteen and more in love with horses than ever. Tall for his age, he was a competent horseman with beautiful hands and large, flat, sticking-out feet. 'After Ternhill,' says Noel, 'I rode work and did quite a bit of schooling over fences and hurdles for Stanley Harrison of Bangor-on-Dee', a trainer who lived close to Noel's mother's home. Harrison won a great many races over hurdles and fences at the little meetings in those days. So many of those grand sporting "gaff" racecourses like the one at Tenby have disappeared.

'It was Major and Mrs Hugh Peel, who made me take the big step. They told me that I was wasting my time with Stanley

15

Harrison and that, if I liked, they would arrange for me to go to their friend Frank Hartigan.' Noel seized the opportunity.

Frank Hartigan was nearing forty at that time and was already a famous name in racing. The son of an army veterinary surgeon, this big red-haired Irishman was the nephew of Garrett Moore who had won the 1879 Grand National on his own horse, The Liberation, on the occasion when the famous four Beasley brothers weighed out together for the race. Despite his size, Frank had ridden successfully under National Hunt rules, first as an amateur and later as a professional. By the time the young Mr Murless joined him as his pupil and amateur rider, Hartigan had trained the winners of many races over fences and on the flat, including the One Thousand Guineas twice, with Vaucluse in 1915 and Roseway in 1919. The former was owned by the fifth Earl of Rosebery, the only man to have won the Derby while holding office as Prime Minister.

Hartigan trained at Weyhill, a little village on the borders of Hampshire and Wiltshire three miles west of the market town of Andover. In my youth the pride of Weyhill was the beautiful big training yard with its immaculate thatched, pink-washed stables. Today the thatch has fallen in, the pink has faded to a dirty white, the walls of the loose-boxes are crumbling and the whole place is a tragic reminder of one-time racing glory.

On a clear day from Weyhill you can look south across the downs to Danebury Ring, made famous by the Days of Danebury, and further to Stockbridge, where Atty Persse was training at Chattis Hill and the ghost of The Tetrarch still lopes along the gallops. Salisbury racecourse perches high on the downs above Wilton, and over to the west are the sacrificial stones of Stonehenge.

Noel worked as a stable-lad at Weyhill, looking after two horses – 'doing his two' – riding schooling over fences and hurdles, having the occasional mount in public as an amateur, and learning the art of training. 'It was a hard life, but a good one,' he says. 'If we were going to, say, Kempton or Hurst Park, I would have to get up at the crack of dawn, make my horse ready, lead him down to Andover Station, unbox at Esher Station and lead him five miles past Hampton Court to the racecourse. Then I'd have his ordinary exercise shoes removed and replaced with racing plates, plait up his mane so that it wouldn't tangle when I changed hands, and then go out and ride him. It was the same performance after the race. Groom him, get him shod up, lead him back to Esher and return in the dark to Andover Station for the long uphill drag to Weyhill, where I had to do up both my horses before I went to bed.'

Jim White, who has been with the Guv'nor for more than fifty years, was serving his apprenticeship with Hartigan when Noel arrived. 'When you had a runner, it was a very long day,' Jim told me, confirming Noel's account. 'When the horses went "out into the country" (to the races), I used to light the candles in the lamps for the pony and trap down to Andover Station with all the tack, equipment, forage, etc. for horse and lad. You could go to Andover and never see a car.' The privately owned railway companies, familiar with the carriage of valuable thoroughbreds from the surrounding stables, were particularly helpful. Water was always provided and the vans which housed the animals and their attendants were warm, confortable and safe.

'When I took my horse to a meeting,' says Jim, 'I would get five shillings (25p) for the day out. So often it seemed to pour with rain. We would box up on the way home at Esher Station by the light of oil lamps, arrive back at about eight o'clock in Andover, where we'd be met by a boy in the trap. He would help us unbox the runners, pick up the luggage and then drive in front of the horses as we led them home. When we got there at nine or ten o'clock, the travelling head lad would stand over us while we, probably soaking wet, took down our braces and strapped the horses for half an hour before we could loose them and let them down. No matter what the time was, he wouldn't allow us to come out until we'd strapped them for half an hour.'

Rigid discipline was enforced by the huge, immaculately dressed Frank Hartigan, by Mr Herbert Arnold, the secretary-assistant, and by the head man, an excellent fellow called Fred Templeton. The boys were normally locked up in the dormitory at 9.30 p.m. and their lights went out when the main switch was turned off quarter of an hour later. The lads slept two in a bed on straw mattresses with straw pillows. Rats abounded in the dormitory and in the stables, so that some of the happiest hours after 'lights out' were spent rat-hunting with pitch-forks. Sharp at six o'clock the next morning they would be called by the head man who would run up the stairs, unlock the door, throw all their

17

B

clothes out of the barred window and chase them out to get dressed, while he fed the horses.

Noel was lodged next to the chauffeur in one of a row of small cottages, known as Brewers Cottages, but as he was about the same age as some of the apprentices, he joined in many of their pranks and struck up lasting friendships.

When he arrived at Weyhill, like every other new boy in the yard, he was sent up into the loft above the feed-house to 'catch the owl'. The other lads would tell the newcomer, 'Mrs Hartigan will give you ten bob for catching the owl. But mind, he's savage. He'll tear your eyes out!' They would dress him up in a mackintosh and a big pair of wellington boots, and put goggles over his eyes and a large sieve over his head. Carrying a bowl of corn to tempt the owl, he would climb gingerly up the ladder to the loft, where, unbeknown to him, another lad was hiding. Just as the new boy was reaching the top of the ladder, he would be drenched by a full bucket of water!

Life was rough and tough, and offenders were rewarded with a sound boxing of the ears or a good boot up the backside. Yet Jim White says, '*Serve* my apprenticeship? I *slaved* it for six years. But I enjoyed every minute of the time at Weyhill.' Noel comments: 'Frank was a very, very good stableman, but a very hard man to work for. Nothing was ever right. The work was never done. In the afternoons I would be sent off farming or laying tracks on the gallops. Nor did the apprentices have any rest in the afternoons. They would either be up on the gallops muck-spreading and stone-picking or helping in the gardens of the big house, picking raspberries and so on. I never finished evening stables until 7.30 p.m. We had to pick up our litters every single day.'

This traditional stable discipline was maintained when Noel came to train on his own. Picking up your litter showed an immaculate floor under a thin carpet of straw, delineated in each doorway by plaited straw – one of the good stable-man's little skills. In the best cavalry regiments, raffia was used plaited in the regimental colours. Now forgotten, it was the meticulous, old-fashioned method of presenting a horse and his box for inspection.

Thanks to his formative relationship with the beloved Mary Jane, Noel already had a deep insight into the mentality of horses and a balanced understanding of their characters. But there were still lessons to be learned. 'The only time in my whole life that I was ever kicked,' he says, 'was by a little chestnut horse that I used to look after at Weyhill. Like many mean, vicious animals, he was no good as a race-horse. I had picked up my litter and put my plait down and was just putting on my jersey when, for no reason at all, he turned round and belted me right in the stomach. As I was getting up, he came at me again, obviously meaning business. So I seized the only weapon to hand, my pitch-fork, and, with the handle, gave him a right crack across the hindquarters. Up he went in the air to try and get round me and came down with his feet in the manger. I said to myself, "This is a fine kettle of fish!"' It was indeed. Noel was trapped.

'As a rule, Frank Hartigan never came round before a quarter to six at the earliest, and it was now just before five o'clock. Of course, on this particular night, who should appear? Suddenly, in the doorway of my box, loomed a huge red-headed figure. He bellowed, "What have you done, boy? What's happened here?" Immediately he sent for the head lad, Fred Templeton, who tried to lift the horse out of his manger and Frank himself went off to summon the yard man and probably the vet as well. There was going to be a very big drama and I, who had only been defending myself, was obviously not going to come out of it particularly well! I said to Fred Templeton quietly, "You get out of the box and I'll get the bugger out of the manger." Fred slipped round the door and as soon as he was out of the way, I gave the horse another couple of belts with the fork. He was so surprised that he leapt out of the manger again and by the time Frank returned, all was completely normal.'

All the lads at Weyhill had nicknames. From the moment they arrived they would be called Belfast, Dublin, Snowy, or perhaps given the name of an old-time jockey whom they might resemble. Jim White's real name is Gordon, but when he arrived at Weyhill he was christened Jim and the name has stuck for the rest of his life.

It is remarkable how the same bad habits appear in generations of stable lads. Living and working amongst them, Noel learned a good deal about stable lads as a breed that was to stand him in good stead in the training years to come.

Two bad habits are particularly common. It is vital that a head man knows if his horses have licked out their mangers. He must know whether they have eaten all the feed which he has carefully calculated that they need. Even a dirty manger can be a sign of approaching sickness so he must be able to warn the trainer. An amazing number of lads, however, believe that, if their horse leaves food, it is somehow a reflection on the lad and so, if they can get to the manger before the head man, they scoop out the leavings into the straw and, when asked, reply that their horses have eaten up. For this reason the head man at Weyhill would try to visit each horse with its breakfast or in the afternoons with its standing feed, at least half an hour before its lad arrived to tie it up.

The other bad habit, which can be even more harmful, is the deep-rooted desire in a lad always to win the gallop, a characteristic which must be checked before it develops. A trainer gives instructions for his horses to work at a nice training gallop – a good three part speed on the bridle – or he tells the stable jockey to work at this speed, instructing the lads or apprentices to lay with him. All too often, some lads will disobey orders and push their horses to win. They can do this quite surreptitiously. For instance if, at the finish of the gallop, they are due to pass the 'Guv'nor' on the nearside, their hands and legs on that side will be deceptively still, while the offside hands and legs will be hard at work.

One of the truest sayings in the sport is that more races are lost on the gallops than on the racecourse. The late Peter Thrale used to say: 'The reason we Epsom trainers win so many races is that we have no proper gallops.' So Frank Hartigan, from his hack on the Weyhill gallops would follow his orders for work with the instructions: 'And no bloody blind heelin' either!'

From his bedroom window Frank could see his gallops – a good straight mile and a fine round gallop – and schooling fences running down to the railway. Noel rode a lot of schooling, and 'I didn't have many falls,' he says. 'Frank's horses didn't fall much because they were too well schooled. But I remember a bloody great black brute called Bruin. It was before the Grand National and we took him, Shaun Goilin and a splendid chaser called Kakushian to Hurst Park for a school. I rode Bruin. He never took off at the first fence, just turned head over heels and buried me. Frank stopped us and sent us back. We came galloping in again and the same thing happened. He just never rose at all!'

Nevertheless it did prove a successful school for the other horses. Shaun Goilin, sired by an unknown colt in a Tipperary field and sold as a yearling for 22 guineas, was now owned by Frank's patron Mr Walter Midwood, Master of the Cheshire Foxhounds for many years, for whom Noel rode his first winner, Zain. At Aintree in 1930, Noel's last year with Frank Hartigan, this powerful Liverpool chaser took part in the greatest Grand National finish since 1882, when Lord Manners on Seaman had defeated Tommy Beasley on Cyrus striking a blow for the amateur. This time, however, it was the turn of the top professional, Tommy Cullinan, who came to the last fence upsides with Sir Lindsey and Millerays Belle. All three made mistakes. Williams on Sir Lindsey lost both irons and the two other jockeys had to ride on with a stirrup empty. The eleven-year-old mare got her head in front briefly, but Shaun Goilin, strongly ridden by Cullinan, fought back to win by a neck. To complete an outstanding double Hartigan's Kakushian won the Champion Chase at the same meeting.

Noel loved schooling but his riding career was not particularly successful. He says, 'I scarcely ever gave orders to my jockeys as a trainer because I was such a moderate one myself!' When he fell at Sandown on a grey call Zorro Gris he walked back disconsolately to the weighing room to be greeted by an irate Frank Hartigan, shouting, 'That horse didn't fall, boy. You threw him into the water!'

Noel says, 'I didn't ride many winners at all. I remember my first was Zain at Tarporley, trained by George Goswell. Zain was a funny old beggar and I should have won the Foxhunters' on him at Liverpool.' In those days the Foxhunters' Chase was run over the full Grand National course and distance of four and a half miles. The fences then were far stiffer and bigger than they are today. 'At the second last,' says the Guv'nor, 'I saw the fence had a great gap right through it. By now my only rival left was Craig Turner riding a horse called Sety. He and Sety had only one eye apiece and Craig was over fifty. He was a great horseman. As we came into the fence, he said to me, "Keep away from that gap!" Of course, old Zain ducked straight into it and down we came!

'I rode several times round Liverpool, but not in the National. The Foxhunters' was a wonderful race to ride in in those days. You had more sensible people competing and it was just like a first-class hunt. Although the fences were very big, you knew everything was jumpable. Yes, certainly the fences were far stiffer then and there

21

used to be a ditch at the Canal Turn. One old-time jockey said to me, "You don't have to worry now. You have platforms to jump off. When I was riding there was nothing in front of the ditches." I don't remember having many falls there, but I did once get stuck on the top of the fence after Valentine's, which I always thought was the biggest fence on the course.'

Although he may have had only a few falls in his riding career, Noel did suffer one appalling accident riding over hurdles at Leicester. One of those long flat feet of his got caught in the wing at 35 m.p.h. and twisted right round. 'At one stage the doctors had to wire it up,' says Noel. 'That effectively put paid to my chances of getting into the army a few years later.'

Fate once more took a hand in Noel's career at that same Liverpool meeting when Shaun Goilin won the National and Kakushian won the Champion Chase. Frank's brother, Hubert Hartigan, had come over for the meeting. Noel says, 'The previous day I had been riding at Colwall Park and at the second last, which was an open ditch, my horse gave me a nasty fall. I went on to Liverpool to ride The Bird for Frank in the Stanley Chase. When I went to weigh, old Manning, the Clerk of the Scales, said, "Are you feeling all right?" '"No," I said, "I feel awful."

'"Well," he said, "I'm not going to pass you. Somebody go and find Frank . . . "

'When Frank arrived Manning said he was not going to pass me. Frank was furious and went off in a huff to find someone else to ride the horse. His brother Hubert was there and, hearing all this going on, he said quietly to me, "You come back to Ireland with me." I did not go right away. I went home for a while and then went over to Ireland to stay with Darby Rogers before I started up with Hubert.'

Noel was not particularly sorry to be leaving Weyhill. 'Frank was a better trainer than Hubert, but Hubert was a wonderful person. He was my greatest friend, the greatest friend I ever had. He had a marvellous personality. He was such a hard worker. He worked hard and played hard.' Today Gwen says, 'Noel was so unhappy when he first went to Weyhill that he never unpacked his suitcase for six whole months.'

Noel had watched Frank trying his horses, when only the big red-haired trainer knew what weight each animal was carrying.

The work riders would be weighed out beforehand so that Frank could make exact calculations. In his car he would have weight cloths looking identical to each other, but loaded with differing amounts of lead; only he knew how much. On the gallops Frank would allow no one else to handle those cloths. He alone would re-saddle each horse, placing the lead cloth underneath and fastening the girth and surcingle. Immediately the work was over, he would whip off the weight cloths and drive away from Kimpton Down, leaving all the lads guessing. Secrecy as to a horse's chances was of paramount importance to a betting trainer. At Weyhill a lad would frequently look after a horse for several months without knowing its real name. In that way there was no chance of any of the lads discussing the horse outside the yard, in the Weyhill pubs or on their weekly trips to Andover in the threepenny Friday bus. These precautions were – and still are – necessary in a betting yard, because there were always plenty of punters around willing to pay for information.

Noel remembers Frank was a stickler for punctuality. One morning the champion jockey, Gordon Richards, turned up three minutes late on the Weyhill gallops and was immediately sent packing, told to get the hell out of it and only to come back when he could be on time.

During his time at Weyhill, Noel formed many attachments, the most significant being a deep and lasting friendship with Gordon Richards who, in 1930 won both the Oaks and the St Leger. Richards was the greatest of all champions, small, sturdy and short in the leg, and a splendid contrast to tall thin Noel, six years his junior. They struck up an immediate *rapport*. They still laugh at the same things, share the same sense of the ridiculous and, as Noel's daughter Julie says fondly, 'They've always been just like Tweedle-dum and Tweedledee!'

Gordon who, by 1930, had already been champion jockey four times, was living at Ogbourne near Marlborough in the cottage belonging to Martin Hartigan (no relation of Frank and Hubert) with whom he had served his apprenticeship. At that time he was riding for Lord Glanely but in 1932 he began his long association with Fred Darling at Beckhampton. 'Once a downsman, always a downsman,' he says – one of the few sentiments of Gordon's with which Noel does not agree.

23

2

Ireland and Penrith
1930–1940

❋

When Noel arrived on the Curragh at the age of twenty, life in Ireland was happy again after the 'troubles'. He found the Curragh steeped in racing memories and thronging with the ghosts of horses, jockeys and trainers. He marvelled at that large, flat plain of turf, with the racecourse, the gallops – and the sheep – surrounded by training stables and stud farms.

The wide galloping track with its long, stiff straight, is probably the finest test of a mile-and-a-half horse in the world.

Newbridge and Kildare are the two towns on either side of the Curragh. Hubert Hartigan was at Ruan Beg on the Kildare side. Noel's brother Stu Murless lives and trains at Newbridge, close by the stands. Close by, at Tully, with its famous Japanese Garden, was the National Stud with which Noel would have a close association in his later life. Tully had been given to the British nation in 1915 by Colonel Hall Walker for the purpose of forming the National Stud. This eccentric, peppery man was a fervent student of the stars and based all his important decisions on whatever they appeared to foretell. To the dismay of his several trainers, who included Atty Persse, this governed the running of his horses. Unfortunately the stars advised him to sell Prince Palatine, who proceeded to win the St Leger and two Ascot Gold Cups. However, he did breed some grand horses, including Minoru, winner of the Guineas and the Derby when leased to King Edward VII, and it was he, when created Lord Wavertree, who persuaded the Aga Khan to involve

ABOVE LEFT   Noel with Mary Jane
ABOVE RIGHT   Gwen Carlow marries Noel Murless, November 1940
BELOW   Early days – a rare afternoon off

24

Sejanus, the old faithful, winning the
Falmouth Handicap at Doncaster, 1946

Closeburn wins the Stewards' Cup at
Goodwood, 1947, ridden by Gordon
Richards

Abernant with Gordon Richards

The Cobbler at Beckhampton – one of
Gwen's better hacks

himself in racing. He did not just donate the magnificent stud at Tully, but included in the gift four stallions, forty-five top class broodmares, foals, yearlings, hunters, carthorses, 600 head of cattle, forage and everything on the land or in the buildings, including valuable furniture and pictures.

During the Second World War, the British and Irish Governments agreed on the Stud's transfer to England. So in 1944 the land at Tully became vested in Ireland while all the livestock were shipped to England, where a new National Stud had been established at Gillingham in Dorset. Later, of course, it moved to its present quarters at Newmarket. That wartime journey across the Irish Channel must have been quite a feat. Once the British had departed, Tully was established as the Irish National Stud which, over the years has given excellent service to the country's breeders. Noel rightly insists that every scrap of credit for the British National Stud go to his great friend, tall, charming Peter Burrell whose vast knowledge and strong personality guided it through the difficult times and established it as it is today.

Ruan Beg belonged to Joe Canty, the stable jockey. Noel was now really enjoying himself. No longer was he forced to live in a workman's cottage and 'do his two', he was one of the family, living in the house with Hubert and Sue Hartigan. 'I had an odd ride or two,' he says, 'but not many. I had quite enough work on my hands. I was a sort of secretary/assistant-trainer/head lad most of the time. Hubert had about sixty assorted horses and we won quite a few races. Every year he used to buy two or three yearlings who were potential jumpers, turn them out until they were three-year-olds and then give them to me to break. I can tell you, some of them used to take some breaking too! He would give them a couple of runs and sell them on at a good profit as store horses.' He added with pride, 'I actually broke Royal Mail.' This magnificent black son of My Prince had been bred by Charlie Rogers, and sold as a three-year-old to Hubert Hartigan, who sold him on to Hugh Lloyd-Thomas, the noted diplomat and amateur rider for whom, in the hands of Evan Williams, he won the Grand National of 1937.

ABOVE Queenpot wins the One Thousand Guineas, 1948, ridden by Gordon Richards – the first classic
BELOW Ridgewood takes the 1949 St Leger with Michael Beary up

After the austerity of Weyhill the gay life of the hunting and racing people in Ireland was a tonic to Noel who was delighted to follow the example of his boss working and playing hard all the time. 'It was tremendous fun!' he says. 'There was the day when we were working horses on Race Hill with Joe Canty. They came up in batches of four. One animal was a furlong behind the others. Hubert kept him back and tried him again with the next lot. He was even further behind with them. So Hubert took off the saddle and bridle, slapped the loose horse over the backside and told it to clear off over the Curragh. He didn't want to see it again. He did though. All through the day people kept bringing the horse back which was promptly sent galloping off again. Finally at tea-time a jockey called Billy Burke turned up with the horse. Hubert gave him £25 and said, "Just take him away and never let me see him again." The horse was christened Sentenced and in later life he won several races.'

One day a horse choked badly on a carrot. Hubert never hesitated. He took a penknife from his pocket, there and then cut a hole in its throat, removed the carrot and saved the animal's life. 'Can you imagine any modern trainer doing that?' asks the Guv'nor. 'Hubert was a real man – a hell of a man.'

At that time, there was a duty levied on Irish horses and cattle crossing to England. Noel recalls, 'We would have runners at Liverpool on each day of the three day meeting. I would put the horses on the boat at North Wall, Dublin, and then get on the mail boat myself. Then I would see them through Customs on the other side and immediately return to Ireland on the next mail, to be back in Kildare at seven o'clock in the morning for a day's work. After I'd done this for three consecutive nights one Liverpool meeting, I came off the mail boat in the early hours and went through the gate to get on the train. Two large fellows loomed up on each side of me and said, "We want you."

"What do you want?"

"You come along with us."

'They thought that I was smuggling sweepstake tickets in the new Irish sweep that had been going for only three or four years. They said to me, "We're going to search you."

'I told them, "Before you do anything, get hold of Mr Morgan, the station master." Old Morgan came along and roared with laughter. He knew me well now from all my to-ing and fro-ing to the meetings in England.'

The duty payable on horses finally decided Hubert to move to England. Although it only had to be paid once on each horse, there was inevitably considerable tax evasion. The incident that finally caused the strict duty enforcement concerned Easter Hero, one of the greatest steeplechasers, winner of two Cheltenham Gold Cups and frequently described as 'the best horse never to win the Grand National'. Noel remembers, 'Jack Anthony and Charlie Rogers got Easter Hero through the Customs as a hunter valued at £100! After that things were tightened up so much that Hubert decided to move to England.

'Hubert's principal owner at that time was a Glasgow book-maker called Jimmy Maclean, who suggested that Hubert should move his stables to Penrith in Cumberland. Much, much later I was to appreciate the worth of this family, when I trained for the old man's son, the late George Maclean. His only idea of having a horse in the south was to have the Maclean colours carried as an adver-tisement and his one stipulation was that the animal should always be trying. Unfortunately, as so often happens with the best owners, the poor creature, however hard it tried, was too slow to get out of its own way!

'Hubert went over to England to reconnoitre the stables at Pen-rith. He liked what he saw, and sent for me. After a couple of days he went back on the Friday, and left me there to try and organize things. I arrived back on the Curragh on Sunday morning and, as we were now due to move in a fortnight, there was plenty of work throughout the day. I worked hard all through the afternoon in the office. But Paddy Cullinan was giving a party that night in Meath, about sixty miles away. At six o'clock, Hubert suddenly said, "We'll go to Paddy's party."

'So we got dressed up and off we went. By midnight Sue Har-tigan and I were dead tired and tried to get him to come home. Not a bit of it. At twelve-thirty, he sat down to play poker. It was about two o'clock when we left. Sue got in to drive, but Hubert said, "No, let Noel drive." They both went to sleep and we went along for a while with me at the wheel trying desperately to keep my eyes open. It was no good. Suddenly there was a bump and a crash and we were up against a tombstone in a churchyard. Hubert jumped up and said, "Where are we?" When I said, "In a churchyard", he said, "Let it graze", and went back to sleep again.'

When the Hartigans and Noel moved to Penrith in the spring of 1933, Jim White had just completed his apprenticeship with Frank Hartigan. As soon as he heard that Noel was returning to England, Jim left Weyhill and made his way north, and apart from the war years, he has not left Noel since. Jim says, 'It was during the Liverpool meeting in March when they arrived. I remember the Guv'nor shipping the horses over because I went to the station three or four times down at Clifton. We used to ride them bareback, dump them in the yard and run back for another one. I went up to Penrith from Liverpool.'

Noel says, 'It was a beautiful place. There were two yards. One was the lovely Clifton Hill and the other was just across the road. We trained in Lowther Park, the grounds of Lowther Castle. There were some excellent gallops. One at the end of the garden ran a straight seven furlongs. We were a long way from anywhere and we won our fair share of races.'

Hugh Lonsdale, the so-called Yellow Earl, now nearing eighty, was in the twilight of his flamboyant life. Time and money were finally running out for the Grand Old Man of English sport, Hugh Lowther, fifth Earl of Lonsdale, who once boasted that you could walk from one coast of England to the other without leaving Lowther land.

Although the staff had been curtailed and the stables at Lowther were filled with Fell ponies instead of carriage horses and hunters, Lonsdale still managed to entertain on a lavish scale and the shooting parties were still as vast as in the good old days. Horses bred at the National Stud were still leased to the Earl of Lonsdale and ran in his colours, and the public image of the glamorous sporting hero remained intact.

The arrival on his doorstep of a famous trainer with a string of thoroughbreds and an enthusiastic young assistant was a thrill for the old man. He could probably imagine that here was his own private racing string. He often came out to watch work, smoking one of the huge cigars for which he was so famous, and he became very friendly with Hubert and Noel, until he left his beloved Lowther Castle in 1935.

Amongst the lessons which Noel learned from Hubert was not to

28

bet. 'He bought a horse called Wild Meadow out of Atty Persse's stable. The original idea was for it to be ridden over hurdles by Bryan Marshall, a highly promising young jump jockey who had served his apprenticeship with Atty at Chattis Hill and had just joined us. Hubert ran this old horse a couple of times over hurdles in selling races, but he did no good, and then started him in a few sellers over one and a half miles on the flat. As he was obviously useless, he gave him to me as a hack. "When he gets handy," said Hubert, "I'll give him to Flossie (his step-daughter)."

'Wild Meadow was a pretty good hack. One day when Hubert was away I had to work some two-year-olds for four furlongs up the straight gallop and there was one filly who always ran off to the right. So I jumped off Wild Meadow and put a kid on him, with instructions to gallop on the right of this filly to try and keep her straight over the first furlong. To my surprise the old horse came up ten lengths ahead of the two-year-olds, cantering on the bridle. I said nothing to Hubert but waited until he was away again and I had the chance to work some older horses. They were fairly useful and included Summary, who was to win twenty-eight races. I jumped Wild Meadow off with this bunch and he treated them just as he had treated the two-year-olds – with complete contempt. So, when he returned, I told Hubert that Wild Meadow was a sprinter – and a useful one too.'

' "No," said Hubert. "Those three and four-year-olds know where they are and won't work at home." I was away one day and later on Hubert came in and said to me, "You were right over that horse." So, having satisfied himself that Wild Meadow was indeed useful over a short distance, he entered him for a six furlong seller at Stockton. He said to me in a fatherly way, "Now don't you go betting. I'll back the horse for you."

'I knew what that would be. I'd get a tenner at 9–4 if I were lucky. So I begged and borrowed about £300 and got a friend to come up from London to Stockton. He went into the "tank" and put our money on at all sorts of prices, right the way down. But at the time we had a somewhat moderate jockey called Dave McGuigan and I had reckoned without the pilot. He got the horse stuck in on the rail and so strongly was Wild Meadow going in the last furlong, that he actually pushed the bloody winner past the post! So I had done my dough. But then, to rub salt in the wounds, Wild Meadow won

29

seven races off the reel and ended up by winning the Final Handicap at Manchester with 9 stone 7 pounds on his back. That showed me that there is no certainty in racing!'

1935 marked the Silver Jubilee of King George V and was the most momentous in Noel's life: he met his future wife and started training on his own.

'When I was with Hubert Hartigan,' he says, 'he bought a yearling by Achtoi. He was very useful, good enough to run first time out in the Fifteen Hundred, the big two-year-old race at Phoenix Park in Dublin, Eagle Hill, as he was now called, was only just touched off and so Hubert decided that he was too good to keep in Ireland. He sent him over to his brother at Weyhill but for some reason Frank did no good with him. He sent him back to Hubert who had him castrated and turned him out. Then he put him in the sales in Ireland and I bought him myself for 45 guineas.

'I was still with Hubert and so I sent Eagle Hill to a farmer friend in Cheshire who hunted him and qualified him for point-to-points and hunter chases. This was my very first racehorse. By the time we came over to Penrith he was a fairly useful performer over fences and my friend Roddy Fenwick-Palmer trained him for me. He won two or three jumping races at courses like Catterick and Derby and then we ran him at Kelso where he won again on Silver Jubilee Day when Hubert had gone to Chester.'

At a party after racing at Kelso with that fine amateur rider Alec Marsh, later to become Senior Starter to the Jockey Club, Noel met for the first time a Scottish girl called Gwen Carlow whose grandfather had once owned a great number of horses. Her horse Golden Crown, bought for only £50, from Alec Marsh, and trained by herself, also won the same afternoon. Five years later they married. After the party Noel had to get back to Penrith, but René Renton had been left behind and he offered to give her a lift. René was the daughter of his friend, the trainer Bobby Renton, the Aintree specialist who saddled the winners of every steeplechase at Aintree during more than fifty years of training and who won the 1950 Grand National with Freebooter. However, going to René's home in Coldstream took Noel out of his way and it was quite late when he arrived back at Penrith. He was told that he must ring the Castle. 'I'll do it in the morning,' he said. 'No,' he was told. 'You must do it now because his Lordship has telephoned twice himself asking for you.' Noel telephoned and was told by the Yellow Earl 'Come up here. I want to see you.'

When he arrived at Lowther Castle at eleven o'clock that Jubilee Day, the two men talked for a while and then the Earl said, 'I want you to drive me round the lakes. The beacons will be lit, and it will be the last time in the history of England. None of us will ever have a chance to see anything like this again!'

Noel says, 'We went everywhere – I don't know where we didn't go. All that night I drove him round that glorious countryside looking at the beacons until finally we got back to Lowther Castle at five o'clock in the morning. There we sat down to beer, ham and eggs. I'll never forget it. It was a fantastic experience.'

The moment of decision about his own career came to Noel in the spring of that year, 1935. He knew at the age of twenty-five that he must soon branch out and start training on his own if he was ever going to do so. He discussed the matter with Hubert Hartigan, who agreed and he also spoke to Jim White. 'Jim, I'm going to start training. Will you come with me?' Jim recounts, 'Of course, there was nothing I wanted more. So he drove me over to Hambleton in Yorkshire to look at the place where he wanted to set up.'

In the North Riding of Yorkshire there is a glorious watershed which separates the moors from those lovely dales, running west from Helmsley towards Thirsk passing the Benedictine Abbey and College of Ampleforth and keeping on to Hambleton which lies right at the western end, high in the sky above the tortuous descent of Sutton Bank. Noel says, 'I think Hambleton is one of the oldest training establishments in the country. There has been a succession of trainers here since 1700. A family called Heseltine lived here for a long time and it was here that they trained one of the most famous racehorses ever, Alice Hawthorn.'

One thousand feet above sea level, Hambleton may be cold and bleak, but it is steeped in tradition and Jim White recalls that first day when they climbed up Sutton Bank in the old pre-war car and walked on the gallops. 'We went right up to the top of the cliffs,' he says. 'I remember the Guv'nor saying, "What beautiful going!" I looked round and could see Helmsley on one side and Thirsk on the other. It was certainly the most lovely place. The Guv'nor said,

31

"We'll get used to it, Jim!" By God we did! I grew to love that place.'

Noel declares, 'There is no turf in the world like that on the Hambleton gallops. There is such springiness in it and peat under the roots. If you were to dig down there, you'd find ten inches of peat before you came to soil. The great John Scott used to bring horses over from Malton to work there.' The unique texture of the seven furlong gallop (which crossed a country road) provided perfect going in the driest summer.

Noel arranged to rent the lodge and the stable yard from old Miss Murray who lived in Hambleton House, and went back to report to Hubert Hartigan. The matter was agreed. Noel was further helped in becoming independent by Hubert's decision to leave Penrith himself and move south down to East Hendred in Berkshire. So on 5 July 1935 C. F. N. Murless moved to Hambleton Lodge with a trainer's licence and five horses.

'My first owners,' he remembers, 'were Lady Maureen Stanley, Dick Taylor (now chairman of Newcastle Racecourse) and Andrew Johnstone.' Andrew Johnstone, later to serve in the Royal Scots Greys, to own the Brickfields Stud at Newmarket and to marry the daughter of the breeding expert Professor Keeloch, was the great grandson of the owner of Pretender who, trained by Tom Dawson at Tupgill, won the Derby in 1869 and is still the last north country horse to win the Epsom classic. (Matt Peacock's Dante won the wartime substitute Derby at Newmarket in 1945.)

Noel owes much to Eagle Hill, his 45-guinea racehorse, apart from the fact that he was responsible for introducing him to his future wife. 'After he had proved himself to be a decent chaser,' he says, 'I put him in the July Sales and Percy Whittaker bought him for Lord Derby for 800 guineas. That was a big price at the time and it was enough to start me off. Towards the end of the season, Lord Derby sent him back to me to train for him.'

This was an astonishing stroke of fortune for a young trainer. The Earl of Derby was at that time not only the most popular but also the most famous racehorse owner and breeder in the world. So many superlative classic horses have carried those famous colours – 'black, white cap', and only two years earlier Hyperion had won the

---

'He carried his own saddle'

Derby and the St Leger. Just before Noel moved down to Hambleton, Lord Stanley won the Oaks with his brave filly Quashed. So, for any young trainer in his first season, to have horses, albeit jumpers, running for that particular owner was at once recognition and advertisement.

Hubert Hartigan had done his job well. Not only had he taught Noel an immense amount about the art of training, but he had also helped him to establish valuable contacts both in Ireland and later in England. As a result, old Jack Rogers, grandfather of Mick and Tim Rogers, who have played such an important part in the Irish bloodstock world since the war, sent the young trainer a three-year-old grey gelding called Rubin Wood who was already a winner.

3 September 1935 was a day to remember. Jim White took Rubin Wood up to Lanark, a little oval course in the Clyde valley which has recently been abandoned. There were only two runners for the Lee Plate, worth just £103 to the winner. It was the last race on the card that day and Noel had chosen Charlie Smirke, a jockey who, at the time, was on the crest of a wave. Like many another fine rider, Smirke was originally apprenticed to Stanley Wootton.

He was almost aggressively self-confident, and never displayed the slightest sign of nerves, and he rode Rubin Wood to win the Lee Plate by four lengths at 11–8 on. For the first time the Racing Calendar carried the words: 'Trained, C. F. N. Murless'.

That was Noel's only flat winner in 1935. The first jumping winner came on 16 December at Carlisle where Intelligent Outlook won a £70 hurdle race in a blinding snowstorm ridden by Bryan Marshall who had also come down with Noel from Penrith. He was a great help schooling and riding the jumpers as well as driving the horsebox.

In the 1935–1936 season there were several jumping winners, but once again only one winner on the flat – a good race nonetheless: twelve months after he had moved to Hambleton Noel invaded Gwen's country and won the Montrose Handicap at Ayr, worth £196 with Mrs Dick Taylor's Outlaw, ridden by Joe Caldwell.

There are so many fond memories of Hambleton Lodge. Noel laughs. 'It was a proper bachelor establishment!' Richard Stanley, Lord Derby's grandson, who now runs his New England Stud at

---

Carrozza, ridden by Lester Piggott, wins the 1957 Oaks for Her Majesty

C

Newmarket, recalls those days in the late thirties: 'I was often there. We used to call Hambleton Lodge "the Ritz" because of its magnificent amenities. When you wanted to have a bath, not only did you put in the plug but you were then warned by Noel that you must get in first and put one heel on each of the two holes in the floor of the bath before you turned on the taps. Otherwise not only would you have no water but the bathroom would be flooded!'

They were all friends at Hambleton. Ben Alder was there and he rode some of the jumpers for Noel. Ben finished second on Mac Moffat in successive Grand Nationals before he was killed in the war. There was Sandy Scratchley, grand company and an excellent amateur rider who was once summoned before the stewards and asked to show his bank pass book. 'As the last entry was £100 from a very well-known owner, I drew myself up to my full five foot seven inches and announced with as much dignity as I could muster, "Gentlemen, I have decided to turn professional!"'

That fine jockey Jack Fawcus, who was later to be made a prisoner of war, was another lively member of the party. Andrew Johnstone was there too, and Dick Taylor and young Scott Plummer who was also to be killed in the war.

Scott owned a very good hunter chaser called March Brown, and Noel remembers: 'We had him entered for the Foxhunters' Chase at Cheltenham National Hunt Festival but we had reckoned without the weather in Yorkshire. It started to snow on the Saturday before the meeting and went on all through Sunday until it seemed to be six foot high and drifting. We had to be at Thirsk station in time to catch the seven o'clock train on Monday morning and we knew that, although the horsebox would get as close as it could, it could not possibly get up Sutton Bank. So Jim White woke me at about two o'clock in the morning and I put on all the clothing I could find. We fastened all the tack on to the horse himself, rather like the old days at Weyhill, and Jim led him. I got a shovel and started to dig through the snowdrifts. I dug so hard that before we'd gone a quarter of a mile, I was in my shirtsleeves. Somehow Jim managed to get him down the Bank and to Cheltenham, only to find that the meeting had been put off for a week. Anyway, the journey was worthwhile. Lester's uncle Charlie Piggott very kindly looked after them and March Brown won the Foxhunters' on the Tuesday and then went in again at Sandown on Saturday.'

Even in those days, Noel was concerned for his owners' interests. Richard Stanley says, 'He had a horse for my grandfather which was not completely sound, and he told him that in charging him £3.50 a week, (or £3 10s as it was then), he felt that he was taking money under false pretences.'

In 1937 the stable won four races on the flat worth £568. The following year the total was increased to seven, worth £1310. 'But at the end of 1938,' says Noel, 'Sir Alfred McAlpine sent his horses to me and so I started to have quite a few winners.' In fact, up to 1 September 1939 before the declaration of war Noel had won ten races in the season worth £2417. The last winner of that momentous year, Sir Alfred McAlpine's Crystal Palace, won the Loom Handicap Plate at Manchester, ridden by the champion jockey Gordon Richards. And the *first* winner of 1939 had been Limace, trained by Noel for Miss Gwen Carlow; given to her as unable to breed by Victor Sassoon.

When war began, Hambleton was requisitioned and turned into a dummy aerodrome to deceive German marauders. For Noel and the boys at 'the Ritz', it was the end of an era. They all, including Bryan Marshall and Jim White, joined the army: except for the Guv'nor, who tried in vain to keep them company but was refused point blank because of that accident to his feet at Leicester in 1930. So, Noel moved with a few horses down to Middleham – to Brecongill, and in November 1940 he and Gwen were married.

3

Hambleton and Middleham
1940–1947

❄

As soon as war was declared on 3 September 1939, sports gatherings were prohibited and racing was not resumed until 18 October at Newmarket. For the rest of the season there were also fixtures at Newbury, Thirsk, Stockton and Manchester. Several courses were used for racing in 1940 until, on 19 June, the Jockey Club announced that, after consultation with the Government, all racing was suspended until further notice. A fixture list was resumed on 14 September but the number of horses in training and at stud was drastically reduced. Racing continued throughout the remainder of the war although in 1942 the number of available courses was restricted. A regional system was introduced, whereby racing at Newmarket, with the exception of the substitute classic races and a few other important events, was confined to horses trained there. The Salisbury and Windsor meetings were only for horses trained south of the Trent (Newmarket excluded), and Pontefract and Stockton were used for those trained in the north.

Events for two-year-olds dominated the programmes, and stayers' races were sporadic. The Second World War affected breeding too, even more adversely than the First and it was responsible for many changes in stud management. Breeders were urged to reduce their establishments so that their pastures could be converted into arable land. When paddocks were ploughed up in this way on the orders of the Ministry of Agriculture, the necessary crowding together of mares and foals greatly increased the risk of infestation by redworm. Breeders had only native stock to consider when normally they would be buying in from abroad. Negotiations took place between influential members of the Jockey Club and relevant Government departments, and what amounted to a gentleman's agreement was effected. Breeders reduced their studs to a minimum; the Government arranged a system of rationing – admittedly inadequate, but the best that could be devised. Scales of food rationing were laid down for all types of stock (e.g. brood-mares, foals, stallions) at various periods of their stud life. Horses in training were similarly rationed, the management and organization of the system being virtually controlled by Weatherby's offices. The Duke of Norfolk, at that time joint Parliamentary Secretary with Mr Tom Williams (who became Minister of Agriculture under a Socialist Government) and the Minister himself, Robert Hudson, cooperated with Lord Rosebery, who, acting in an official capacity, was an invaluable adviser and ally.

The reduction process was effected largely by culling the older and unprofitable mares, and, as a result of this policy, the whole of the thoroughbred population temporarily diminished. By 1942 the foal population had fallen to 2282. (In 1939 3675 foals had been born.)

Noel, who spent the first half of the war farming at Middleham, watched a revolution in farming take place on practically every stud farm in the country. Even the smallest breeders were compelled by their local War Agricultural Committee to plough up a proportion of their grasslands reducing to a minimum the acreage necessary for maintaining their stock. In the early stages of the war many injustices occurred due to the inability of the Committee executives to understand the needs of breeders. In some instances owners were told that they only needed pasture for their stallions regardless of the fact that in the covering season each breeder had to provide accommodation for around forty mares and their foals!

Matters, however, were gradually smoothed out and breeders made the best of what many of them regarded as a bad job. It is hardly surprising that there was virtually no National Hunt racing, and indeed, from the middle of 1942 until the autumn of 1944 there was no jump racing at all. Help was needed to convince austere wartime officialdom that racing and the thoroughbred are essential parts of Britain's heritage.

The Royal Racing Manager, Captain Charles Moore, a shrewd, highly intelligent, witty Irishman, had realized when he took over in 1937 that the Royal Studs were at a very low ebb. He seized on the war as an ideal opportunity to cull the stock, then, following the example of Lord Marcus Beresford thirty years earlier, he arranged for a number of yearlings to be leased from the National Stud and raced in the King's name, and returned to the Stud at the end of their racing days.

These animals, all bred in the purple, were to be trained at Beckhampton in Wiltshire by Fred Darling, who had already won five Derbys before the war. In 1940 and 1941 he won the substitute classic run at Newmarket with Pont l'Eveque and with Owen Tudor, a horse who was later to play a significant part in Noel's life. Darling knew the National Stud families well. He had had plenty of opportunity to study their idiosyncrasies when he trained for Lord Lonsdale, in whose name and colours the leased horses ran before the war.

By great good fortune among the yearlings leased by King George VI from the National Stud in the autumn of 1940 were Big Game and Sun Chariot. The former, a massive heavy-topped colt, was by the Aga Khan's Triple Crown winner Bahram out of the brilliant mare Myrobella, a daughter of Tetratema. Sun Chariot, a robust, well-balanced, long, low filly with a faultless action, was by Hyperion out of Clarence, by Dilligence. By nature she was unpredictable, quick-tempered and self-willed, giving grey hairs to all those who were closely connected with her, particularly to her rider, Gordon Richards. She was, however, undoubtedly one of the greatest fillies of the century. Big Game won the Two Thousand Guineas by four lengths at 11–8 on, but failed to stay in the Derby, which was his only defeat. Sun Chariot, on the other hand, won not only the One Thousand Guineas, but the Oaks and the St Leger as well. In the Oaks she was in a thoroughly difficult mood. She spoilt three starts and when at last the starter got them off, she darted away to the left. She had covered about fifty yards after the others had gone a furlong, but she won. She gave her finest display in the St Leger, winning with contemptuous ease from the colts that had the first three places in the Derby.

So, inspired by the King's example and fortified by the turn of the tide of war, racing began to make a slow but steady comeback.

Noel and Gwen started now to collect a few horses again. It was a joint effort from now on and there is no doubt that in training, possibly more than in any other walk of life, two heads are better than one.

Every successful trainer can look back on one horse which can be said to have given him a start, to have ensured that its name and that of its trainer became sufficiently well-known in the racing world to attract other owners with more horses.

No one who hears the story of Sejanus as told by Jim White could doubt that Noel Murless did the right thing when he bought a mare called Senna Tea as a potential jumper at Hambleton in 1939. Jim remembers Bryan Marshall riding Senna Tea on the Hambleton gallops. 'The Guv'nor told him he couldn't understand why he couldn't get the stomach off the mare. Where she should have been getting hard and fit, she just stayed fat. Then they discovered the reason. She was in foal!'

Senna Tea foaled down a brown colt in the spring of 1940 and Noel discovered that she had been covered by the Ascot Gold Cup and Goodwood Cup winner, Tiberius, a top-class stayer by Foxlore who, racing for Sir Abe Bailey, had also been placed in the Derby and the St Leger. Noel and Gwen called the little foal Sejanus and on 26 June 1943, he provided Noel with his first wartime victory in the £117 Brecongill Plate over one mile at Stockton. Two months later he won the August Handicap at Pontefract, ridden by Joe Taylor, who was to be the stable's chief jockey for the next few years. How appropriate that that first winning race should have been named after the place where Sejanus was foaled and where Noel and Gwen had made their home when they were married.

Noel's and Gwen's only child Julia (Julie), was born at Brecongill in February 1942. The snow was so thick on the Yorkshire moors that the doctor had to walk across the fields to get to the house. It is a family joke that the proud father went to register the birth and, when asked the date of his marriage, insisted vehemently that it was November 1941. 'I bloody well ought to know, oughtn't I?' Even in wartime the Yorkshire registrar was shocked until it was established that Noel and Gwen had in fact been married a year earlier!

Julie once asked her mother what was the secret of Noel's success. Gwen answered that, from time to time Noel would look at a horse on his evening inspection and say, 'My word, that's doing well now.' Gwen said, 'I would look and look, but I just couldn't see it. Nor could anyone else. Then ten days later, I would see what he had meant.' Also, wherever they have been living, there has been a calm, relaxed atmosphere which must have had a beneficial effect on the horses. Julie says, 'I have never known any hurry, feeling of rush or urgency about the place.'

During the lean years Noel and Gwen had not been idle. They had invested in a few mares. They sent Cuddlededee to Bellacose, the well-known sprint sire; and they sent Congo to Bobsleigh, who had raced for Lord Derby and was at that time producing a number of fast horses. This choice was deliberate. As most two-year-olds are run over five and six furlongs, it is obviously best to use sprint sires if you want juvenile winners. And winners were what the Murlesses needed to put themselves on the map as soon as racing revived. Both mares foaled down safely in 1944, the year Ocean Swell won the Derby and Noel won five races worth £1642.

The first of his winners that year was Mashallah, owned by their old friend Andrew Johnstone, who had joined the Greys in Palestine. Noel chuckles as he remembers. 'Before he left, he sold his car to Sim Feversham and Dick Taylor. After he had gone, they went outside to drive it away, only to find that it had three flat tyres!' It was good for Noel and Gwen to have Andrew back again when asthma forced him to return home, and they had also made friends with a charming old Yorkshireman called Roland White, a retired wholesale grocer, who lived in Wakefield. Starting with a very useful handicapper called Aprolon, who won the last race for the stable in 1944, White bought the two foals which Noel and Gwen had bred, Closeburn, out of Cuddlededee, and Julius, the grey colt by Bobsleigh.

At this stage, as the Allied tanks were rolling through Belgium and Holland into Germany, Noel and Gwen took The Cliff Stud near Helmsley at the other end of that Yorkshire watershed on a long lease from the Feversham estate. The Cliff is acre upon acre of rolling paddock and pasture land and, as Noel says, 'We bought it because it is right on the limestone.' For Noel, who had grown to adore Yorkshire, The Cliff became much more than functional farmland. It became a haven, an emotional release from the day to day racing pressures.

'I loved getting back to Yorkshire,' he muses. 'I loved getting up to Helmsley among these young animals.' The Cliff saw the start of Noel and Gwen's breeding enterprises and many famous horses have been bred or reared, including Closeburn, Caerphilly, St Chad, Lowna, Caergwrle, Adios, Gospill Hill, St Paddy, Twilight

Alley, Sweet Moss, Sucaryl, Attica Meli, Mysterious, Owen Dudley, Millymoss and Mil's Bomb.

Discussing the whole question of breeding, Noel says now, 'The problem of planning a horse's pedigree is difficult. It adds up to the class and type of animal you're trying to breed. It depends on what mares one has at one's disposal and more, perhaps, on what sires you can get into. Breeding is not an exact science. One has always got to be planning a couple of generations ahead, but then, if a colt comes up instead of a filly, you're back to square one and you've got to start the operation all over again. Many good horses are bred by chance. To figure out a balanced pedigree: the stamina principally comes from the sire and the speed from the dam. So often things don't work out as you had planned. There are more disappointments in this business than anything else, as everyone who is connected with horses knows. But it is very, very rewarding when your plans do work out and a really good horse turns up.' Even now, after so much experience of other studs, Noel says firmly, 'I have always thought that the pick of the studs was The Cliff.'

In 1945 the war ended and racecourses began to open up again and bloodstock sales to do good business.

That year Noel went over to Dublin where he bought a yearling colt by another sprint sire, Khosro, for 220 guineas, and called it Oros. That year Noel won nine races worth £3429 including the Clifton Welter Handicap at York with Drummond, and the Stansfield Handicap at Newmarket with Sejanus.

The family had returned to Hambleton but this time to Hambleton House. The days of 'the Ritz' were over. Jim White was demobilized and hurried back to take over as travelling head man, a position he held until the Guv'nor's retirement. There was also Jack Russell, head man until he died at Warren Place, Johnny Mack, head lad in the fillies yard, who is still at Woodditton, and Billy Rea who was later to look after Royal Palace.

Those who had been abroad during the six years of war and who had yearned for British racing, came home expecting to find it as they had left it. But there had been a great many changes. There had for instance, been no racing at Ascot, vulnerable as it was to bombing action so near to London. Ascot would never really be the same again. Although few realized it immediately, the holocaust had completely altered the social structure of the country. For a while there was sufficient money about to foster the illusion that all was just as it had been before, but it was a sad, dangerous illusion.

Possibly Noel was affected less than most. He was always a realist, and a tremendously hard worker. 'I was never a very keen racegoer,' he says. 'So much hanging about. You could be more use at home. I liked watching my horses run, certainly, but I loved the training part, especially in the spring when you start to find out how your two-year-olds have progressed, or how they haven't! They would start going out on to the gallops halfway through March and doing quiet work. It was wonderful. Halfway through April they would be striding along, sorting themselves out a bit. I always liked to work them in small batches of three or four. When I classified them, it depended really on the individual horse, with some horses I could tell very early on whether they were useful. For example, I told Jim Joel in the spring of his two-year-old season, long before he had ever run, that Royal Palace would be a classic horse. By the middle of April, I would know what was what. When I started off, I always split up what I thought were my best two-year-olds so that they were not working together. I normally galloped my horses two days a week. But again, of course, it depended on the horse because some needed three days' work. I generally galloped them on Wednesdays and Saturdays and, if they were going to do a good gallop on the Saturday, they would have a little half-speed pipe-opener on the Friday. I seldom needed the racecourse to tell me how good they were: when you've been watching them for a long time, you have a pretty good idea at home how good they are. It's the way a horse moves, the way he moves up to his lead horse. No, I don't enjoy the atmosphere of the racecourse at all.'

Noel had to go to the races much more in 1946 when he won thirty-four races worth £15,326. Julius won three, Oros two and Closeburn four, and Sejanus boosted the total with another two victories. Noel had his first doubles – two races in one day – in June at Redcar, in July at Stockton and on 12 September at the Doncaster St Leger Meeting when he won Rous Stakes with Oros and the Princess Mary Nursery with Lady Dandy. Two of his winners that year – Delville Wood who took the Great Yorkshire Handicap at Doncaster and Julius in the Clearwell Stakes at Newmarket – were partnered by Gordon Richards.

From the beginning, the Murless hallmarks were patience, attention to detail and a deep understanding and regard for a horse's nature. Noel started as he meant to go on and, for longer than any other trainer, he insisted on the old, thorough routine, particularly at evening stables. As modern labour has sadly compelled a relaxation of discipline, and litters are no longer picked up at evening stables, horses being inspected instead on their normal beds, it is as well to note here how it was, and how indeed it ought to be, done.

A fully-trained experienced lad would tie up his first horse and muck out, picking up the clean litter and heaping it in a smart rectangular pile against the long front wall of the box. He would then spread a thin carpet of straw over the floor and plaited the edge by the door, brushing clean the remainder of the sill. Leaving his first horse tied up, he would move on to the second and repeat the process. He would then fetch the necessary hay and new straw for each animal and pile it neatly on the end of the litter. He would have to take his turn with the hoof oil and would use it on the hooves of both his horses as and when the oil was free during the evening. This meant that the horses' hooves would have to be picked out ready. Some trainers used a sophisticated mixture containing Stockholm tar, but most thrifty old trainers used sump oil. The hoof is a living thing and the reason for oiling hooves above and below is not so much for smartness as to ensure that the hooves are picked clean and inspected for risen clenches and loose shoes, and for any sign of thrush or cracked heels. If necessary the hooves would be treated with medicaments such as Stockholm tar.

Then, going back to the first horse with a bucket half full of water, he would sponge out the eyes, nose and dock, in that order. He would now untie the rugs in the reverse order from that in which he had fastened them, starting with rearstraps, then the girth and the breaststrap, and proceed to groom his horse in quarters, starting on the nearside and always using the hand nearest the horse's head to do the sponging, rubbing or brushing, having rolled the rug back so that it would rest over the animal's loins and quarters. First he would sponge the whole area from the head down the neck to the point where the rug was resting, paying particular attention to sponging out any remaining sweat marks or dung marks which the horse might have collected while he was lying down. Once he had damped the whole area, including the near foreleg, he would dry it briskly with his dry rubber and then, with

43

bodybrush in the left hand and curry comb in the right, scraping out dirt from the brush at regular intervals, he would brush firmly with a circular motion and then sleek down the coat before throwing the rug forward to cover the part that he had just strapped. He would then repeat the performance with the nearside hindquarter, and then putting his horse over, he would repeat the performance on the offside. The good stableman, when strapping a colt or a gelding, would probably remove the rug for a few minutes to whisp him thoroughly with a hay wisp to help the circulation. After he had completed the process and put in whatever quarter marks the trainer approved – normally one large sweep was the most effective – he would probably place a clean rubber over the quarters as he replaced the rug, refastening the breaststrap and lightly readjusting the girthstrap so that it would not mark.

With his dandy brush he would brush out the mane, foretop and tail. Only the head man would use the comb and scissors to bang the tail to the required length. Then he would hurry off to repeat the drill with his second horse. By a quarter of an hour at the latest before the time of the trainer's inspection, he would be finished and both his buckets, now full of clean water, would be lined up with those of the other lads opposite their respective boxes on the other side of the wall. The head man would now ensure that the yard was swept and that each lad, himself now clean and tidy, was with his first horse. His grooming kit would be laid out neatly on a stable rubber on top of the litter. Both headcollars would have been polished. After the trainer's inspection, the lad would bundle up his kit and hurry to his second horse to await the Guv'nor.

It was an education to go round stables with Noel. As he gave each horse its tit-bit of carrots, and had a quiet word with the lad, his eyes absorbed so much more than anyone else's would have done. He seemed to know instinctively just how the horse was feeling. When the trainer, after a few words with the head man, left the yard, the horses were done up for the night, watered, fed and let down.

By 1946 there were no more jumpers in the yard at Hambleton. The last jumping winner had been Vain Knight who, ridden by Frenchy Nicholson and carrying 12 stone 7 pounds, had won the three mile Danby Chase at Catterick Bridge. But by the end of the year's flat racing season, he was tenth on the list of all British trainers, above such famous men as Matt and Harry Peacock, Jack Colling, Charles Elsey and Walter Nightingall.

Second on the trainers' list to Frank Butters was the famous Fred Darling of Beckhampton, whose jockey, Gordon Richards, was champion yet again with no less than 212 winners. Son of Sam Darling, who trained two Derby winners, Fred Darling was widely held to be the outstanding English trainer of the century. He won nineteen classic races and magnetized the racing world. He had served as an apprentice for a brief time, but had never held a jockey's licence and had begun training at Kentford near Newmarket with a few horses owned by Lady de Bathe (otherwise known as Lillie Langtry). He next trained for the Weinburg brothers in Germany, returning to England just before the start of the First World War to take over the Beckhampton stable from his father. Though often handicapped by ill-health, his record was one of remarkable success. Taciturn, secretive and quick-tempered, he had no time for fools. He was a ruthless martinet in the stable, insisting at all times on the highest standards and the closest attention to detail. His discipline with horses was rigid and he demanded utter obedience from them. At evening stables the colts were always tied up by three rack chains. When Fred Darling came round each colt had to stand to attention. If any horse moved he felt the trainer's stick. Gwen says, 'The first thing we did at Beckhampton was to remove two of those chains.'

The sheen on the coats of Fred's horses made them stand out from all their rivals in the paddock before a race. Noel says today: 'I learnt a great deal from Fred Darling and will always look back on his memory with affection.'

Few of Fred's horses were to reproduce themselves at stud. Exceptions were Fair Trial and Darling's 1941 wartime Derby winner, Owen Tudor. He was responsible for Tudor Minstrel, the immensely powerful bay who was unbeaten as a two-year-old in 1946 and won the Two Thousand Guineas the following year by eight lengths. Gordon described him as 'the best miler on the day that I rode in my whole career'.

Noel, looking back, says, 'Tudor Minstrel was a right-handed horse,' and by now the Derby had returned to Epsom, a sharp left-handed track. Gordon recalls that Tudor Minstrel had been quietly practising on the replica Derby course at Beckhampton, cantering round with a lead horse as all the Derby runners had done before at least twice a week for a fortnight. The stable jockey rode Tudor Minstrel in the last of these canters. He was badly shaken. 'On pulling up,' he remembers, 'I went straight to Noel and said, "This fellow's not right. He can't get on his other leg. If he does, he's all at sea."' Darling was just as disturbed. The left-handed course might cause Tudor Minstrel to lose the Derby. In the final workout, Michael Beary rode the stable's other Derby candidate, Blue Train. They galloped up the one mile three furlongs of the nearly straight trial course and, as Tudor Minstrel went so much better, their trainer scratched Blue Train. But neither he nor Gordon knew how to ride the favourite.

On the day, Gordon confessed that he had never had such an uncomfortable ride at Epsom. Every time he tried to restrain Tudor Minstrel, the horse fought him. Every time he allowed him his head he veered sharply to the right. 'Either way, he was making certain that he lost the race,' said Gordon. 'The whole race must have been a nightmare, but Tudor Minstrel finished fourth and went on to win the St James's Palace Stakes at Ascot in 1947 in a canter, a mile on a right-handed course. He proved his brilliance at stud but, of course, he also showed that although his sire. Owen Tudor, won a Derby he himself was unquestionably a ten-furlong horse at the outside.'

That same year Gordon established an all-time British record of 269 winners.

Fred Darling was by now very ill and decided to retire. He planned to sell Beckhampton to Tudor Minstrel's owner, 'Lucky' Arthur Dewar, the whisky tycoon, and to find a trainer to take over and to persuade all the other owners to stay on. At breakfast one day Darling said to his jockey, 'Gordon, I'm very impressed with that friend of yours, Murless. That fellow is on the job. He doesn't let his head lad carry his saddles for him.'

Royal Ascot that year was the most momentous race meeting for Noel, who was challenging for the biggest race of his career to date, the £1864 Britannia Stakes with Buckthorn and Oros, ridden by Gordon Richards. Imagine the surprise in that elegant, top-hatted crowd when these two colts from the little-known Yorkshire stable finished first and second. Noel takes up the story. 'I was in the weighing room waiting for Gordon to pass the scales,' he says, 'when I felt a tug on my sleeve. I looked down and saw a face that I knew well, although I had never met its owner.

'"I'm Fred Darling," he said. "I'd like a word with you."

'"Certainly, sir," I said. "We'll meet after this race."

'He told me that he was going to give up and asked whether I would consider moving to Beckhampton to take over from him. He said he thought that if I did, Dewar would buy the place and lease it to me. I would go back to Hambleton and make arrangements to move down south in October.'

Despite a tempting offer from the late Aga Khan, Gordon decided to stay on as first jockey to his beloved Beckhampton with its famous gallops on the rolling Wiltshire Downs. He and his wife Margery were still living on the Ogbourne estate which belonged to Norah Laye, daughter of impresario George Edwardes of 'Gaiety' fame. She was very knowledgeable about horses, having been married first to Paddy Hartigan, and then on his death to his brother Martin. Both trainers had been buried in a little plot of consecrated ground fenced with white racecourse rails up by the starting gate, on the glorious Ogbourne gallops, looking north to the Bristol Channel and south to the south coast of England. Norah's third husband was another trainer, Captain Billy Laye, his black patch over one eye earning him the nickname 'The Burglar'. Noel remembers, 'Gordon was always pulling Billy's leg. He would say, "You want to watch out, Cap. She'll have you up there with them!" Gordon and I felt distinctly uncomfortable and could hardly look at each other at Billy's funeral when this prophecy came true.'

Noel was still winning bigger and better races. Closeburn was improving all the time and, although he had been allotted 8 stone 10 pounds in the Stewards' Cup, Noel reckoned that he could win the big Goodwood sprint. It was 29 July 1947. Joe Taylor, his usual jockey, was very ill and, in any case, Gordon was now riding most of the runners that came south from Hambleton. Noel recalls, 'It was a very, very hot day, and Closeburn was stabled at the village of Singleton down at the bottom of the hill. They started to let the traffic come down the hill just as he was coming up in the horsebox, which therefore got hopelessly stuck. Gwen started to run down the hill to see where he was. Luckily a policeman gave her a lift on the back of his motorbike and she found the box. The only way that they could get the ramp down to get him out was on to the bank of a hedge by the side of the road. They ran him up the hill to the course, and the sweat was pouring off him and all of us when we arrived. Gordon and I were the only people in the paddock. All the other horses had gone down to the start. I slapped the saddle on, legged Gordon up and away they went. They came back like an express train, Gordon riding a tremendous race to win by a neck.'

At Doncaster Sales that September Noel bought two colts, one by Bois Roussel for 4000 guineas, and another by Nearco for 5000 guineas. Both had been bred in Yorkshire by Sir Richard Sykes at his Sledmere Stud. The Nearco colt was called Krakatao and Bois Roussel's, Ridge Wood.

When he returned to Hambleton, Lord Feversham telephoned to ask Noel which of the pair had been bought for him. 'You didn't ask me to buy you one,' protested Noel, Sim Feversham swore that he had, and said that he would ring back.

Noel says, 'I had definitely been asked to buy one for Geoffrey Smith, the Tadcaster brewer. The next day, the first person I saw on the racecourse was Geoffrey, so I had to avoid him. However, Sim did not ring so I had to keep faith with Geoffrey, who chose Ridge Wood.'

Among the owners whom Noel was to inherit from Fred Darling were Sir Reginald Macdonald-Buchanan of the Scots Guards, and his wife Lady Macdonald-Buchanan, who had inherited and maintained the wide bloodstock and breeding interests of her father, the well-known whisky distiller, Lord Woolavington. He had won the Derby with Captain Cuttle in 1922 and with Coronach in 1926, both sired by Hurry On, whom he had bought for only 500 guineas. Lady Macdonald-Buchanan had bred and owned Owen Tudor, the wartime Derby and Gold Cup winner, who had, of course, been responsible for Tudor Minstrel.

At about the time when Closeburn won the Stewards' Cup, Major Macdonald-Buchanan said to Noel, 'We'll go up to Lavington and see what yearlings you want.' Noel remembers, 'We were a bit late arriving and found Fred Darling and Harry Cottril already there. There were three colts walking round the yard and Fred said

---

ABOVE Lester Piggott with Crepello after their 1957 Derby triumph
BELOW Petite Etoile at Warren Place with Lester Piggott, 1958

that in his opinion the nicest horse was the yearling by Mieuxce, whose produce was doing very well in those days. 'I said, "What about the grey?"

'Fred said, "You don't want him. He's just a little rat."

'I asked if I could see him turned out in the paddocks and watch him move. Away they went, and it was then that I saw that wonderful action. I said to Fred, "We couldn't possibly leave him behind!" He agreed.'

The name of the grey colt was Abernant. In the hands of Noel Murless, Fred Darling's 'little rat' was to become one of the fastest horses of the century.

ABOVE   Prima Aly Khan leads in Petite Etoile, with Lester Piggott after the 1959 Oaks

BELOW   Juliette McLeod's portrait of Petite Etoile

D

4

Beckhampton: 'It's Cold and It's Damp' 1948–1952

❋

Noel started the 1948 season with fifty-one horses, including Closeburn, Oros and Sejanus. It was, of course, a tremendous challenge to succeed the legendary Fred Darling and the critics were ready to pounce. Throughout his career, Noel was never worried by criticism however, concentrating instead entirely on his horses. As he went round the stables or rode out with his string, he had every reason to be satisfied. The classic horses looked to be The Cobbler, Colonel Giles Loder's handsome dark bay colt by Windsor Slipper, unbeaten in five races the previous season, including the Coventry, the National Breeders' and the Middle Park; Sir Percy Loraine's Queenpot, a charming little filly who had won at Salisbury, Goodwood and Newmarket; and Goblet, a filly by Owen Tudor, bred and owned by Fred Darling.

Noel recollects, 'Fred went out to Kenya, which didn't suit him, and so he came back to Beckhampton where he lived in the big house for a while. His TB was undoubtedly getting worse all the time. Then he went to Midhurst for treatment and came back again. He was in and out of hospital. He was a very tough man, as far as his work went, with his owners and with his horses. Yet away from racing he could be the nicest person in the world. But I'm afraid he had no love of animals, and his horses really had to go through it.'

Noel never hurried his two-year-olds, allowing them to come to themselves naturally, and they were, therefore, a little backward compared with some others, but the old horses and the three-year-olds were in such good form that Noel started the 1948 season well. Queenpot, who had wintered really well, won her first race of the season in the Katheryn Howard Stakes at Hurst Park, an ideal curtain-raiser for the One Thousand Guineas three weeks later. The

50

Cobbler, looking superb after his winter's rest should also have run at Bath in preparation for his bid for the Two Thousand Guineas. Unfortunately, a few days earlier he had bruised a foot and was unable to run which meant that Noel could not race him before the Newmarket classic. There he had to take on My Babu, the Maharaja of Baroda's French-bred Djebel colt who, trained by Sam Armstrong, had won the Woodcote Stakes and the New Stakes as a two-year-old, and had the benefit of a previous outing and victory in the Craven Stakes over the classic course and distance at Newmarket. The Cobbler's bruised foot probably just foiled a classic double for Noel in his first season as Master of Beckhampton.

The ground was hard and fast for that Newmarket Spring Meeting. My Babu, ridden by the irrepressible Charlie Smirke, was favourite at 2–1 for the Two Thousand Guineas with The Cobbler second favourite at 100–30. Edgar Britt, the likeable Australian, jumped Pride of India off into the lead and made his best way home. Gordon Richards tucked The Cobbler in behind him and hit the front running down into The Dip. Smirke challenged almost immediately and two great jockeys on two superb classic colts fought a tremendous battle up the hill to the winning post, where My Babu won by a head. Gordon is convinced that, if The Cobbler had been able to have that previous race, he would have won. The Guv'nor agrees: 'The Cobbler was a lovely horse, very brave. He was highly strung and always ran his races right out.'

The One Thousand Guineas was due to be run two days later, on the Friday. Fred Darling liked to have his runners stabled in the middle of Newmarket town instead of at The Links on the other side of the London road, mid-way between the two courses where 'provincial' horses are usually accommodated. This arrangement nearly cost Noel his first classic success, for on Thursday night a fair opened just behind the Beckhampton boxes and Queenpot, accustomed to the calm of the Wiltshire Downs, nearly sweated away her race. Stable confidence was undoubtedly shaken but Gordon jumped her out of the gate and, just sitting against her, letting her run in his hands, was always up with the leaders. At halfway Queenpot hit the front and in another desperate battle, reminiscent of the Two Thousand Guineas, she held on gamely to win by a head from Ariostar. It was Noel's first classic success and it gave him great pleasure to win for Sir Percy Loraine, who had also

51

bred the filly. As fair as ever, Queenpot's trainer says, 'She was lucky to win at both Hurst and Newmarket. The Aga Khan's Masaka, trained by Fred Butters, was a better filly but she was left at the start in both races.'

At the next Newmarket meeting on 11 May, Fred Darling's Goblet won the Haverhill Stakes so impressively that she became the stable's selection for the Oaks, since it was clear that there was no chance of Queenpot staying one and a half miles, even at Epsom.

By now at home at Beckhampton the two-year-olds were beginning to show signs of tremendous ability. The dark grey Abernant, in particular, was about to reward the instinctive faith of the Guv'nor. After careful thought, Jeremy Hindley, who learned his job with the Guv'nor, and is now a successful Newmarket trainer, says, 'I believe that a great part of Noel's secret was that he could identify a classic horse incredibly quickly, far earlier in its life than anybody else could. As a result, having identified it, he would point it in that direction and start training him with the classics in view at an incredibly early stage. A lot of people get a good horse but fail to recognize its potential, and work him and run him so much as an ordinary run of the mill animal that by the time he gets to the stage where he should be being prepared for the classics, he lacks the ability to win that sort of race. Of course this particularly applies to stayers, the sort of horses that could be trained for the Derby or the Oaks, or other top-class events. Having spotted such an animal, Noel always gave it a tremendous time to develop.' Jeremy quotes a later filly called Parmelia. 'It was quite obvious at stables in the evening which animals the Guv'nor fancied and which he didn't. I thought this filly was an appalling mover with a nasty round action and I thought she had very little class about her. But long before she had done any work, Noel was always very high on her. Of course, he was quite right. She turned out very good indeed. I've never stopped wondering what the hell he saw . . . If you have this sort of uncanny intuition in a top-class stable, you can be like a schoolmaster and place the animal in the right stream.'

The big betting trainers like Atty Persse galloped their youngsters before Christmas, albeit only for two and a half furlongs in batches 'upsides' to assess their potential. Noel never did this. 'We never started working fast with the two-year-olds until the beginning of April,' he pronounces. 'Nevertheless, I just knew that

Abernant, with his glorious low sweeping action was terrifically fast and he confirmed this when I first started to get him into a bit of decent work.'

The grey colt seemed sufficiently forward in condition to run at Lingfield in the middle of April, but the clay turf of the pretty Surrey course was hard that spring. Abernant was slowly away and, even though he ran very green, looking about him in this his first appearance on a racecourse, he made up a lot of ground to finish second, beaten a head by Potentate. He would undoubtedly have won in another stride. This was the only occasion Abernant was beaten as a two-year-old. He won the Bedford Stakes at Newmarket, the Chesham at Royal Ascot, the National Breeders' at Sandown, the Champagne at Doncaster and the Middle Park at Newmarket.

'We never really tried Abernant at home,' says Noel. 'The only time we galloped him at Beckhampton was before he won the Champagne to see if he would get the six furlongs with a three-year-old called Gold Mist. The weight-for-age scale said that in September a three-year-old should be giving 22 pounds to a two-year-old over six furlongs. On this occasion Abernant, the two-year-old, was giving at least 10 pounds to Gold Mist and so was meeting him on 32 pounds, worse than weight-for-age terms. Believe me, Abernant won that gallop as he liked. He trotted up. Doncaster gave us some idea of his phenomenal speed.'

Royal Forest, who also belonged to the Macdonald-Buchanans, was another high-class colt. Noel regarded this bay son of Derby winner Bois Roussel as a probable Epsom winner in 1949. 'He was a very good horse, but very highly strung,' he says. First time out at the end of May, Royal Forest won in a common canter at Salisbury. He went on to Royal Ascot where he won the Coventry Stakes, beating Nimbus among others.

Just before Ascot, Gordon Richards broke some ribs in a nasty fall at Brighton when a horse of Noel's old boss Frank Hartigan came down with him in the middle of the field. The stable jockey had to miss that Royal meeting and the three Beckhampton winners were ridden instead by his brother Cliff and by Charlie Smirke. After an unaccountable defeat at 25–1 on in a small field for the Clarence House Stakes at Ascot in September, Royal Forest went to Newmarket for the Dewhurst Stakes which he won comfortably, trouncing horses that had beaten him in his previous race and proving that he was indeed a worthy classic candidate.

That year, Noel met King George VI for the first time – as his trainer. He won five races with horses leased by His Majesty from the National Stud, starting with a double on 11 August at Bath – with Gigantic and Royal Blue. Gigantic, who was superbly bred by Big Game out of Sun Chariot, went on to win the £2335 Imperial Produce Stakes at Kempton Park. He had not much scope, however, and probably the best Royal prospect for 1949 was Berrylands, a colt by Bois Roussel out of Snowberry. After an introduction at Salisbury, Beckhampton's other local downland course, Berrylands went on to Ascot in October and won the Duke of Edinburgh Stakes.

Arthur Dewar had a useful two-year-old at the time called Faux Tirage who, after winning the Granville Stakes at Ascot, won the Rous Memorial Stakes at Newmarket. Sir Percy Loraine, in this, his classic year, was also entitled to hope for a good season in 1949 after his two-year-old Wat Tyler had won both the Champagne Stakes at Salisbury and the Rous Memorial at Goodwood.

All this success with two-year-olds produced an amusing sequel. One day Noel was approached by eighty-year-old Atty Persse, who had earned a reputation as the greatest of all two-year-old trainers. Leaning on his two sticks, cigar clamped between his teeth, Atty looked over his bifocals, large bright blue eyes twinkling and said, 'Young man, I like to win with my two-year-olds first time out. I don't want to run up against any of your hotpots. You'd better give me plenty of warning, tip me off!'

At the end of the season, Beckhampton horses filled the first, third and fourth places in the Two-Year-Old Free Handicap. Abernant was top with 9 stone 7 pounds, Royal Forest was given 9 stone 3 pounds and Faux Tirage two pounds less. Noel was champion trainer for the first time, having won sixty-three races worth a total of £67,046. Of these, sixty-two had been ridden by Gordon Richards, who finished 1948 as champion jockey for the twenty-first time with 224 winners.

The French were by now plundering British big races and the second name on the British trainers' list was 'in France'. Horses trained on the other side of the Channel had won the Derby and the Oaks in 1947 and in 1948 French colts filled first and second places in the Derby. My Love, owned in partnership by the Aga Khan and Leon Volterra, trained at Chantilly by Richard Carver, had won the colts' classic at Epsom from his compatriot, Volterra's Royal Drake with Noor third, owned by the Aga Khan and trained by Frank Butters, the first of the home contingent to finish. The Aga Khan won the Oaks as well, with his filly Masaka.

The extent of Noel's triumph during this, his first year in top international competition, can be measured by the fact that seventy-year-old Frank Butters finished third on the trainers' list with nearly £10,000 less than the newcomer in winning stakes. When asked to name the greatest racehorse trainers of his time, Noel listed Alec Taylor, Dick Dawson Fred Darling and Frank Butters. It was an interesting choice.

Frank Butters was one of the most successful and respected trainers of his time. He was born in Vienna, the eldest son of Joseph Butters and, after being educated in England, he returned to Austria, where he helped his father train for some years before becoming private trainer to Mautrer de Markham. During the First World War he was interned in Austria and, after the Armistice in 1918 he trained successfully in Italy. In 1926 he succeeded the Honourable George Lambton as Lord Derby's trainer, with a four-year contract. He won the St Leger and the Eclipse Stakes with Fairway, the Eclipse with Colorado, the One Thousand Guineas with Fair Isle, the Oaks with Toboggan and the Gold Cup with Bosworth. All four belonged to Lord Derby and he won the Oaks for Lord Durham with Beam. However, in August 1930 Lord Derby informed him that, owing to the world economic crisis, he was reducing his racing commitments and that the trainer's contract would not be renewed. Thus, at the age of fifty-two, at a time of acute financial depression, Frank Butters found himself out of a job. However, he was not unemployed for long and, after the Aga Khan's break with Dick Dawson, he was asked to take the Aga's horses. He agreed to do so and trained them with immense success. At the start of the 1949 season Butters had already been champion trainer seven times and although sadly this was to be his last season, he was to prove that even in his seventy-first year, he had lost none of his great skill.

1949 was another tremendous year for Noel and the Beckhampton stable. Of the older horses The Cobbler had remained in training and was to justify the decision of keeping him on as a four-year-old by winning the Wokingham Stakes at Royal Ascot under 9 stone 4 pounds.

Noel's bargain yearling purchases, Ridge Wood and Krakatao, now began to justify their trainer's faith, winning in April at Sandown, a meeting which Noel often used as a stepping stone to greater things.

Abernant was so impressive when he won his first race at Bath on 6 April, that Noel decided to run him in the Guineas. 'I did not think that he would stay the mile,' he says. 'But Gordon believed that he would last out.' The decision was confirmed by Royal Forest showing signs of temperament. Furthermore neither Faux Tirage or Wat Tyler, good as they were, clearly had any chance of defeating Abernant.

Although the colt he was riding was only a sprinter, albeit the best in the world, Gordon so nearly stole that Two Thousand Guineas at Newmarket on 27 April. Noel's eyes light up as he recalls the day. 'Gordon rode the most wonderful race,' he says. 'He slipped Abernant out of the gate and let him run. He was about three lengths in front coming out of the Dip and Nimbus was picking him up quietly all the way. Gordon dared not move on the horse and he sat as still as a mouse until the last stride. Nimbus just collared him and beat him a short head. If anyone but Gordon had been on him it would have been four or five lengths. It was yet another education in race-riding by a great champion.'

It is amazing than even at that early stage, our quiet north country trainer seemed to have no difficulty in making that most difficult of decisions – which horse to choose for the greatest test of all, the Derby. Atty Persse used to joke that he once had four runners in the Derby but the nearest that he ever got in fifty years of training was fourth. But the Derby never held much significance for Atty. He said, 'I'll leave that race to the idealists. Me, I want to make money for my owners and myself.' Noel, unlike Atty, was never a betting man, yet he always managed to combine idealism and profit.

In 1949 the process of elimination must have been more difficult than usual. There was no question of running Abernant over a mile and a half, and Faux Tirage and Wat Tyler were no more than first class milers. The King's Berrylands had won a little race at Salisbury in May but was clearly not good enough for the Derby. There might have been a temptation to run both Ridge Wood, and Krakatao (who had won again at Newmarket) but not for Noel. He knew that they had not yet come to their best and he decided that Royal Forest would be Beckhampton's representative in the Epsom classic.

For a fortnight before the big race Noel followed Fred Darling's example and worked the colt twice a week round the replica Epsom gallop at Beckhampton. He went splendidly and appeared to be an ideal type for the Derby. This impression was confirmed when Gordon rode him round Tattenham Corner the day before the race. As was to be his practice throughout the years in races big and small, Noel produced Royal Forest trained to the minute for the Derby. At Epsom the blaring funfair and the screaming crowds so close to the runners as they parade and then make their way to the start, make the Derby as much a test of temperament as of galloping ability and stamina. And on this occasion, Noel remembers that 'although he was so highly strung, Royal Forest would have won the Derby, but Bobby Jones had a horse in the race, just because his owner wanted to have a runner. The bloody thing put its foot through the reins when it got down to the post and it took them twenty minutes to get it out. By then, what with the parade and all the other preliminaries, it was as though Royal Forest had run four races. The sweat was pouring off him and his chance was gone. Even then he started favourite, was in a good position throughout the race and still finished fourth behind Nimbus, Amour Drake and Swallow Tail, who were divided by heads in the first Derby photo-finish.'

He added, 'Royal Forest proved what a decent horse he really was at the end of July when he won the Gordon Stakes at Goodwood with the greatest of ease from a pretty good field.'

Now it was Abernant's turn to prove that he was the real sprint champion. At Royal Ascot where Faux Tirage won the St James' Palace Stakes and The Cobbler took the Wokingham, Abernant turned out for the last race of the meeting, the five furlong King's Stand Stakes. He started at 6–4 on and never gave his supporters a moment's worry. Gordon had him out of the gate like a flash and won unchallenged by four lengths. Now followed all the other jewels in the crown of the sprint champion – the July Cup at Newmarket, the King George Stakes at Goodwood and the

Nunthorpe at York. His trainer rembers that 'Abernant was a wonderful horse, the kindest animal in the world. He used to stand in his box with his tongue hanging out and, when Julie was a kid, she would lie under him playing with his tongue. But he could be a monkey on the racecourse and he would have a good jump and a kick in the parade ring. He never dropped Gordon – not many did – but we had to have him ridden and led round the paddock.'

Gordon recalls the Nunthorpe Stakes at York. 'Abernant was a great favourite of mine, a tremendous character with a pronounced personality all his own. He was immensely interested in all that went on around him. He would canter quietly down to the start and then, when he got to the other side of the gate, he would give a great big sigh, prop himself lazily on three legs and have a look round at everything and everybody. That day at York we had to wait two or three minutes down at the starting-gate. There were four kids playing marbles down there and I was talking to the other jockeys. I gave Abernant his head and he raised his near leg and started playing marbles with them. He was just like a big faithful old dog. Then the starter said, "Come on jockeys, line up". I felt him suddenly tense up as usual and he was off like a bullet. You would never think he could be so relaxed one minute and then off like a machine right away. And he was indeed a real machine over six furlongs. He was a great horse.'

By the beginning of September Noel had a strong hand for the St Leger. Not only was Royal Forest fit again and justifiably a short price ante-post favourite for the final classic at Doncaster, but both Ridge Wood and Krakatao had come to themselves as Noel had known they would. Each of the colts that Noel bought at Doncaster as yearlings had won five good races and all three Beckhampton St Leger candidates worked well and came through their final preparation perfectly.

Noel says: 'I had arranged for Gordon to ride Royal Forest, Michael Beary for Krakatao and Willy Nevett for Ridge Wood. But a few days before the race I discovered that all was not well with Royal Forest. He had a slight bow in a tendon and could not possibly run.' Given the choice between the two remaining candidates, the stable jockey chose Krakatao leaving Ridge Wood for Beary. But that extra one and three-quarter miles on Doncaster's course was too much for Krakatao. Gordon had him up with the leaders turning into the long straight but he faded to finish fifth just behind the Derby third, Swallow Tail.

But all was not lost for Beckhampton. As Krakatao came to the end of his tether, Michael Beary sent Ridge Wood smoothly into the lead and stayed on well to win by three lengths from the Aga Khan's Dust Devil. It was Noel's second classic triumph and it gave him a particular satisfaction because from the very beginning it had been 'all my own work'.

On 22 October when Gold Mist won the Round Oak Handicap at Newbury, Noel had completed his second season at Beckhampton, and he closed the doors for the winter. He had won sixty-six races worth £62,523 which had placed him second on the list to Frank Butters.

During the 1949 season the stable jockey Gordon Richards had won 261 races, been placed second 144 times and third 82 times. Gordon's winning percentage was incredible – 33.67 per cent of all his 775 mounts. The champions of today win a hundred less races in a season.

Noel, whose lungs have never been strong, was not particularly happy at Beckhampton. 'It was so cold and damp that I never really felt well and, although Fred Darling's lads were good stable men, they were, in general, not the type that I like very much.' But he and Gwen were so happy to have retained so many of their old friends from Hambleton – Jim White, Billy Rea and Johnnie Mack from Ayr, now retired but still with them now at Woodditton.

The Murless owners in 1950 included King George VI, Colonel Giles Loder, Arthur Dewar, Fred Darling (who was still living just across from the stables), Sir Percy Loraine, Captain Arnold Wills, Major H. P. Hold, Colonel Basil Hornung, David Hely-Hutchinson, Major and Mrs Macdonald-Buchanan, Lord Feversham and Geoffrey Smith.

Noel's older horses at the time were Abernant, Wat Tyler, Krakatao, and Ridge Wood who was retired to stud. He had won seven races, including the St Leger, and more than £21,000. Krakatao, the second of those bargain yearlings, proved to be one of the best four-year-olds of the season, winning the Rous Memorial at Ascot, the Bottisham at Newmarket and the Chesterfield Cup at Goodwood carrying 9 stone 7 pounds, in a common canter.

Krakatao was the stable's only Royal Ascot winner that year though there were two narrow defeats for Abernant and Wat Tyler. In this, his final season, Abernant was once again to cover himself with glory retiring as the undisputed sprint champion having won the Lubbock Sprint Stakes at Sandown, Newmarket's July Cup, the King George Stakes at Goodwood and the Nunthorpe at York. He was only defeated at Ascot in the King's Stand Stakes when he was set to concede no less than 23 pounds to Tangle, the fine three-year-old trained by Bill Payne at Lambourn. Bill Payne told me, 'The horse that could give mine 23 pounds has not yet been born.'

There were only three runners in this the last race on the programme of the Royal Meeting, the third being Skylarking II, trained in France and ridden by Doug Smith. This was the year when British racing began fully to realise the significance of French horses, who won four of five classic English races – the One Thousand Guineas with Canaree, the Derby with Galcador, the Oaks with Asmena and the St Leger with Scratch II. The last three were owned by the late Marcel Boussac and ridden by Australian jockey Rae Johnstone.

All the same the French horse was rightly considered not to be in the same class as either Abernant or Tangle, the latter ridden by Eph Smith, a fine jockey in the English classic style. Intrepid punters made Abernant favourite at 11–4 on with Tangle at 3–1 and Skylarking unconsidered at 12–1. It was a memorable race. Abernant slipped out of the gate fast as usual but Eph was with him and the grey never really came away from his rival. Tangle challenged below the distance and won, hard driven, by half a length and Gordon said, 'It was a very tough assignment and Abernant did not seem to have his usual sparkle that day.' Noel's comment, 'It was both our faults that he was beaten. Gordon wanted to hold him up and I said that if he did so and got beat, he would be blamed. I told him that he had better let the colt run his own race. In the end we compromised and didn't do one thing or the other. I am sure that if he had been allowed to step out as he liked, the other horse would never have got him.'

In addition to the French classic successes, 1950 was also notable for the arrival in England of Arthur ('Scobie') Breasley, who must rank with the best jockeys from Australia who have ever ridden in Britain. Scobie rode his first winner in Australia in August 1928, came to England later that year to ride for Noel Cannon, the Druids Lodge trainer, and swiftly made his reputation. Level-headed, businesslike, unemotional, a dedicated professional, Scobie was a superb judge of pace and excelled in split-second timing. He was a master at winning on two-year-olds or highly-strung fillies without giving them a hard race and, throughout his career, although never as popular as Lester Piggott, he gave racing connoisseurs continual pleasure.

Sir Percy Loraine's topping little chestnut Wat Tyler, a son of Lord Derby's wartime Derby winner Watling Street, won two races for Noel that year and in the Royal Hunt Cup he was set to give 8 pounds to Hyperbole, a very useful five-year-old from Druids Lodge. Gordon Richards who later as a trainer was to employ Scobie as his stable jockey, now learned to his cost the strength of the newcomer. There were twenty runners for that famous handicap run over Ascot's straight seven furlongs, 155 yards and Wat Tyler was favourite at 100–30. Knowing that his mount was carrying the steadier of 9 stone 2 pounds, the champion jockey decided to give him a chance and hold him up for a late run. A superb judge of pace, he knew that the leaders would not be able to keep up with the fast early gallop at which the race is always run. He was correct in his estimation, but, as they began to come back to him a quarter of a mile from home, Gordon found himself uncharacteristically boxed in. At the same time, Breasley, another wonderful judge of pace, made his effort and, by the time they reached the distance he had Hyperbole in a commanding lead. Gordon finally extricated himself and fought back with tremendous power but though little Wat Tyler stuck out his neck it was just not good enough and on the line they were beaten by a short head.

Noel did remarkably well in 1950 to finish fifth on the list of British trainers because the three-year-olds were decidedly moderate and so, too, with the possible exception of Giles Loder's Seraphin and Crawley Beauty, were the two-year-olds. Noel remembers working the two-year-olds with Gordon before the Epsom summer meeting. 'Each lot worked worse than the one before and by the time we had finished and got back to the house both Gordon and I were feeling so depressed that I decided to open a bottle of champagne. By the time we had finished the second bottle the two-year-olds seemed considerably better. At the end of the

61

third we decided that there were definitely some very high-class animals among them. As we downed the fourth bottle there were classic prospects among them, Gordon was standing on the arm of a chair singing as he usually does at a party and I was laughing my head off helplessly. We sent for Herbert Blagrave to help us finish off the fifth and sixth. All this time Gordon's private aircraft was standing by waiting to fly him down to Shoreham where he was staying for the Epsom meeting and where his wife Margery was waiting for him. I am afraid she had to wait for nearly five hours, and when the plane finally arrived and the door was opened, Gordon fell out on his head. Just the same he rode three winners and a second at Epsom the next day.'

Early in 1950 Noel returned from a holiday to find in his yard a colt by Persian Gulf and Precipitation belonging to Mrs Vera Lilley. Noel had no room for the colt – Supreme Court – and he was sent back, to be subsequently trained by Evan Williams at Kingsclere for whom he won the Horris Hill Stakes in 1950. Supreme Court was unbeaten as a three-year-old in 1952, winning the King George VI and Queen Elizabeth Festival of Britain Stakes, the King Edward VII Stakes and the Chester Vase. The Guv'nor was later to train many winners for Mrs Vera Hue-Williams, as she became, vice-chairman of Berger, Jenson and Nicholson Ltd., who with her husband Colonel Hue-Williams, owns the Woolton Hill Stud at Newbury and the Rathasker Stud in County Kildare.

In the spring of the same year Fred Darling's mare Pasqua had foaled a big, powerful, slightly coarse bay colt by the high-class French stallion Chanteur II. Noel says, 'Fred never liked him at all and, when he was weaned, he refused to have him running with his own colts. So we had to send a colt down from our own stud in Yorkshire, The Cliff, to keep him company.' The Chanteur II colt was to be named Pinza.

There had been no Royal winners so far that year, but now Noel was delighted to win six races for the King with Deuce, Good Shot and Fair and Game, and the season ended with a total of forty-five wins worth £22,799, all ridden by Gordon, who was once again champion with 227 winners compared with 117 scored by his nearest rival Doug Smith.

By the end of 1951 Noel was becoming disenchanted with Beckhampton. By now the Guv'nor's reputation was so formidable that there was no shortage of owners keen to obtain his services. He says, 'The Aga Khan wanted me to come to Newmarket to train some of his horses and Sir Victor Sassoon, who had originally wanted me to train for him at Hambleton after the war, was again anxious for me to take his horses over.' Noel had had no room to train for Sassoon at Beckhampton but, when Fred Darling sent Pinza to the yearling sales of 1951 it was Noel who persuaded Sir Victor to buy the colt for only 1500 guineas. 'I would have trained him, too,' he said, 'but Fred Darling, who was sitting beside Sassoon, called to me and by the time I had turned back, the new owner had arranged to send the colt to Jack Clayton for whom Norman Bertie, Fred's former travelling head man, held the licence.'

Back in 1938, after dancing with Gwen at the Turnberry Hotel in her native Ayrshire, Sassoon gallantly presented her with the aged Massine mare Limace who had failed to breed at stud. Gwen had sent Limace to be trained by Noel and, as we know, Miss G. Carlow's mare was the young trainer's first winner of 1939 in the Wolviston Handicap Plate at Stockton.

A member of a famous Jewish family that emigrated from Baghdad to India early in the nineteenth century, Sir Victor Sassoon was educated at Harrow and Cambridge and succeeded to the baronetcy in 1924. In the First World War he served in the Royal Flying Corps, and his business interests were mainly concerned with E. D. Sassoon and Co., bankers, merchants and mill owners. He came into racing almost by accident. While in India he had met Jimmy Crawford, the son of an Ayrshire blacksmith and a successful amateur rider on the Indian turf. In 1922 Crawford went to England to train for Mr M. Goculdas, a Bombay cotton magnate and when Goculdas got into financial difficulties, Sassoon took over his racing interests, consisting of over a hundred horses in India and a number in England. In India he raced as 'Mr Eve' and, when he started a stud in Newmarket, he called it the Eve Stud. In 1925 Sassoon really began to launch out on the English turf when he spent what was then considered a fortune on yearlings. He also bought Fitzroy House Stables in Newmarket and installed Jimmy Crawford as his trainer. Those 1925 yearlings included Hot Night who, ridden by Harry Wragg, ran second to Call Boy in the Derby of 1927. When Jimmy Crawford died Sassoon divided his horses between Basil

Jarvis, Joe Lawson, Matt Peacock, and Jack Rogers, Noel's and Gwen's great friend in Ireland.

Jimmy Crawford must have served his owner mighty well. In 1935 Sir Victor won the Irish Triple Crown with Museum, and two years later he won the One Thousand Guineas and the Oaks with Exhibitionist (who was by Solario out of Lady Wembly – a mare bought by Crawford for only 750 guineas), the Irish Two Thousand Guineas and the Irish Derby with Phideas.

The 1952 season started well enough for Noel. Agitator trotted up in the Two Thousand Guineas Trial at Kempton, and Refreshed won the Lambourn Stakes at Newbury, a race now renamed the Fred Darling Stakes. These two were clearly a long way in front of the other three-year-olds at Beckhampton, but two successes were not good enough for Noel. Agitator ran a good race in the Two Thousand Guineas but only finished fourth, and Refreshed was third in the One Thousand. Most of the maiden three-year-olds won but, with the exception of Buckhound who was to train on into a high-class four-year-old, their careers were finished. Two-year-olds like Cyrus the Great and Turbulence performed well at Salisbury, only to disappoint at Ascot. In the words of the old racing adage even the best trainers and jockeys, among whom Noel and Gordon could undoubtedly be counted, 'cannot come without the horse' and the horses of Beckhampton in 1952 could not match their standards.

Early in the year Noel had acquired a new, knowledgeable, enthusiastic owner. King George VI had spent Christmas with his family at Sandringham and, at the end of January Princess Elizabeth and her husband Prince Philip represented him in East Africa, Australia and New Zealand. A week after their departure the King died peacefully in his sleep after a day's rough shooting at Sandringham. The new Queen and Prince Philip heard the news in Kenya and came back to London. In due course it was announced that the Queen would race on the same lines as her father and that the horses leased from the National Stud would continue to be trained by Noel.

ABOVE   The Guv'nor with Jim White leading in St Paddy after the 1960 Derby win
BELOW   Pinturischio ridden by Lester Piggott, winner of the Wood Ditton Stakes, Newmarket, 1961

While the Court was in mourning, Her Majesty's horses carried the colours of the Duke of Norfolk, so that Noel's first winner for his Royal patron, Ardent at Chepstow on 2 June, ran in the Duke's name. He won seven races for the Queen that season with Ardent, Infernal Machine, Black Bee, and High Service.

1952 was remarkable in racing for the Triple Crown victory of the Aga Khan's Tulyar, a little bay colt by Tehran out of the Nearco mare, Neocracy. Runner-up to him in the Derby and in the King George VI and Queen Elizabeth Stakes was Gay Time, son of Rockefella, owned by the widow of Mr J. V. Rank and ridden by the sixteen-year-old prodigy, Lester Piggott. During Goodwood week the National Stud bought Gay Time for £50,000 – then a record price for the stud – and, after he had won the Gordon Stakes, ridden by Gordon in the Queen's colours, he came to Beckhampton. Noel soon discovered that those hard races against Tulyar had left their mark on Gay Time and this was something that not even Noel's skill could counter. Gordon said later, 'We used to have to coax him on to the gallops and he did not work as a high-class horse ought to. We hoped he would be different on a racecourse and he ran in the St Leger, running well for one and a quarter miles, but then there was nothing left. Smirke on Tulyar nearly got into trouble over this, he was trailing me, naturally thinking that as an old rival, Gay Time was the danger. But he saw in a flash that I was done. He just got out in time to go on to win.'

A few weeks earlier, while in his beloved Yorkshire for the Festival meeting at York, Noel had finally made up his mind about the future. His father and mother were looking after the Cliff Stud for him and Gwen, and together with Gordon, they discussed the Aga Khan's offer and the prospect of moving to Newmarket. There was no doubt that the Guv'nor had had enough both of Beckhampton and of Arthur Dewar. So he flew to Paris to talk the matter over with the Aga Khan and with his son Prince Aly, that admirable and delightful character who had long been Noel's and Gwen's great friend. Apart from his immense charm, Prince Aly was also highly intelligent, a first-class judge of a horse and of form and breeding. It is probably fair to say that, with his experience of international racing, he was the best judge of collateral form in the world, and his

Aurelius, winner of the St Leger in 1961, with his owner, Mrs Vera Lilley flair for pedigrees was unique. He was immensely popular with the racing public because of his perfect manners and his sense of fun.

It was arranged that Noel should take over some of the Aga's yearlings to train for the next season, so Noel and Gwen went to Newmarket and bought Warren Place. Arthur Dewar was somewhat surprised when he learned that Noel was not going to renew his lease at Beckhampton and, says the Guv'nor, 'Fred Darling, who was still there, was rather annoyed about it.'

The last winner from Beckhampton was Geoffrey Smith's Cavour who, ridden by Gordon, won the £242 Stayers' Handicap at Folkestone on 6 September.

Says Gwen, 'It was some move. We, our lads and more than fifty horses all slept at Beckhampton on Sunday night and on Monday night we were in our own beds at Warren Place. But there was very little furniture in the house itself and, when the Press arrived asking "Where are the staff?", Cathy and I looked at each other and I said "We are the staff!"'

5

First Years at Warren Place: 1952–1955

❀

Warren Place dominates the headquarters of racing. Most of the other yards lie within the town itself, but Warren Place is outside, raised above it all on Warren Hill. After three-quarters of a mile at the top of the slope is a wooded area and there on the right are the studs and on the left is Warren Place, surrounded by its cottages and the covered ride built by Noel. The house itself was built by Fred Darling's brother, Sam. It's a rambling place, roofed with tiles that are now unobtainable and built with old seasoned timbers.

Warren Place immediately became home to Noel, Gwen, Julie, Cathy, Jim White, Old Mack, Billy Rea and all the others. With the predictable exception of Dewar, every single one of the Beckhampton owners, including the Queen, came with Noel to Warren Place. Even Gordon, with his love of the downland country, refused a retainer from Arthur Dewar and joined the team.

There were five more winners that year and appropriately the last, on 4 November was the Queen's High Service in the Queen Bess Plate at Birmingham.

Gordon had won 231 races in 1952. He was champion jockey for the twenty-fifth time and he was getting very excited at the prospect of winning his first Derby. The Epsom classic had always eluded him but now the giant bay Pinza had shown the most promise, rounding off the season by winning the seven-furlong Dewhurst Stakes at Newmarket by five lengths in most impressive style.

During the winter months Noel was able to relax, stretching his long legs in the space around Warren Place, enjoying his family and playing with his dogs. In training were a likely-looking bunch of yearlings which included Princely Gift, a promising bay colt by

67

Nasrullah out of Blue Gem by Blue Peter bought for only 4000 guineas at the sales on behalf of Sir Victor Sassoon. There was also Queen's Landau, a handsome colt by Derby winner Dante out of Sun Chariot, the Aga Khan's Bara Bibi and a lovely filly called Queen of Hind, by Nearco out of Queen of Baghdad. Elopement, the full brother to Gay Time seemed likely as did Key and Rashleigh, though the latter, a son of Precipitation, was still very backward.

Noel had worked wonders with Gay Time and it gave him great pleasure to make a strong start to the season by winning the March Stakes at Newmarket with the big chestnut on 30 April in the Coronation year.

The day before the Coronation the entire country was en fête. After a lovely fresh hazy start to the day, the sun was already blazing down when I opened my newspaper to read that racing had been honoured by the inclusion of Gordon Richards, in the Coronation Honours List, the very same Gordon who happened to be riding my own little filly Mirabelle in the second race at Leicester that very afternoon. A week earlier, ridden by my apprentice, she had finished second at Warwick. Now she was tipped by all the papers to win the Billestone Plate for the new knight. As always Gordon was complete master of the situation. Any excitement he may have felt was quite hidden behind the big, twinkling eyes and the charming self-deprecating smile as he received the congratulations that were showered on him. He finished fourth in the first race and, when I put him up on Mirabelle, he admitted that he would dearly love to ride at least one winner during that memorable afternoon. My little filly and her jockey were admirably suited. Starting at 5–2 on, she flew out of the gate, made all the running and won by eight lengths to tremendous cheers.

Fred Darling was dying at Beckhampton, but he lived long enough to know that Gordon had at last won the Derby on Pinza, the horse that he had bred and which, as his successor, Noel had persuaded Sir Victor Sassoon to buy.

Despite all Noel's efforts, Gay Time never recovered his courage and, after he had been well beaten into third place in the Hardwicke Stakes at Royal Ascot, it was decided to sell him to Japan. Despite his disappointment over Gay Time the Guv'nor won three races for Her Majesty with Landau and the first season at Warren Place ended with Noel seventh on the trainers' list, with forty-four wins worth

£28,182. He had won races for all his new owners, including the Aga Khan and Sir Victor Sassoon, whose Elopement and Princely Gift held considerable promise for the future. Gordon finished the season with 191 winners, champion jockey for the twenty-sixth and, as it was to turn out, the last time. He says now that, although he had told no one, he had already decided to retire at the end of the 1954 season.

Just as he had done at Beckhampton, the Guv'nor had taken no time at all to acclimatise himself to Newmarket and to adjust to its gallops. He discovered that horses need more work at Newmarket, not because of the flat terrain compared with the hills of Yorkshire and Wiltshire, but because of the *texture* of the gallops. The grass turf of the heath takes far less out of a galloping horse than the matted moorland of Hambleton or the springy virgin downland of Beckhampton. But, cautions the Guv'nor, 'In the hottest, hardest weather you could work two-year-olds up that summer gallop at Hambleton getting them really fit, so that when you brought them out on to the hard ground at the racecourse, they would win first time out. But the next time they met hard ground they did not like it so much!'

So much is heard nowadays about watered racecourses, watered gallops and all-weather surfaces, that Noel's views are relevant and interesting. He loves Newmarket's traditional summer gallop, The Limekilns, where for many, many years racehorses of the highest calibre have galloped in the hottest summer droughts. He explains, 'The Limekilns is right on chalk and in sunny weather the chalk comes to the top so that you get an almost powdery surface there. That only happens in the summer heat. It's an ideal surface. A horse coming off The Limekilns on to a hard racecourse is quite happy. I have always been against watering. It makes the ground so false. The grass grows up instead of down to look for moisture. What's more, with the watering systems they have in this country, one spot will get fifty gallons and ten yards away the course will be lucky to get five.'

Gordon's Derby ride in 1954 was to have been Landau. Part of the prejudice against the colt was due to his colour. Blacks have always been unpopular in racing, regarded as temperamental, unreliable and even unlucky. Gordon rode Landau in the Derby Trial Stakes at Lingfield and thought he should have won instead of finishing second, beaten by a length. 'It was the same old tale again,' he said, 'when you asked him to do something, he either would not or could not.'

Soon after, while riding Misty Night at Salisbury, Gordon was brought down when an apprentice fell in front of him after touching the heels of another horse. The champion was badly concussed and remained unconscious until he woke up in Salisbury hospital. Reluctantly Gordon decided that he would not be well enough to ride Landau in what was to have been his last Derby, so Landau went to Willie Snaith, a grand little jockey who had been apprenticed to Sam Armstrong and who has been with the Guv'nor ever since. They finished eighth. Elopement, ridden by Charlie Smirke, was fourth. And the winner was Never Say Die, a big liver chestnut, son of Nasrullah, trained by Joe Lawson and ridden by eighteen-year-old Lester Piggott.

Never Say Die had finished third in the Dewhurst Stakes as a two-year-old and second, ridden by Lester, in his first race of the following season, the Union Jack Stakes at Liverpool. Then the late Manny Mercer, Joe's brother, had the mount in the Newmarket Stakes and was third behind Noel's Elopement. Suddenly out of the blue a telegram from Joe Lawson arrived at Piggott's Lambourn home. 'You ride Never Say Die in Derby.' One of the oldest trainers had selected the youngest jockey. He had no cause to regret his choice. Young Lester handled the colt with all the cool of a veteran to win comfortably by two lengths from Arabian Night, with Mercer on Darius a neck away third.

Gordon, still shaken from his fall, was at Sandown's weekend meeting before Royal Ascot. He rode Sun Festival for Noel to second place on Friday and was back in the winner's enclosure again on Saturday. The Warren Place horses were in great form and on the third day of the Royal meeting Gordon won the Cork and Orrey on Key. Then came the King Edward VII Stakes, in which the Warren Place candidate Rashleigh was due to take on the Derby winner. As opposed to Epsom, Ascot is constantly turning to the right and Lester Piggott knew that he would have his work cut out to keep Never Say Die balanced in this one and a half mile race, in which he was giving 8 pounds to the Epsom runner-up. So, at the weights, Arabian Night was favourite at 13–8 with the Derby winner at 7–4. Rashleigh was third in demand at 5–1.

The jockeys' accounts of this controversial race, which sparked off one of the racing sensations of the decade, are interesting.

Gordon: 'Coming into the straight, Blue Prince and Dragonfly were making the running, with Rickaby on Garter third, Gosling on Arabian Night fourth and I was fifth. Dragonfly dropped out and Rickaby and I began to move up to the leader. All of a sudden, Lester Piggott on Never Say Die started to make a move. I was on the outside, so I do not know whether Never Say Die was hanging or not. Lester claimed he was. At any rate, Never Say Die charged into Garter, hit my quarters and practically turned me round. Then Never Say Die charged Garter again, and Garter turned me broadside on. I suspect that it did look, from the stands, as if my horse was doing the damage; but, if another horse hits yours in the rump, it will throw you into him, and that's what happened. Rashleigh recovered marvellously and he and Tarjoman – ridden by that splendid French jockey Poincelet – went on to challenge Arabian Night, who had taken up the running with Blue Prince. Arabian Night dived twice, first of all putting Blue Prince on to Tarjoman and then Tarjoman on to me. But Rashleigh would not be beaten whatever happened to him and he went on to win. Of course it was a most unsatisfactory race and the Stewards objected to me. But immediately they had heard the evidence, they withdrew their objection. They did, however, stand Lester Piggott down.'

Lester told them, 'It all happened soon after we entered the straight. I was lying handy on the rails. As there were three horses in front of me, who were beginning to weaken, I decided to switch to the outside to give my horse the chance of a long unimpeded run with that great style of his. As I started to move, however, one of the leaders dropped back and, at that moment Gordon came from behind further outside and proceeded to ride in. First he lay on the other horse. Then, although looking across he could see I hadn't much room, he pushed the other horse (I think it was Lord Rosebery's Garter, ridden by Bill Rickaby), right on top of me. Of course there was a big bump and the other horse was half turned. My horse was hanging towards his favourite left-hand side which, of course, didn't help matters. Anyway Gordon went on and won by a length. I finished fourth. As soon as we got back the Stewards objected to Gordon – rightly, in my opinion – but, when they heard the evidence of the other jockeys, they withdrew their objection and turned their objection to me, claiming that I had been trying to force my way out.'

The Ascot Stewards, with no film to guide them, completely exonerated everyone but Lester. They listened to the evidence of the other jockeys, such as it was, and heard the eighteen-year-old boy's stumbling version. Then they suspended him for the rest of the meeting, and reported him to the Stewards of the Jockey Club. The Duke of Norfolk headed the Cavendish Square enquiry. There was no question of a caution or a fine, the normal punishment in those days, even though the issue was so controversial. They suspended Lester for six months and ordered his father to send him to another trainer.

Today Lester says, 'I was absolutely dumbfounded. I just couldn't believe it. Again I felt that everyone was against me and I still insist that this was an unnecessarily savage sentence which did no good at all.' And Noel agrees. 'It was a damned shame that Lester was stood down like that,' he says. 'It was most unfair.' Lester was ordered to leave home and go to Newmarket to 'do his two' and ride out under the instruction of Lord Rosebery's trainer, Jack Jarvis. 'As the old man was sick in bed the whole time I was there,' says Lester, 'that was a fat lot of good!'

Few people realized what suspension meant to the dedicated boy. 'My life stopped,' he says, 'because racing is my whole life. It is my work and my pleasure at one and the same time.' The blow was struck at the height of the season. Apart from all the other winners, he missed riding Never Say Die in the St Leger. Charlie Smirke substituted for him and won by twelve lengths. The same Racing Calendar that carried the official announcement of Piggott's six-month suspension reported that Manny Mercer had been fined £50 for striking Davy Jones with his whip in a race. How could the two sentences be reconciled?

The following day Noel and Gordon had another victory at Royal Ascot in the Rous Memorial Stakes with Landau who went on to win the Ellesmere Stakes for the Queen at Newmarket's July Meeting a fortnight later. Gordon was still riding all the Warren Place winners but not for much longer. At Sandown on 9 July he rode Princely Gift to win the Ditton Sprint Handicap for Noel and Sassoon, the same Princely Gift who, when Noel had bought her as a yearling, had caused Sir Victor to complain fretfully: 'next time you buy a rabbit for me buy the hutch as well!' By the following day Gordon had ridden fifty-four winners overall and was once again well ahead in the jockeys' list. He was due to ride a two-year-old filly called Abergeldie in the Star Stakes and this filly, like Landau who had just finished third in the Eclipse, belonged to the Queen.

Gordon was riding in a one-pound dock (a tiny saddle) and the filly may have felt it a bit cold on her back. The accident happened as Gordon was walking her up the pathway to the stable yard. Abergeldie half reared up and then went right up on her hind legs as they went down the gravel track past the grandstand to the course. A colt will not come over backwards unless he is pulled over, but a thoroughbred filly will sometimes suddenly flip over on to her back. Unfortunately, on this occasion, Gordon was underneath. When he was X-rayed in hospital, it was found that he had fractured and dislocated his pelvis. It was the end of the champion's racing career.

Noel always liked to have a stable jockey who could ride out at home and get to know the horses' idiosyncrasies. Gordon had excelled in this capacity and Noel missed him terribly. For the next three months the rides were shared by Willie Snaith, who was part of the team at Warren Place, and Charlie Smirke, already retained by the Aga Khan, and who had ridden a number of winners for the Aga and Prince Aly. Noel had three winners at Goodwood that year – Sir Percy Loraine's Baba Ali in the Craven Stakes, the Queen's Landau in the Sussex and Mrs D. M. FitzPatrick's Key in the Nassau Stakes.

A fortnight after Lester Piggott's first classic winner, Never Say Die, won the St Leger in the hands of Charlie Smirke, the Jockey Club realized that they had overstepped the mark. They lifted their ban after Lester had served over three months of his suspension, and on 4 October 1954 he was appointed to succeed Gordon as first jockey to the Guv'nor.

Gordon holds the record total of winners with 4870 from 21,834 mounts. He himself says that the secret was the will to win, and concentration on the job at all times.

Noel believes that balance is the great thing in jockeyship. 'Gordon had this immense strength in his legs and in his knees. He could hold on to an animal and keep it balanced whatever he did on top, riding with a loose rein, half turning round to drive it home.

Whatever he did, his horse was always perfectly balanced and running for him. I had to find a jockey to replace Gordon. One or two of the top ones approached me and I looked around. Then the old Aga suggested Lester or Manny Mercer. Apart from the fact that Mercer was not available in any case, I had always had leanings towards Lester. After all I had known both his father Keith and his grandfather Ernie for many years before. That was the way Lester came into the stable.'

Looking back Lester's own explanation of the trouble which started when he was fourteen and was to follow him through his career is typically simple. 'Old jockeys riding for old trainers and old Stewards.' Noel confirms this: 'The Stewards were on to Lester for any little thing at all.' Instead of fining him for minor infringements, as was the normal practice in those days, they would suspend him and report him to the Stewards of the Jockey Club – a sentence traditionally reserved for only the most heinous offences. It was like sending a little boy to be tried at the Old Bailey, and in the eyes of the law, Lester was just that – a boy of fourteen.

He says, however, 'I was not afraid then and I have never been afraid since when I have been summoned before the Stewards. Come to think of it, I don't think that I have been afraid of anyone or anything.' Nonetheless, he felt that the atmosphere was all wrong. 'Everyone was against me,' he said. 'It was a nasty feeling.' Lester has never lacked courage, moral or physical. He survived the vindictive suspensions and also a broken leg from a Lingfield accident – to come out hardened and more determined to ride winners and assist his trainer who, at that time, was the Guv'nor.

Elopement proved himself a good horse. After finishing second in the St Leger he won the Cumberland Lodge Stakes at Ascot. Princely Gift, whom Noel had allowed plenty of time to mature, justified this faith by winning the Challenge Stakes at Newmarket ridden by Lester. Four days later Lester won the Wheat Sheaf Stakes at Sandown on Rashleigh, the same colt which, in the hands of Sir Gordon, had brought about his unjustified downfall at Ascot.

Forty-four races worth £41,240 and fourth place on the trainers' list was a fair ending to the muddled season of 1954. Highlights of the 1955 season, in which Lester rode all but three of the thirty-six winners for Warren Place, were the victories of Elopement in the Hardwicke Stakes at Ascot and, on the following day of the

Queen's Jardinière in the King George V Stakes. But the race that gave Noel the greatest pleasure was undoubtedly the tremendous triumph under 9 stone 4 pounds of Princely Gift, after Abernant one of the highest class sprinters in the Portland Handicap at Doncaster. Like nearly all Noel's top-class colts Princely Gift proved himself a consistently successful stallion, passing on the Nasrullah blood to So Blessed, King's Troop, Floribunda and Faberge II, sire of Rheingold, the Arc de Triomphe winner.

Hubert Hartigan, Noel's greatest friend and Julie's godfather, died in 1955. He had done so much for Noel and even in his death Hubert was able to help his protégé. With bitter sweet feelings Noel took into the yard at Warren Place a horse of tremendous quality called Hugh Lupus. Bred by the late Duke of Westminster and raced by his daughter Lady Ursula Vernon, Hugh Lupus was foaled in 1952. He was born in France and his pedigree was essentially French, as he was by Djebel out of a mare by Goya. He was trained in Ireland by Hubert and on Hubert's death went first to Jimmy Lenehan and then to Noel. He was an unlucky horse who, after winning the Irish Two Thousand Guineas would have probably won the Derby at Epsom but for injuring himself just before the race. Noel trained Hubert's horse with the supreme skill that he had learned from his old friend. He won five races with him in 1956 – the Fryston Stakes at Pontefract, the March Stakes at Newmarket, the Hardwicke Stakes at Royal Ascot, the Scarborough Stakes at Doncaster and finally his greatest triumph, the Champion Stakes at Newmarket. On every occasion he was ridden by the Australian Rae ('Togo') Johnstone, who had partnered him in France.

Noel says, 'He came to me at the end of his three-year-old days after he had run in the Arc. I thought I'd give him an easy race for a change. So I decided to run him at Pontefract. Julie and I drove up and hit a car on the way; still, we got there in time. Rae Johnstone had never been to Pontefract and he came round that elbow with the reins in three double handfuls, let him go to the front and he was winning so easily that he dropped his hands to canter home. Hugh Lupus almost stopped! As a result, one of Rufus Beasley's horses which would normally have finished a long way behind in second place, found itself beaten only a head by the classic horse. Poor Rufus. The handicapper never forgot and kept his animal right at the top of the handicap so that it never won again!'

75

6

The Classics
1955–1957

❖

In 1955 Noel took over the management of Sir Victor Sassoon's studs. Like all good trainers he has always attached tremendous importance to the correct breaking of yearlings. Balance, control, impulsion, trust and confidence in human beings, upon which will hang success or failure and the possible destination of millions of pounds all depend so much on the tuition that the highly-strung youngster receives in those few weeks. Unlike most other trainers, however, the Guv'nor always studied each animal from the very beginning. 'I never lay it down as standard drill,' he says. 'It depends on the yearling himself. I never liked driving them too much on long reins because I believe that the weight of the reins was very heavy on their mouths. That weight would harden their soft mouths. So some I did not drive at all and others I did not drive too much. I formed my own breaking staff, who were experts at the job of breaking yearlings.'

In the autumn of that year the yearlings who had been broken included a big, handsome, all-quality chestnut colt by the Italian champion Donatello II, whose son Alycidon, winner of the Ascot Gold Cup for Lord Derby, was in 1955 champion British sire, and whose daughter, Picture Play, had won the One Thousand Guineas for Mr Jim Joel and was to be the great granddam of Royal Palace. The yearling's dam was Mieuxce out of Red Sunset by Solario. The colt was called Crepello. The Guv'nor said, 'From the moment we started breaking him I knew that Crepello would be a champion. He had such tremendous pride and presence.'

The yearling fillies included Carrozza, a tiny bay by Dante out of Calash leased by the Queen from the National Stud, then under the management of Noel's life-long friend Peter Burrell. By the middle

76

of May, Carrozza was ready to have her first outing. Noel remembers, 'I ran two fillies in the Rosemary Plate at Hurst Park. I wanted Lester to ride my own filly, Shaken Bridge, as she was more forward than Carrozza. I tried to get hold of the Queen's racing manager, Captain Charles Moore, to get permission for my stable apprentice Lines to ride Carrozza, but he was abroad and I couldn't contact him before the race. So I felt that Lester had to ride for the Queen. Carrozza beat Lines and Shaken Bridge by half a length.' Shortly after her début, Carrozza reared over backwards, badly damaging her withers and had to be rested for nearly two months. After two unsuccessful runs later in the year she retired for the winter.

In 1956 Victor Sassoon was seventy-five. He still loved to have runners at Ascot. It was a good Royal Meeting for Noel that year winning the Queen Anne for Sassoon with Kandy Sauce, the King Edward VII Stakes for Vera Lilley with Court Command, and the Hardwicke with Hugh Lupus.

Over the winter Crepello had grown into a most impressive colt, standing over 16 hands 2 inches, powerfully built with a nice short back, lovely quarters and a strong second thigh. He had plenty of depth, splendid heartroom and spring of rib, and a fine head set on a good neck. He was already by far the best-looking horse of his age in the country. He had just one fault. Looking back now Noel says, 'Crepello's leg trouble was really my fault. I was to blame for it. Like all Donatello's colts he was a bit straight in front. I hadn't anything much to run for the old man at Ascot and Crepello had been working with the two-year-olds. I had never really galloped him but in his work he went exceptionally well. So I thought I would give him a run in the Windsor Castle Stakes at Royal Ascot. I told Lester, "Whatever happens, don't touch him with the whip, don't even show it to him." He was beaten a short head by a fast precocious colt trained by Geoffrey Brooke called Fulfer. Five or six days afterwards I felt the tiniest little notch, not as big as the end of a match, under his suspensory. I always hated anyone other than myself touching my horses' legs. Even the best head lads cannot help running their fingers down, feeling the animal's fore legs and, as often as not, they are responsible for breaking the horse down. So I had a pair of "Newmarket cloths" – sort of box cloth bandage – sewn on to his legs to stop anyone from feeling them. He wore

77

them all the time he was in training. Of course that little notch was always there in the back of my mind.'

Crepello was now given a long period of rest but he won the seven-furlong Dewhurst Stakes at Newmarket, on 1 November 1956, most impressively. Noel had won forty-seven races to the value of £37,872. He was full of quiet hope and some confidence as he left for a holiday in the sun.

There is a side to the Guv'nor known only to his relations and close friends. To the outside world he has always appeared shy, withdrawn and worried, carrying his responsibilities somewhat heavily. In fact he has a lovely twinkle and a tremendous sense of fun. Julie elaborates, 'Everyone thinks that Uncle Stu is the funny one of the two brothers. We were staying with the Sassoons in Nassau when Stu arrived with no swimming things. Dad lent him some shorts, which came down to his knees. They had some extraordinary cork chairs which floated on the swimming pool especially made with all sorts of fitments. Stu was floating around luxuriously in one of these chairs. He had a scotch in one hole and an ashtray in another and a dirty old pipe in his mouth. When he least suspected it, Dad jumped in and tipped him over backwards. Barney Sassoon was furious because there were bits of tobacco floating around in the pool for days afterwards. Dad has a wonderful sense of humour. He always sees the ridiculous side of everything.'

Unlike some Newmarket trainers Noel never kept his horses cantering through the winter. 'I always stopped them,' he says. 'I broke up their routine, stopped them at the end of October and let them down. They would then start trotting in January and cantering in February. I liked to break their routine and cut their feed and put them on a bit of soft hay. But I always gave my horses a very firm conditioning grounding before they started to do any fast work at all. That's very important. As I said earlier I had found that horses trained at Newmarket need more work than those trained on downland or the sort of ground we had at Hambleton. Beckhampton is downland and Newmarket is heathland. It is like bowling on a slow wicket and a fast wicket. A horse has to be really fit if he is going to run in the classics and I never spared Crepello.'

Jeremy Hindley says, 'It was an education to watch him working classic horses. When they set out on a classic campaign, they really went through it. Of course, most of the horses that he trained were so big that they would not have won if they had not had plenty of strenuous work. The galloping tackle would consist of good older horses to whom the three-year-old was giving weight. They would go a good gallop and then the classic horse would quicken up nicely and stride on in his own time while the other tried to stay with him.'

Soon after the Guv'nor returned home from Nassau old Martin Benson the bookmaker came up to Warren Place for a drink one night. Noel says, 'We were talking about the Classics over a whisky and soda. I said that, although I never had a bet, I would on this occasion like a £100 double on Crepello for the Two Thousand Guineas and the Derby. He gave me 66–1 for the double. I worked Crepello over the full mile before the Guineas, ridden by Lester. He worked with decent older horses like Kandy Sauce who had won at Royal Ascot, Riseborough and others, giving them weight. Crepello just trotted at them. He was so impressive that I decided that there was no need to give him a run before the Guineas.'

Noel had been able to report to the Queen that Carrozza had improved hugely since her two-year-old days. She had not grown much and indeed was a real pony standing barely 15 hands, but she was doing particularly well in that mild spring. Noel decided to run her on the final day of the Epsom meeting in the Princess Elizabeth Stakes for three-year-old fillies for which the Aga Khan's Rose Royale II, trained in France by Alec Head, was a hot favourite. Although he had won the 1954 Derby and several long-distance handicaps on the course, Lester's reputation as the greatest Epsom specialist had yet to be made. Now he rode a perfectly judged race in the Princess Elizabeth Stakes on Carrozza, winning cleverly from Rose Royale II. A few days earlier the Sassoon filly Sijui had won the Fred Darling Stakes at Newbury and was Noel's intended runner in the One Thousand Guineas but, after Epsom, he decided to saddle Carrozza as well.

First the Two Thousand Guineas and on that May Day Crepello, who had not had a race beforehand, was made second favourite at 7–2 behind Pipe of Peace, a colt trained by Sir Gordon that had previously won the Greenham Stakes at Newbury, a race traditionally regarded as a Guineas trial. Well fancied also at 100–8 in the betting was Quorum, the grey northern colt who had won the Free Handicap Stakes on the same course by a comfortable three lengths carrying 8 stone 7 pounds. Two good French colts, Tyrone, owned and bred by Madame Elizabeth Couturie, and Wayne II, were ridden respectively by Roger Poincelet and Freddy Palmer.

Poor Noel. Whenever he had a top-class classic horse, there always seemed to be a series of scares, and he and Gwen were pestered day and night before the race by a continual stream of telephone calls from the press checking to see if Crepello was fit to run. The bare result and the distances do not give a true indication of the impressive ease with which Crepello won. Lester held the big colt together well, joined Pipe of Peace and Tyrone at the distance, ran on into the lead 200 yards from home and had no difficulty in holding off Quorum's late challenge up the hill. Crepello won by half a length and a head from Quorum and Pipe of Peace, but, if Lester had let him down, it could have been so easily ten lengths.

The One Thousand Guineas was two days later. The Guv'nor recalls, 'Carrozza had got over her Epsom race so well and I knew that the fast ground at Newmarket would suit her. Lester chose to ride Sijui and I booked Bill Rickaby for Carrozza.' The Murless family and the Heads had been good friends for years. 'That filly of Alec's, Rose Royale II, whom Lester had beaten at Hurst Park, came back to Newmarket, stayed with me at Warren Place and duly won the One Thousand,' he says. 'Carrozza ran very well indeed to finish fourth well in front of Sijui.'

All the horses at Warren Place were now in tremendous form. Gwen's 'hack', Arctic Explorer, was already making a name for himself having won the Hastings Stakes and the Fen Ditton Stakes both at Newmarket.

Crepello was preparing for the Derby as expected. 'Once again I did not spare him,' says his trainer. 'He galloped brilliantly over the full distance of one and a half miles but, in the back of my mind, I still had that nagging worry about the notch on his suspensory.' A few days before the Derby rumours began to circulate that Crepello was going to have to miss the classic for which he was now firm favourite. He even drifted in the market to 11–4, only to go to 6–4 on the day of the race. It was also suggested that there were to be attempts to nobble him.

The going on that undulating, one-and-a-half-mile Derby course

Noel inspecting the new starting stalls at Newmarket, 1964

was hard and rough, with broken bottles on the track. With the roads and paths that he had to cross it was a nightmare for a bad-legged horse. Perhaps the worst hazard of all was the tarmac road, crossing the course by the pub a hundred yards past the winning post. This was covered with a light sprinkling of dirt or tan but was disturbed between every race by pedestrians and traffic. Any classic colt that had given his utmost in the greatest test of his life would be starting to pull up, still leading on his near fore-leg when he came to this road and inevitably he would lean towards his stables over on the right and change with a sickening jar on to his off fore. It is normal to give any horse a decent rest after running in the Derby and therefore damaged legs can pass unnoticed until the colt has got back into strong work and runs again. The number of horses in those days that developed leg trouble after running in the Derby must have been legion. Now, happily, an underpass has been built and the ground turfed over past the winning post.

It was a brilliant feat of Noel's to get Crepello to the post in the Derby. 'Lester was very easy on him in the race,' he says, 'but damage to the tendons was inevitable.' Lester rode Crepello with the cool tenderness of a veteran. The Irish challenger Ballymoss, ridden by T. P. Burns, took the lead two furlongs out but Lester was just biding his time, saving the legs of his great horse by keeping him on a tight rein. As soon as he met the rising ground he allowed Crepello to quicken and, still hard held, the champion swept past his rival to win by the easiest possible one and a half lengths. Pipe of Peace was third a further length away. Ballymoss, who had been defeated so convincingly, went on to win the Irish Derby and St Leger at Doncaster, the Coronation Cup, the Eclipse Stakes, the King George VI and Queen Elizabeth Stakes and the Prix de l'Arc de Triomphe. What sort of a horse was Crepello? Lester says of his mount that day, 'He was a really great horse. We never saw the best of him because of his legs. I could never let him down, you see, and so I am sure he was quite a bit better than he even showed.'

So Noel had landed his 66–1 double and there was even more triumph to come. He says, 'I didn't go racing on the Thursday but, when I arrived at Epsom on Friday, I bumped into old Benson, who

---

Busted, ridden by George Moore, wins the 1967 Eclipse Stakes at Sandown

81

congratulated me on my win. On the spur of the moment I said, 'I'll tell you what you can do. You can put me £50 on Carrozza. That was one of the best bets I ever had. She won at 100–8!' The Queen was represented in the Oaks that year not only by Carrozza but also by Mulberry Harbour, who was well-fancied by her trainer Cecil Boyd-Rochfort. Mulberry Harbour carried the first colours and was a firm second favourite behind the Aga Khan's One Thousand Winner Rose Royale II, on whom Charles Smirke had been replaced by the French jockey Jean Massard. Lester on Carrozza wore the Royal colours with a distinguished white cap. The northern-based Australian Edgar Brit rode Taittinger, trained by old Charles Elsey for Sassoon, and James Eddery, father of the future champion Pat, was on Silken Glider, the McGrath filly and the more fancied of two Irish challengers.

Carrozza's classic race was thrilling. Round Tattenham Corner Taittinger led from Mulberry Harbour with Carrozza lying about fifth as they entered the straight. Just as the Royal colours with the black cap on Mulberry Harbour started to go backwards, Lester's white cap somehow slipped through on the rails. He reports, 'I got through on the inside of Edgar Brit and Taittinger about two furlongs out. Taittinger had led into the straight and, as she weakened, I squeezed though with over two furlongs to go. I got the better of Rose Royale II who failed to stay, but up the final hill Jimmy Eddery on the Irish filly Silken Glider came at me, finishing very fast. Carrozza was only tiny and a bit lazy but she was game as a pebble. She was dying in the last hundred yards, but she gave everything she had and as we passed the post I didn't know whether we had held on or not. I did know that after a couple of strides after passing the post Jimmy Eddery was definitely in front.'

In those last desperate strides Lester had ridden with the inspiration of a truly great jockey and indeed as the two fillies passed the post seemingly locked together, no one knew which had won. Although King George VI had won a substitute race at Newmarket with Sun Chariot during the war there had never been a royal victory in the Oaks. It seemed an unconscionable time of waiting before the outcome of the photo-finish was declared. There was a stupendous cheer when it was announced that Carrozza had won and then the Queen, looking sublimely happy, emerged to lead in her filly. Noel says, 'I think it was the most brilliant race of Lester's entire career.' And Sir Gordon, summing up his successor, says, 'The secret of Lester's success is his confidence in his own genius. For he is a genius, as Steve Donoghue was before him. From the very beginning of his career he has instinctively known what to do and when to do it. Take Epsom, the trickiest course of them all. Lester never worries about the bends or the crowding or what the other jockeys are doing. Like Steve he gets into exactly the right position – about fourth or fifth – and then at the psychological moment he goes. That is how he was in that Oaks on Carrozza, one of the best races he has ever ridden. Just think of it! – He was only twenty-one. . . riding for the Queen. . . and it was the Oaks. But it made no difference to Lester. He behaved just as if it had been a selling race and, at precisely the right moment, before the other jockeys knew what was happening, he went. Believe me, he stole that race.'

Three classic winners in a season, including the great Epsom double, was an extraordinary achievement. But Noel was not finished yet. He enjoyed another good Ascot, winning the Queen Mary with Colonel Bernard Hornung's filly Abelia, and the King George VI Stakes with Arctic Explorer, who then went on to win the historic Eclipse Stakes at Sandown.

Suddenly, in the middle of this marvellous year, came a crisis that had been unforeseen. The Guv'nor is absolutely frank about the event that shook the fickle, jealous racing world. 'After the Derby Crepello was definitely jarred up and I did not want to run him again until Doncaster in September where, after a decent rest, I think I could have brought him back to win the St Leger and thus the Triple Crown. Though I wanted to cut him out until them I also had to consider the owner, Sir Victor Sassoon. The old boy was seventy-six and he wanted the horse to run in the King George VI and Queen Elizabeth Stakes at Ascot.'

Noel tried so hard to bring Crepello up to form for Ascot. 'The trouble was that I had nothing else of Sassoon's to run at the meeting,' he says. 'I thought, Well, he's *his* horse,' and I allowed myself to be overridden so we took him down to Ascot.' Right up to the eleventh hour the favourite was expected to run. 'Then a terrific thunderstorm produced the false ground that would have been fatal for him,' says the Guv'nor, 'and on the morning of the race it rained and rained.' He was severely and most unjustly criticised when Crepello failed to appear. Noel has never misled the public but has always tried to study the interests of his horses and of his owners, and it is a great pity that the Press feel bound to recommend the public to bet on every race as in case like this it would have been far better for me to tell their readers not to have a bet at all. From the point of view of the racing public the result of the big Ascot race could not have been worse. The French challenger Montaval, starting at 20–1, won the prize and cross-Channel invaders filled the first four places. Nevertheless Noel still entertained hopes of getting Crepello ready for Doncaster. 'I started to prepare him for the Great Voltigeur at York in August,' he says, 'but his legs started to go and I stopped him and retired him to stud.'

Noel ended that year as Britain's champion trainer for the second time, having won forty-eight races and set up a new record of winning stakes £116,908. He was the first man to break the £100,000 barrier and the extent of his superiority in 1957 can be shown by the fact that his nearest rival Cecil Boyd-Rochford won £75,227.

Sadly, in the midst of all this triumph Noel and Gwen heard of the death at the age of eighty, of the Aga Khan. The Aga had been the outstanding figure in European racing from 1922, the first year he raced in England, until his death. He enjoyed tremendous success on the English turf and shares with Lord Egremont the distinction of having won the Derby five times. His winners were Blenheim (1930), Barnham (1935), Mahmoud (1936), My Love (1948) and Tulyar (1952). He won the Two Thousand Guineas twice, the One Thousand once, the Oaks twice and the St Leger seven times. When Firdaussi won the St Leger, the Aga Khan was the owner of four of the first five horses to finish. For Noel and Gwen the blow was personal rather than professional because, in 1954, owing to the lower costs and higher stake money across the channel, the Aga Khan had transferred his racing interests to France and most of his later horses had been trained at Chantilly by Alec Head.

All the Aga Khan's horses in training and at his studs in Ireland and France were shared with his son, Prince Aly Khan. Noel remembers, 'When the Aga sent most of his animals to France, Aly left most of his own share with me. The Aga was dead before Petite

Etoile came along. She was bred in Ireland and at the time nobody had any idea just how good she was. In the autumn of 1957 she just arrived in a draft of other yearlings. We knew she looked pretty good, but she was an awful monkey!'

7
Triumphs and Tragedy
1958–1960

❊

Petite Etoile was destined to be a star. She owed the first part of her name to her sire Petition and the second to the name of her dam, the Bois Roussel mare Star of Iran, a descendant of The Tetrarch's flying daughter, Mumtaz Mahal, the grandam of Mahmoud and of Nasrullah. Noel remembers, 'She was a peculiar animal. She was a grey and she loved to have a grey in front of her in the string, and more particularly, a grey behind her when she went out to exercise. In my experience this was unique but then Petite Etoile was unique in every way.'

He gave Petite Etoile plenty of time to mature and to the outside world the two-year-old career of the lean, athletic, greyhound-like filly makes strange reading. Her first outing was in the £612 Prestwich Stakes at Manchester's now defunct Castle Irwell track on 30 May 1958. Her trainer recalls, 'There were only two runners. She got loose twice on the way up from the stables to the course and then she got loose again in the paddock. I am not sure whether she didn't get loose again at the start! Anyway she was beaten eight lengths by her solitary opponent Chris, ridden by Billy Nevett. She won her next race in the Star Stakes at Sandown. Then we ran her in the Molecomb Stakes at Goodwood and Lester missed the start on her. He was half turned round when the gates went up and she was just beaten.'

Finally Petite Etoile won again in the Rose Stakes at Sandown on 13 August. She was allotted 8 stone 6 pounds in the Free Handicap, 15 pounds behind the top two-year-old, Tudor Melody. She progressed during the winter and on 15 April 1959 showed the official handicapper what she thought of his insult. 'I had two in the Free Handicap,' says the Guv'nor, 'and we thought that of the three-year-olds Collyria, a Sassoon filly, was our best runner. Lester and I really thought that she was going to be a better filly than Petite Etoile.' She had been out once as a two-year-old and had just been beaten by a short head by Saint Crespin, Aly's top-class French colt, in the Imperial Produce Stakes at Kempton. They were both running for the first time. This was to be a great year for Prince Aly for whom the Australian champion George Moore was currently riding in France. He and Alec Head hoped to win the Two Thousand Guineas with Taboun and complete the double with Paraguana in the One Thousand.

Says Noel, 'Aly asked if I would give George Moore a ride over the course before the Guineas. My other runner in The Handicap was Short Sentence owned by the Queen. I discussed the matter with Lester and told him that we couldn't put Moore on to the royal filly as they had not been working together.'

So many of the top horses had defected from the Free Handicap that the weights were raised 8 pounds and Petite Etoile carried top weight of 9 stone. She was easy to back at 9–1 and the Tote returned nearly 12–1 after she had won by three lengths.

Taboun duly won the Two Thousand for Aly and Alec Head. The only danger in the One Thousand was thought to be Rosalba. Lester was given his choice of the Warren Place pair. Their trainer says: 'Although Collyria had not done well through the winter, and had not had a race, she had been working well enough and Lester said he would stick to her. So I got Doug Smith for Petite Etoile.' It was a lucky spare ride for Doug who said, 'I had ridden her in her final gallop and had formed the opinion that she was a really high-class filly. Fortunately Lester did not ride her in the same gallop and failed to realize just how good she was.'

Petite Etoile was backed from 100–8 to 8–1, at which price she was third in demand behind the two favourites. Noel told Doug to keep her covered up and not to show her the front too soon, but Doug said afterwards, 'I was not prepared for her fantastic acceleration as I picked her up when we started to run down into The Dip . . . once I had begun my run I had to go on.' The filly shot away from her rivals as soon as Smith asked her, but in the last hundred yards up the hill Rosalba was catching her and Petite Etoile had only a length to spare at the line. Her time in almost identical conditions was two seconds faster than that recorded by Taboun in the colts' classic but till then nobody had realized that this was a truly great filly. 'She was always on the go,' says the Guv'nor. 'She was like quicksilver under you.'

Noel did not run Petite Etoile again until the Oaks on 3 June. Two days earlier Colonel Loder's colt Carnoustie, who had finished third behind Taboun in the Two Thousand Guineas, had run into fifth place in the Derby won by Parthia, who was to be Cecil Boyd-Rochfort's only winner of the Epsom classic. There were three Warren Place runners in the Oaks, Petite Etoile, Rose of Modena and Collyria. This time Lester did not make a mistake. He chose to ride the One Thousand Guineas winner and the other two were ridden respectively into third and fourth places by the Smith brothers, Eph and Doug. Bookmaker-owned Cantelo, winner of the Cheshire Oaks, was installed favourite at 11–4 with the Sledmere filly Myrnya at 2–1 to complete the double for Boyd-Rochfort. Petite Etoile started at 11–2.

This race saw the partnership that was to make history. Lester, bottom high in the air, still had the filly on a tight rein as he took the lead from Cantelo a furlong out and came away smoothly up the hill to win the 1959 Oaks by three lengths. Again the time was faster than the colts'. Petite Etoile went on to win the one-mile Sussex Stakes at Goodwood, the mile-and-a-half Yorkshire Oaks and finally on 17 October the mile-and-a-quarter Champion Stakes at Newmarket, earning top rating in the official three-year-old Free Handicap.

'Lester rode her so brilliantly all the time,' says the grey filly's trainer. 'She never really got more than a mile and a quarter. We knew that if anyone took her on from start to finish in a mile-and-a-half race that she would not stay. How Aly loved that filly and how she loved him too, but my word, how she hated strangers. I remember Cyril Hall, who was Aly's stud manager in those days, coming into Warren Place one December Sales and walking into her box. He said, "You're getting a bit fat, old girl!" He pushed his finger into her neck and she turned round like lightning and got hold of the lapels of his coat and lifted him off the ground! Frightened the life out of him!'

Mr Jim Joel leads in Royal Palace, ridden by George Moore, after winning the 1967 Derby

Her Majesty's Hopeful Venture, with George Moore, winning the 1967 Hardwick Stakes.

Above Aunt Edith's King George VI and Queen Elizabeth Stakes, Ascot, 1966, Lester Piggott in the saddle

Opposite above Fleet's One Thousand Guineas with George Moore, May 1967
Opposite below Lady Sassoon's Sucaryl takes the News of the World Stakes at Goodwood, July 1967, ridden by George Moore

There were some grand staying horses at Warren Place that year including Primera, whom Noel had bought for Stanhope Joel from his previous owner Charleston George, the Queen's Pinza colt Pindari, winner of the King Edward VII Stakes at Ascot and the Great Voltigeur at York; and of course Collyria who, although not as good as her grey stable-companion, was still good enough to win the fillies' St Leger as it is called, the Park Hill Stakes.

Primera, who had been foaled in 1954, was bred by the Maharaja of Baroda by Mr Babu out of Pirette by Deiri. He raced until he was six, improving with age. Altogether he won eight races worth over £18,000, including the Churchill Stakes, Ormonde Stakes, Prince and Princess of Wales Stakes (twice) and the Ebor Handicap with 9 stone. In that year, 1959, he finished fifth in the Prix de l'Arc de Triomphe.

The Hindleys also had a very useful filly called Rose of Modena, who won the Princess Elizabeth Stakes at Epsom and the Princess Royal Stakes at Ascot. And at the same Ascot meeting on 25 September Sir Victor Sassoon's home-bred bay colt St Paddy, by the Queen's stallion Aureole out of Edie Kelly appeared second time out in the prestigious Royal Lodge Stakes over a mile to win in impressive style by five lengths.

But there was no doubt at all that Petite Etoile was the big star of 1959, a year in which Noel was champion again, winning sixty-three races and breaking his own prize-money record with a total of £145,725. In addition to his wonderful horsemastership Noel was now proving himself an outstanding businessman and, what with the studs, stallions and animals in and out of training he was making a lot of money for Sir Victor Sassoon. 'Unlike some trainers,' he says, 'I never got presents – just my ten per cent of winning stakes.'

Julie was now old enough to drive a car so one day Noel went off and bought her a Mini. Sassoon was at Warren Place when he drove the little car back. Eyes twinkling, Gwen gave a wry smile. 'I wish someone had bought me a car when I was a girl,' she said. Sassoon retorted, 'It's about time you and Noel had a decent car. You'd better get one.'

Noel examines Royal Palace's legs after winning the King George VI and Queen Elizabeth Stakes, 1968

'What sort of car?' Noel asked. The old man answered, 'I don't know. Choose whatever you like. You have all these garages here at Warren Place so perhaps you could have two or three of those Jaguar things.' Noel went off and bought the most beautiful car in the world – a drop head coupé Continental Rolls-Bentley. He laughs today, 'I don't think old Victor was all that pleased when he got the bill!'

Noel and Gwen were very friendly with the painter Sir Alfred Munnings, and his wife Violet who was besotted with her little black Pekingese, Black Knight. She used to carry the dog like a fur muff every time she went to the races and claimed that he barked when he saw a horse that he wanted to back. She always took his advice and would promptly invest ten shillings on the particular horse on Black Knight's own account with a bookmaker. Letters kept arriving at Warren Place addressed to Crepello and signed Black Knight, one of Julie's least favourite chores as a young girl was replying to them! The story had a macabre ending. When Black Knight died, he was taken by Lady Munnings to the best taxidermist who stuffed him so skilfully that the little dog was still able to accompany his mistress wherever she went. He must have been the only dead holder of a current account with a bookmaker!

That autumn at the sales Noel bought a fine big colt by Aureole. 'I had nobody to buy him for,' he says, 'but I just bought him because I liked him. When I got home, before I had time to sit down the telephone went. It was my old friend Tom Lilley. I told him, "I bought a horse this morning. Do you want to have him?" He said, "Right." Unhappily poor Tom was dead before Aurelius won the St Leger.'

That year Warren Place enjoyed a splendid York. They won the Ebor Handicap with Primera, the Great Voltigeur Stakes with Pindari and the Yorkshire Oaks with Petite Etoile. Prince Aly, having watched his filly win the latter in a common canter, was about to leave the course when Noel suggested he might like to wait and see his next year's Derby horse St Paddy have his first run in the Ancomb Stakes. The big bay colt's reputation had travelled fast and he opened at 5–1 before being backed down to be 3–1 favourite. 'The trouble was,' says Noel, 'that he ran away with Lester going down to the start. We had been trying to settle him and so when they jumped off Lester had him stuck in behind a wall of horses and they just couldn't get out. When Aly told me he had lost £4000 on the race I could only say, "I never told you St Paddy was going to win the race; I just thought you would like to see him have his first outing." Aly had an enormous bet on him in the Derby but unfortunately, he wasn't there to collect.'

In 1959 Aly's racing career was at its peak. He was the first owner in the history of the British turf to win over £100,000 in stakes, and adding all his winners to those of his late father he succeeded in reaching six figures that year as a breeder too. He had also set a new record as an owner in France, with winnings of 212,314,631 francs. In 1959 his horses won the Two Thousand Guineas, the One Thousand Guineas, the Oaks, the Champion Stakes and the Middle Park Stakes in England; in France the Prix de l'Arc de Triomphe and the French One Thousand Guineas; and in Ireland the One Thousand Guineas.

On 7 May 1960, Petite Etoile won the Victor Wild Stakes at Kempton Park. Before the race she had been at her fieriest knocking Johnny Mack down and injuring him. Although delighted with this victory, typically Aly's only concern was for Mack's health. He rushed to the ambulance room and sat there with the lad until he was certain he was all right. On the following day two of Aly's horses were short-headed in successive races at Longchamp. Surveying the photographs of the two finishes displayed outside the Weighing Room, Aly observed with a rueful smile that his luck was beginning to run out.

Four days later Aly was killed in a car crash in the Bois de Boulogne. It was a shattering blow to his intimate friends who included Noel and Gwen, and the entire racing world suffered a grievous loss. Prince Aly Khan was the second son – the first died in infancy – of the Aga Khan and of his second wife Teresa Maglioni. Educated privately, he took a keen interest in racing and bloodstock breeding from an early age and in addition became an extremely confident rider on the flat. On his father's death he bought out the inherited interests of the Begum Aga Khan and his step-brother Sadruddin, assuming sole responsibility for an immense racing empire. When he died, he owned six studs in Ireland, four in France and roughly a hundred broodmares. He was also part-owner of a dozen mares in America. Most of his horses were trained by Alec Head but he always kept some with Noel.

Viscount Astor wrote in his obituary in *The Times*:

'If one knew Aly Khan only by repute it was easy to preconceive a dislike towards him. When one met him it was impossible not to be stimulated and attracted by his charm, his perfect manners, his vitality, his gaiety and sense of fun. But if you were fortunate enough to know him really well and had him as a friend you aquired a friendship which was incomparable – generous, imaginative, enduring and almost passionately warm. He was curiously defensive towards the world and intensely sensitive to real or imagined slights but, if he was sure of your friendship, he returned it a hundredfold. All over the world in all classes of society from high to low, thousands of people will feel a sense of loss and the closer one knew him, the more irreparable the gap.'

It is an obituary that Noel and Gwen still keep filed away, under the heading 'Shah Aly Khan'. After each Ascot they would spend a few days with him at his villa outside Cannes.

Even the greatest of trainers have been daunted by the thought of campaigning with a four-year-old filly especially one who has run so well as a three-year-old. Petite Etoile was such a filly. Noel says, 'It depended on the filly. I found that top class three-year-old fillies will hold their form until about next June. They did not come on at all afterwards. I found that later with Aunt Edith and Lupe.' So in 1960 he grasped the nettle firmly and won with Aly's Petite Etoile over a mile and a half at Kempton and then returned to Epsom to trounce Parthia, the previous year's winner in the Coronation Cup over the Derby course and distance. It was an historic meeting between the Derby hero and the Oaks heroine. Lester held Petite Etoile up, and was last of the three runners coming into the straight but then a hundred yards out, he asked her for an effort. She quickened to take the lead and won in an easy canter, hard held, by one and a half lengths from Harry Carr on the Boyd-Rochford colt. The Queen's Above Suspicion was the same distance behind. The smooth, easy style in which these victories were gained led everyone to believe that Petite Etoile was winning over a mile and a half with consummate ease. As it turned out, this was a false assumption.

Noel says, 'I think that, if Aly had lived, Petite Etoile would probably have finished after the Coronation Cup as a four-year-old. But we kept her on, for the sake of the new Aga Khan.' He added, 'You've got to string mares up if you are going to keep them on as four-year-olds and if they are going to take on the colts. I think it is against the run of nature, although in the case of Petite Etoile she didn't need a lot of work.'

The kind, lovable spirit of Hubert Hartigan, who had done so much for the Guv'nor in the early days, continued to influence him. 'When Hubert died, I persuaded Victor Sassoon to buy his mare Edie Kelly. He had to pay 3000 guineas for her and, at the time, he cribbed a bit at the price! After being mated with the Queen's horse Aureole, Edie Kelly came back to my own stud, The Cliff at Helmsley, where she produced St Paddy.'

Noel classes that burly colt among the greatest horses he trained. 'He never gave me a moment's anxiety through his life, never sick or sorry except for one small cough. He was one of the best doers I have ever known. It was no good giving him a clean straw bed or that went the same way as his oats and hay – straight down inside him! But I don't think he was too fond of the battle.'

After his first run in the Two Thousand Guineas, in which he finished fifth behind Paddy Prendergast's Martial and Venture VII, Noel sent St Paddy up to York for the Dante Stakes, run over one mile, two and a half furlongs and here he was backed down to 11–8, firm favourite by the Yorkshire punters. Lester came into that long straight third, but took the lead over a furlong out and won by three lengths. Surprisingly St Paddy was not favourite for the Derby. Once again the rumour gremlins were at work, and the night before the Epsom classic word spread that St Paddy would not run. The bookmakers believed these stories and betting on the Derby was delayed until Noel and Gwen arrived and confirmed St Paddy's participation.

On that glorious June day in 1960 St Paddy was the best horse in Europe. As it happened the French favourite Mme Stressburger's Angers, trained by George Bridgeland and partnered by Gerard Thiboeuf, caused a sensation when he broke his fetlock six furlongs out and had to be destroyed. He was running in blinkers and was well behind St Paddy. Lester, once again riding Epsom in his copybook manner, had come fourth into the straight, had taken the lead more than two furlongs from home and St Paddy had quickened nicely inside the final furlong to win by three lengths from Scobie Breasley on Prendergast's Alcaeus. Prendergast's Kythnos was half a length behind in third place.

Noel's Primera went on winning that year and Exar, an Italian colt, proved himself a grand stayer by winning the July Stayers' Stakes at Sandown, followed by the Goodwood Cup, the Poulson Stakes at Sandown and the Doncaster Cup. St Paddy coughed slightly in the middle of the season but Noel produced him again at York to win the Great Voltigeur Stakes over one and a half miles on 17 August.

The Guv'nor considers that St Paddy's gallop before the St Leger was the most exciting work of his whole career. 'It stands out in my mind,' he says, 'Paddy was a very stuffy horse and he had to be really opened out before the St Leger. I put some top-class older horses into that gallop. There was Red Pins as a lead horse and then Off Key, Sunny Way, Exar and Primera. You couldn't find much better trial tackle than that, could you? Paddy gave them weight and ridden by Lester, just slammed them.' In the St Leger at Doncaster on 10 September, St Paddy started favourite at 6–4 on. He never gave a moment's anxiety. Lester took the lead two furlongs from home and won with the greatest ease from Vincent O'Brien's Die Hard and Sir Winston Churchill's Vienna. Off Key who, ridden by Eph Smith, had acted as pacemaker to his stable-companion, leading until three furlongs from home, was still good enough to finish fifth.

Noel was top trainer again in 1960 and this time Lester was Champion Jockey with 170 winners. There was only one disappointment that year and that was the defeat of Aly's great filly, Petite Etoile, in the King George VI and Queen Elizabeth Stakes at Ascot.

It poured with rain and the ground was heavy and sodden. The Derby winner of 1959, Parthia, was in the field as well as Kythos, who had run third to St Paddy at Epsom, and Sir Harold Wernher's big strong mudlark Aggressor, a five-year-old who had won the Harwicke Stakes at the Royal Meeting and was ridden by Jimmy Lindley. Despite the ground, Petite Etoile was installed favourite at 5–2 on. Lester, who knew the filly so well, held her up and was last coming into that short straight. He tried to bring her through on the inside but was given a hefty bump a quarter of a mile from home. Then he switched her to the outside but, hanging right, the grey was unable to quicken inside the final furlong and was beaten half a length by Aggressor on whom Lindley had made his best way home from a furlong out.

The Guv'nor says, 'A lot of people blamed Lester, but I never did. In my view he did just the right thing, sticking on to the rails and he might just have scraped through. What's more, after that bump I am quite certain he did the only possible thing in coming to the outside.' The pundits blamed the soft going, they blamed Lester for lying out of his grounds, and they blamed that interference in the straight which caused her to be switched. There were so many excuses, all of which seemed valid at the time. But Lester rode a superlative race on a filly who, according to her trainer, did not really get a yard more than one mile and a quarter.

Petite Etoile did not run again that year, but she was to play her part in kindling the spark of racing interest lying dormant in her new owner, Aly's son Karim, the new Aga Khan. When the gates of Warren Place closed that October, Noel had won forty-two races worth £118,297. And there was in the yard a big, powerful, unraced two-year-old by Pinza – Pinturischio.

8

Years of Achievement
1961–1966

❋

The Guv'nor was leading trainer in 1961 for the third successive season. Nevertheless it was not the happiest year for the Master of Warren Place though it had begun so well. At the Craven Meeting he won the Craven Stakes with Aurelius and then took the Wood Ditton most impressively with the big, backward Pinturischio who looked another certain Derby winner for Sir Victor Sassoon.

Such was the reputation of that colt, nicknamed 'Pint of Sherry' by the bookmakers that before he had ever been *seen* on a racecourse, he was backed down to 4–1 for the Two Thousand Guineas and 5–1 for the Derby. Describing this state of affairs as 'quite fantastic', a spokesman for William Hill said that his firm had laid Pinturischio to lose £20,000 in the Guineas and £15,000 in the Epsom classic. One client had £10,000 to £2000 for the Newmarket race and the same man's Derby bet was £10,000 to £1000. On the first day of the Newmarket meeting even the bookmakers were stunned into silence as Pinturischio's workmate Aurelius, hard ridden by Lester, cantered in at 8–1 to a two-lengths victory in the Craven Stakes. But that did not stop them from cutting Pinturischio's Guineas price from 4 to 3–1. For, in a one-mile gallop on the previous Saturday Aurelius, Noel's first runner of the season, had impressed the spectators on the Heath as being at least a stone behind the unraced Guineas and Derby favourite. Of course, as Noel reminded them at the time, neither horse had been seriously tried. Nevertheless, as with all Noel's runners, Aurelius was of course, fit and in great condition.

Two days later Pinturischio made his first appearance in the

Noel with Colonel Giles Loder during the Beckhampton years

Wood Ditton Stakes. In the parade ring all eyes were on the tall, rich bay novice. He looked superb. From the start Allenby led the field at little more than half-speed. Three furlongs out Doug Smith sent Nicodemus on, but coming down into The Dip, Pinturischio drew smoothly upsides and, taking the lead with no effort, strode up the hill to win by a length.

Noel was very pleased. 'Pinturischio couldn't have done it better,' he commented. The colt was now down to 5–2 for the Two Thousand Guineas. Staying-bred as he was, he should never have been such a short-priced favourite for the Newmarket mile classic. In the circumstances he did particularly well in the race to finish fourth behind the 66–1 northern outsider Rockavan trained by George Boyd at Dunbar. When Lester drew his whip in The Dip, the big bay favourite could do no more and finished two lengths and two short heads behind the winner. The champion jockey made no bones about it. 'It was not lack of experience. Over that distance Pinturischio was purely and simply not good enough.' Nevertheless, it was a great training feat by the Guv'nor to get the big colt as close as that over such a short distance so early in his career.

By now doping had become widespread in England – Rule 176 (II) of Racing, which was feared by every trainer, read, 'If in any case in which the Stewards have ordered a horse to be examined it shall be found that any drug or stimulant has been administered to a horse for the purpose of affecting his speed in a race, the licence of the trainer shall be withdrawn and he shall be declared a disqualified person.' In 1961 this rule was still in operation when a bookmaker-inspired gang broke into Warren Place on the night of 7/8 May and nearly killed Pinturischio, by now 6–1 favourite.

Noel says, 'I was warned a few days beforehand that he would be nobbled, but I didn't think that anything would happen until the horse had run in the Dante Stakes at York on 16 May. Later some woman wrote an article in one of the Sunday papers saying that they had sat up in the big tree at the back of the yard and waited until everything was closed up at night and that they then got in through the skylight in Pinturischio's box. Of course they did not get in

---

ABOVE   Caergwrle's One Thousand Guineas, Newmarket, 1968, Sandy Barclay up
BELOW   In the winner's enclosure, a pat from a proud owner

G

through the skylight. They just picked the locks on the door. Then they gave him a very strong physic, the stuff, I believe, that they give to elephants. It must have been terribly powerful. He was never the same horse again and although for a short while I hoped that I would be able to get him right again to run in the Derby, they broke in a second time and made no mistake. They really finished him off. In fact, from their point of view, they did such a good job that he was never able to run again.'

Pinturischio was finally scratched from the Derby at 10.30 a.m. on Saturday 27 May, just four days before the classic. Lester says, 'He would have won it all right.' Not even the Guv'nor could overcome the effects of that; and during those weeks of tension, hounded by the Press day and night, with every movement of himself and his horses followed by long-range cameras hidden behind all the bushes on Newmarket Heath, he still remained his calm, cool, courteous self.

Psidium, trained by Harry Wragg, won the Derby at 66–1 so that the bookmakers' cup must have been overflowing. Later that week Sweet Solera won the Oaks for old Reg Day and Bill Rickaby, a victory so richly deserved and accorded a very warm welcome in certain contrast to the stony silence which greeted the running of the Derby.

However, the Guv'nor and Lester had a splendid form of consolation when Petite Etoile won the Coronation Cup for the second time. Of all the cheeky races that Lester had ridden, this was undoubtedly his cheekiest. Sir Winston Churchill's Vienna was leading from Proud Chieftain. The pace, slow at first, gradually increased but Piggott, lying third, made no move until a furlong from the post. Even then he just let the filly glide up to the leaders. As she passed Vienna to win by a neck, he still had her on a tight rein. Petite Etoile was running for the first time in the presence of the young Aga Khan. Her winnings now stood at £65,061, a record for a filly in Britain at that time.

Warren Place enjoyed an excellent Royal Ascot in 1961 with five winners. Vera Lilley's Favourite won the Jersey Stakes, the Queen's Aiming High the Coronation; Aurelius, also in Vera Lilley's colours, won the King Edward VII; Petite Etoile the Rous Memorial; and St Paddy the Hardwicke.

The Aly Khan Memorial Gold Cup on 4 July might almost have

been designed for Petite Etoile and Noel, as one of Aly's oldest friends and greatest admirers, was determined to win with his favourite grey mare. But the distance was one and a half miles. This was the flat, tight Kempton circuit and Lester's bluff was called at last. Sir Winston Churchill's High Hat, with a display of courage and stamina worthy of his great owner, beat the champion grey mare fair and square. Riding to a plan, Duncan Keith jumped off in front and set a fast, true gallop throughout the mile-and-a-half race. Lester was sitting still on the grey filly two lengths behind. Two and a half furlongs from home Petite Etoile started to make her move. It looked as though once again she was to sweep by to an appropriate victory. Piggott urged her on, she ran to within a length of High Hat but she could produce no more. She had shot her bolt and High Hat drew further away to win by two lengths. Noel was typically the first to congratulate Sir Winston Churchill's son-in-law and racing manager Captain Christopher Soames, the then Minister of Agriculture, and now Lord Soames.

The Aga Khan was perplexed and bewildered at the defeat of his champion. 'What happened?' he asked Lester. 'Why didn't you come away and win?' His head tilted slightly to one side, Lester looked steadily at this dark handsome young man of his own age, and answered simply, 'He ran me into the ground.'

Noel too discounted stories that Petite Etoile was amiss, and Lester said after the race, 'She was better than she has ever been, and battled on as well as ever.' Duncan Keith, the rider of the winner, said, 'I was told to set a fast gallop, to give High Hat a breather at the stables on the far side and let him go on again on the turn. That is what I did. Lester got to within a length of me, but as soon as High Hat heard him, he kept pulling out a bit more. He's a really brave, gutsy horse.'

Both Noel and Lester had bluffed quite brilliantly. They had always known that Petite Etoile did not get more than one and a quarter miles in a true run race. At the time Noel was doubtful about running her again. 'She had done marvellously well to have kept going as long as that. A five-year-old mare is not an easy proposition. The reason why we kept her on as a five-year-old was because Alec had not much for the Aga to race in France.'

Noel gave the third of his great champions one more race, the Scarborough Stakes at the Doncaster St Leger meeting, which she won very easily, bringing her winning stakes to £67,785.

After his Ascot victory Aurelius was rested until 23 August at York, when he ran an excellent trial for the St Leger in the Great Voltigeur Stakes finishing second beaten three-quarters of a length by Just Great, an Epsom-trained colt ridden by Scobie Breasley. But staying was Aurelius' forte and in the St Leger Lester was always going well. He cruised into the long straight in third position, took the lead below the distance and galloped on strongly to win by three-quarters of a length from Bounteous and the Derby runner-up from France Dicta Drake.

Aurelius had now brought his total to six victories, including the St Leger, King Edward VII Stakes and Hardwicke Stakes. He retired to stud in 1963 but unfortunately proved useless as a stallion, and was eventually brought back into training in Berkshire, running with mixed fortune over hurdles and fences.

'He was a fair horse,' the Guv'nor affirms, 'not a bad horse. He had a lot of Aureole about him. He was a bad worker at home. When I galloped him at Newmarket, the sweat used to roll off him. Get him on the racecourse and he wouldn't turn a hair. You couldn't pull his mane or foretop or anything like that at home, but on the racecourse you could do anything you liked with him! He ran a good race in the King George VI and Queen Elizabeth Stakes at Ascot when he was beaten only three-quarters of a length by the top-class French colt Match III.'

The Kempton Park defeat of Petite Etoile was nicely avenged at Newmarket on 30 September 1961 when St Paddy defeated High Hat in the Jockey Club Stakes over one and three-quarter miles at Newmarket. Five days earlier, Noel and Gwen's home-bred two-year-old Caerphilly had won the Lavant Stakes at Goodwood.

It is interesting to note that in 1962, when the camera patrol was introduced, the third most valuable race in another championship year for the Guv'nor was the £10,460 Vaux Gold Tankard at Redcar which he won with Off Key, ridden by Lester and carrying 8 stone 5 pounds to beat the course record by no less than $4\frac{1}{5}$ seconds. Leslie Patch, the clerk of the course at York and Redcar said, 'Noel Murless was once opposed to handicaps for classic horses, but now he finds classic horses can win handicaps he is all in favour of them. He thinks that the handicap should have a limited weight range from, say, 7 stone to 9 stone 7 pounds.'

The close of the season saw Noel champion trainer for the third successive season and for the fourth time in five years. His winning stake total was not as large as it had been: thirty-six races worth £95,972. Although he headed the list it had been a troubled year with the doping of Pinturischio and the deaths of Tom Lilley and Sir Victor Sassoon. Noel had also bought Woodditton stud, just outside Newmarket, where he now lives; sold Thornton-le-Street stud near Thirsk in Yorkshire to Lord Howard de Walden; and advised Jeremy Hindley to buy the 100-acre stud at Cartoft in Kirby Moorside in Yorkshire's North Riding.

Lady Sassoon's Twilight Alley, Crepello's big three-parts brother by Alycidan, took a long time to come to hand and did not run as a two-year-old. At the age of three in 1962 he ran once, winning the Cranbourne Chase Stakes at Ascot, and three times the following season, finishing second in the Henry II Stakes and winning the Ascot Gold Cup.

Another of Lady Sassoon's horses, The Creditor, a grand chestnut daughter of Crepello, was so small, that Noel would not even break her until the August of her two-year-old season. Then she showed that she was very fast indeed as a three-year-old. 'The first time she ran at Chester, I thought she was a certainty for the Stewards' Stakes. Our good friend from Wiltshire John Sutton, decided to have a really big bet. But he left it too late and came across the course from the paddock to the stands where the book-makers operate. The horses had gone down to the start and the officials had closed the gates so that John was locked out. Unable to have a bet, he fumed and ranted helplessly behind the bars, watching the filly romp home. Poor old John! We were laughing our-selves silly. I've never heard such language!'

The Creditor became the top miler until she broke a blood vessel. 'I thought she'd never stop bleeding. But we found she had a growth in one ovary, had it removed, and she proved a wonderful broodmare, dam of Abwah and Owen Dudley.'

Even as champion jockey, Lester was still having occasional brushes with authority but Noel always defended him. When he started pulling up his stirrup leather further and further, all the other jockeys tried to imitate him. 'I've been pulling them up all the time and I'm still pulling them up! Although I may not look very comfortable, I feel more comfortable . . . everybody has to ride the way he feels most comfortable. One of the disadvantages of being tall is style. Style is the way you look. If you are small, it doesn't matter so much how you look because there isn't so much of you to be seen and your legs don't take up so much room. If you're big you can be seen better and there's less horse showing. I smile when people ask me why I ride with my bottom in the air. I've got to put it somewhere, haven't I? Anyway, it works and I'm comfortable.'

Noel says, 'It's difficult to tell who was the finest jockey of my time. You've got to look at the records. There is none finer than Lester. Steve Donoghue must have been brilliant. Gordon, Steve and Lester must compare with the best there has ever been. I think the short stirrups have done a lot of harm. Lester and Yves Saint-Martin are artists and can do it, but none of the others who try to ape them can. Gordon, of course, rode a good length. Balance is the essential thing for a jockey.'

Noel won good races including the National Stakes at Sandown for the Aga Khan with Zahedan, but it was Aunt Edith who was to prove the best horse at Warren Place in 1965 and the early part of 1966. After only two easy runs as a two-year-old this chestnut daughter of Primera and the Hyperion mare Fair Edith won the Nassau Stakes at Goodwood and then followed with a spectacular eight-lengths victory in the £30,485 Prix Vermeille, frequently referred to as the fillies' Arc de Triomphe, at Longchamp on 19 September. It was a spectacular contest and was by far the Guv'nor's biggest success to date across the Channel. The field included four individual Oaks winners and two runners-up. Three fillies fell, but Lester kept clear of trouble and brought Aunt Edith, with a well-timed run to win from Dark Wave, ridden by Jean Deforge, with the Australian Jack Purtell third on the English Oaks winner, Long Look.

Once again in 1965 Warren Place enjoyed a good Royal Ascot winning three races, including a real thriller for the Royal Hunt Cup with the grey colt Casabianca who, carrying 8 stone 7 pounds fought out a tremendous battle in the final furlong with Weepers Boy ridden by Bill Williamson, Zaleucs, Blazing Scent, Balustrade and Old Tom. Lester, who had been holding up the fine grey Murless four-year-old, brought him with a strong run inside the final furlong and just got up on the line to win by a head from Williamson. The remainder were divided by half a length, a head, a short head and a short head. It was one of the most sensational blanket finishes ever seen at Ascot.

Certainly one of the most momentous events in Lester's life – and in racing generally – was his break with Noel in May 1966 after a ten-year partnership which produced two Derbys, two Oaks and two St Legers. Since Lester had taken over from Gordon as first jockey for Warren Place, Noel had headed the trainers' list four times and Lester had won three jockeys' championships. The retainer system had become so much a traditional part of the English racing scene that the very idea of a break was a tremendous shock to everyone. Lester says today, 'Noel was very easy to ride for and he never gave you any orders. As you had ridden most of the horses at home, of course you knew them. He never told you what to do, so you could do what you liked. This was a big help.'

Lester came in for such harsh criticism that it is only fair to let him tell his own version of these events, which the public first heard of on 18 May just nine days before the Oaks, for which Charles Clore's Irish One Thousand Guineas winner Valoris, a half-sister to the French Derby winner Val de Loir, was favourite.

Lester had been toying with the idea of giving up his retainer for some time. He has never made any bones of his admiration for Noel – 'a wonderful trainer, equally good with colts and fillies. A great man at his job. I told Noel towards the end of 1965 that I had decided to go freelance next season. He tried to dissuade me but I was determined and, when I refused to accept the retainer for the first time, he must have realized I was serious. Certainly we carried on as though nothing had happened but I knew things were bound to come to a head sooner or later. This was Charlottown's year, the year when French horses were banned owing to swamp fever, a year when Noel had some moderate horses at Warren Place. Since he had no classic colt worthy of the name, I had been booked for Charles Engelhard's big black Right Noble in the Derby, a soft disappointing animal, who was often likened to a Life Guards charger. His stable companion, Valoris, engaged in the Oaks had proved herself, as I thought, a very good filly indeed by winning the Irish One Thousand Guineas first time out that season. She would be worth a great deal of money if she won the Oaks at Epsom, bred as she was. And what was to beat her? Noel had a filly called Varinia who was a fair performer, but just not in the same class. I had won the Chester Cup on that splendid tough stayer, Aegean Blue, and wanted to ride him again in the big race at Ayr on Saturday 14 May.

'This was the day, however, when Varinia was due to run in the Oaks Trial at Lingfield. Noel let me off and put Stan Clayton up on his filly, which duly won. Incidentally I broke the course record on Aegean Blue at Ayr. I hinted to the press that at the weekend I might not be on Varinia in the Oaks. Unhappily, Noel seemed to take it for granted that I was still stable jockey and that I would automatically ride his filly at Epsom on 27 May. When he said that to me, I replied, "Stan won on her yesterday. He can ride her again." Like all the top English trainers Noel had always been accustomed to having his stable jockey riding the horses both in their home work and on the racecourse. The whole thing was a shock to him. It upset all his arrangements and disturbed his way of life. The papers, of course, made a sensation of it. My judgement proved right when I won my third Oaks on Valoris. It would have been ironical indeed and would have delighted my many critics at the time if I had been parted from Valoris before the race. It so nearly happened. I wonder how many officials would have bothered to catch her! She was shying so badly that I took her back to the paddock and dismounted. Then I led Valoris all the way through the crowds down the hill and up the other side to the start.

'Stan Clayton jumped Varinia off in front and made the running while I lay handy in about sixth place. Down Tattenham Hill I moved up fourth. When I let Valoris go to the front one and a half furlongs out it was all over. After the dust had settled, apart from the fact that I had made Noel unhappy which did worry me, I was so glad that I had turned freelance. Noel and I patched up our differences and I rode a winner for him at Newmarket on Mr Joel's Pink Gem on 13 July. I saw him through to the end of that season when he engaged George Moore for the following year.

'Some jockeys prefer the retainer system. They know exactly where they are. But I love riding freelance, which entails a great deal more work and travel to ensure the right rides in the right races.'

And Noel says today, 'I think Lester was quite right. The best jockey deserves the best rides and he was undoubtedly the best jockey.'

In all other aspects 1966 was a very happy year at Warren Place, ending as it did with forty-nine races won worth £92,282. The stable had been joined by one of the most popular men in the sport, Mr Jim Joel who said of Noel, 'He is a wonderful man and a magnificent trainer. From the breeding point of view he has no equal. He really understands all those families.'

George and Patsy Pope also joined the stable that year. George, a delightful man and a crack polo player, bred and raced on the top scale at his famous El Peco Ranch in California. At the time he had a very good horse of his own breeding called Hill Rise. Noel says, 'George asked me if I would train the horse for him. He would not send him to England unless I would take him. So the horse came over but he was wrong in his back. He seemed to be a cripple coming out in the mornings. He would just scratch along like an old hen. One morning I was on Long Hill talking to Harry Wragg. I said, "That American horse will be coming up in a minute. I'm going to send him back home. I'm not going to have it said that I broke down a really good horse like him." So Harry, who goes out to California every winter, said as Hill Rise cantered past, "Oh, he's always like that in his slower paces. Put Bill Rickaby on him on The Limekilns and tell him to give him a tap down the shoulder." I did that and I nearly fell off my hack the way he came up there.

'I ran him at Ascot first time in the 1966 Rous Memorial Stakes. I had Sweet Moss, ridden by Scobie Breasley in the same race. He and Silly Season were hot favourites. Hill Rise started at 30–1 but Bill Rickaby came up and beat them both. Hill Rise was five then. In September he won the Queen Elizabeth II Stakes at Ascot. He was a good horse. But he was not a very good stallion, although he did get one or two decent foals.'

The Guv'nor's charm, skill, personality and integrity have always attracted the best owners, amongst whom there is no doubt that Wiltshire farmer John Sutton had long been one of his firmest friends. John, who loves a bet, was particularly discomforted one day at Newbury when Noel thought that a horse called Magicote would win his race. The Guv'nor says, 'I think it was the first time I ran him. He got loose at the start and galloped round the course only to pop over the rails by the bend just between the mile and five furlongs and the mile and a half start – he went into a bit of a corn field. I heard someone puffing and blowing behind me and there was John Sutton coming up with a lad. John was very anxious because he had apparently had a very big punt on the horse. We caught the horse and, just as we were coming back on to the racecourse, his foot went into a hole. He went right down and suddenly a swarm of wasps came out. They were all around him, stinging him everywhere. John was trying to pull his coat over his head, jumping about and screaming like a pig. I couldn't do anything. I could only sit down on the grass and laugh and laugh and laugh!'

On 16 October of that year Julie Murless married Henry Cecil, twin stepson of Sir Cecil Boyd-Rochfort whom he was assisting. There could obviously be no finer recipe for racing success than this alliance.

At the end of 1966 the victories of Mr Joel's Royal Palace in the Royal Lodge Stakes at Ascot, and of Bob Boucher's Fleet in the Cheveley Park Stakes at Newmarket, foreshadowed the greatest season that Warren Place was ever to know.

9

Vintage 1967

✺

One of racing's most controversial years had ended in universal sadness, when Arkle, the superb steeplechaser, who had elevated the winter sport to new heights, suffered a final crippling injury at Kempton Park on Boxing Day.

At Warren Place, however, there was an air of optimism and subdued excitement, despite the fact that Lester had decided to ride freelance. So, for the year in which starting-stalls were to be used officially for the first time in Britain, Noel had to look elsewhere for a retained jockey.

At the beginning of November he announced that he had signed up the eighteen-year-old Scot, Sandy Barclay, whose indentures had been transferred from Harry Whiteman, who then held the licence at Cree Lodge, at Ayr. Harry said at the time, 'I'm delighted. Barclay's an absolute genius. I have been in racing for sixty-five years as jockey and trainer and I have never seen anyone like him. He rode his first winner, Sarouis, for me at Hamilton a year ago last May. Sandy finishes his apprenticeship in May. This is a wonderful opportunity for him. Given good health, he will go to the top. I don't expect him to be first jockey at once. That will come later.'

The problem of who would be first jockey for what promised to be a vintage season still had to be overcome. He had to be the best in the world. So Noel followed Prince Aly's example and sent for George Moore. In his home town of Sydney the Australian champion, described by Aly as the world's greatest rider, was delighted with the offer of Noel's retainer. 'One of the big factors,' he said, 'is that I'll have the great honour of riding for the Queen. I would only have to do nearly as well as I did in France for Prince Aly Khan for this to be better than that job.'

Moore, who combined immense power with gentle persuasion in his riding and was a superlative judge of pace had gone to France in 1959 to ride for Aly, and his victory on Taboun in the Two Thousand Guineas that year was his first ride in an English classic race. He also won the French Derby and the Grand Prix on Charlottesville; the Prix de l'Arc de Triomphe and the Eclipse on Saint Crespin III; the Grand Prix de St Cloud and the Ascot Gold Cup on Sheshoon; the French One Thousand Guineas on Ginetta; the Irish One Thousand on Florentina; and the Gimcrack and Champion Stakes on Paddy's Sister.

George had acquired over the years the reputation of a wayward, temperamental genius and it was hoped, too, that he would not be over the top at forty-four. As it was George Moore was to streak across the English racing firmament like a turbulent meteor, and produce a unique record of one winner in every three rides. Even Sir Gordon Richards was mesmerized by George in that season of 1967. 'This George Moore's the greatest today because, like Steve Donoghue, he's got something the rest of us haven't got – and Steve was the greatest I ever knew or rode against. It's unfair really. The rest of us, Lester, Scobie, Saint-Martin or I – have our horses perfectly balanced, ready to slip through a gap the moment it opens up, always ahead of the next fellow. But this chap, like Steve, is different. With a wall of horses in front of them, they go for a gap which isn't there. But always, just as they go for it, it opens up.'

George was a natural horseman and he rode, like Steve, in the classical English style. Soon after his acceptance of the Murless retainer, George was summoned before the Australian Stewards, following an alleged changing-room brawl with Athol Mulley. The *Sydney Sunday Telegraph* reported that an argument had broken out as the two jockeys were pulling up after the Frank Underwood Cup at the local Canterbury track. George had finished unplaced on the odds-on favourite and Athol Mulley was third. Subsequent blows in the changing-room, stated the report, resulted in scratches on the chest for Moore, a cut lower lip for Mulley and a report of the 'scuffle' to the Stewards by the Jockeys' Room supervisor. George was seldom out of the news for long. Wherever he was, something always seemed to be happening.

George arrived in England on 14 April, with his beautiful wife Iris and three children. He had 1973 winners to his credit when he arrived and an inspection of the Murless horses had revealed that he would not be long in passing the 2000 mark.

In the spring of 1967 Britain's racing world was faced with a strange and somewhat embarrassing situation. While Noel had already been champion British trainer on five occasions, in the last four years the title had gone to Ireland. In 1963 Paddy Prendergast had become the first Irish-based trainer to finish at the top of the British table. He had held the champion position for three successive years and then, in 1966 had come the turn of his compatriot, Vincent O'Brien. Vincent O'Brien, the man from Tipperary had given Lester Piggott the winning ride on Valoris in the Oaks, the ride which had finally ended the partnership between the Guv'nor and his champion jockey: 'bred in USA, trained in Ireland' was beginning to be a formidable recipe for success. But it was not a threat at Warren Place where the horses of England's top trainer had wintered better than any other string in Europe. They looked superb. Noel had built a covered ride designed to defy all extremes of British weather and to allow horses to walk, trot and canter round 280 yards of raked, salted sand. This has now been copied a number of times, but at the time it was unique. Nearby as befitted one of the prime movers in the starting stalls campaign, stood a well-used set of practice stalls.

Noel's two classic stars had improved enormously since the previous season. Mr Jim Joel's Royal Palace, rated second, only 3 pounds behind Bold Lad in the Free Handicap, had always beeen a handsome colt. Now the bay son of Ballymoss and Crystal Palace had strengthened considerably. 'I don't think he could have done better,' said his trainer with pride.

As for Bob Boucher's tall, dark bay Fleet: alert, bright of eye and carrying a coat that shone like high summer, she looked a perfect racing machine, full of the joys of spring and ready to run. 'She's as well as she looks,' said Noel, 'as you'd know if you rode her out in the morning. Her lads have to sit tight.' An 11,000 guinea yearling, Fleet had a family reputation to maintain. Display, one of her sisters, had been narrowly beaten in the One Thousand Guineas; a second, Pourparler, had won the fillies' classic for Paddy Prendergast; Democratie, was soon to uphold the family tradition in France.

Hopeful Venture, a strongly-built bright bay with black points, was the best colt of his generation by the Queen's Aureole. He was out of White House, who had won for the Queen and whose dam was Snowberry, one of the National Stud's best mares, who had produced Chamossaire, the St Leger winner. Noel recalls, 'Hopeful Venture was ill as a yearling and had a touch of pneumonia. So he was very backward and we didn't run him as a two-year-old.'

Sucaryl, the Sasson three-year-old, a bay by St Paddy out of the Honeyway mare Sweet Angel, had won as a two-year-old, over seven and a half furlongs at Chester in September, ridden by Bill Rickaby.

Mr Joel's Pink Gem, a big chestnut filly by Crepello out of Topaz, had won her only race, the six-furlong Princess Stakes at Newmarket's July meeting from twenty-nine rivals in fast time. The same owner's Golden Reward, a chestnut daughter of Major Portion and his brilliant but unlucky classic filly West Side Story, had also won her only start, the five-furlong Ilsley Stakes at Newbury in June.

Gwen Murless' St Chad, a chestnut colt by St Paddy out of the Abernant mare Caerphilly, was obviously going to be very speedy. He had run four times, finishing second on three occasions and winning the five-furlong Ladykirk Stakes at Ayr in September. Vera Hue-Williams' Royal Saint, a good-looking chestnut filly by Saint Crespin III out of Bleu Azur by Crepello, had won her only two starts, the seven-furlong Saddlescombe Stakes at Brighton at the end of August and, a month later, the six-furlong Chertsey Stakes at Ascot by five lengths from Pertinacity. Colonel John Hornung's good-looking Crepello filly, Cranberry Sauce, inherited her grey colour from her dam Queensberry, a daughter of Grey Sovereign. She had been placed once in two outings and showed promise. King of the older horses and indeed of the whole yard was Stanhope Joel's magnificent bay four-year-old Busted, a son of Crepello, who had arrived at Warren Place from Ireland the previous autumn and was to play a big part in this important year.

When George Moore arrived in England connoisseurs, as far as the first classics was concerned, favoured Bold Lad from Ireland and Alec Head's Taj Dewan as opponents for Royal Palace in the Two Thousand Guineas and Howell Jackson's Fix the Date, a daughter of the One Thousand Guineas and Oaks winner Never Too Late as the rival for Fleet. Fix the Date had won the Prix Imprudence at Maisons-Laffitte. Five days after his arrival, in his first ride as Noel's stable jockey, George Moore achieved a lifelong ambition in winning a race for the Queen at Newmarket. Although he claimed that he was not yet really fit he had Hopeful Venture first out of the stalls in the Wood Ditton Stakes, pulled his whip through smoothly when the colt started to sprawl, and won comfortably. 'It's too good to be true,' he said. And the following day, in his second ride of the season, he galvanised the grey Cranberry Sauce to sprint away with the Nell Gwyn Stakes. The following day Lester substituted for Moore on Royal Saint in Newbury's classic trial, the Fred Darling Stakes, and succeeded in getting Vera Hue-Williams' filly home in the last strides of a blanket finish between the first four.

Up at Thirsk in Yorkshire, Noel and George Moore suffered a setback in the Tor Anglia Thirsk classic trial which her trainer had chosen for Fleet's preparatory race for the One Thousand Guineas. The classic filly who started favourite at 2–1 on was left at the start and took no part. That race was still started by the old-fashioned barrier. Noel was justifiably incensed when Fleet was left; there was a Stewards' enquiry after the race.

'The sooner they get stalls the better. My filly goes out of them like a bullet. Even with this gate she would have gone all right if the starter had given her longer.' Fleet was broadside on to the gate and being held by the assistant starter when the tapes went up. Moreover the starter should unquestionably have waited more than three minutes for this odds-on favourite, who represented Britain's best hope of keeping the One Thousand Guineas at home. Nevertheless, despite the lack of a vital preparatory race, it seemed sure that she would win at Newmarket on 4 May.

This apart, everything went smoothly for the new Murless-Moore partnership. In the Princess Elizabeth Stakes at Epsom on 27 April Golden Reward was beaten only a short head by Pytchley Princess with Pertinacity two and a half lengths away third.

At Sandown the following day Noel scored a double with John Hornung's St Padarn in the Tudor Stakes and Lady Sassoon's Cathey III in the April Stakes. Moore gave racegoers a glimpse of true star quality when keeping the still ungainly St Padarn beautifully balanced to win by three lengths and then he gave the unraced chestnut filly Cathey a lovely ride, coming smoothly through the field to win at the generous odds for any Murless runner that season of 10–1. The glass was set fair for Newmarket.

Royal Palace was the quiet champion. He never radiated power or star quality, was in no way flamboyant. But he was a great racehorse, whose speed, stamina and supreme courage did much to boost Britain's prestige in the bloodstock world. Bold Lad for Ireland and Taj Dewan still looked formidable obstacles to Royal Palace's success in the Two Thousand. Moreover, unlike the Murless colt who was being aimed specially at the Derby, these two had both been laid out for the mile classic. If Paddy Prendergast's young Australian jockey Des Lake had allowed Bold Lad to run in his hands he might have finished closer. As it was, he pulled back the big bay with disastrous results. At the Bushes, Golden Horus went on, followed by Taj Dewan. Running into The Dip the French colt took the lead, inadvertently squeezing Golden Horus on to Bold Lad who had nevertheless already shot his bolt.

Meanwhile, George Moore had switched his mount and 100 yards out, he took the lead from his former pupil, nineteen-year-old Freddie Head. Taj Dewan fought back but George kept his colt going, to win by a short head. 'Freddie had first run,' he said, 'and my horse lost half a length down the hill, but then I just wore him down.' Noel said immediately that Royal Palace, like Crepello, that other Guineas winner, would not run again until the Derby.

The luck was changing at last for Royal Palace's owner, Mr Joel. Although his father had won the Derby with Sunstar in 1911 and Humourist ten years later, Jim had still not been successful at Epsom. In fact, despite all the money he had lavished on breeding, he had won only one previous classic – the wartime version of the One Thousand Guineas with Picture Play in 1944. Now his colt was 2–1 favourite for the Derby.

The first-ever British classic to be started from the stalls was a resounding success in every way and there was more to follow. The next day Noel and George completed the Guineas double at Newmarket when Fleet defeated the best that Ireland and France could offer.

It was a great training achievement for Noel. His Beckhampton

---

ABOVE   Mr Jim Joel's Connaught, ridden by Sandy Barclay, wins the 1970 Eclipse Stakes, Sandown
BELOW   Ascot 1970 – Welsh Pageant wins the Queen Elizabeth II Stakes, ridden by Sandy Barclay

predecessor Fred Darling, had won both classics with Big Game and Sun Chariot, but these were wartime events and Noel himself had gone nearest to duplicating this with The Cobbler (second) and Queenpot in 1948.

Fleet, Regality, Royal Saint, who was ridden by Lester, and Jadeite, looked best in the paddock before a pathetically small crowd reduced, no doubt, by the rain and strong wind. Noel was proved right when he said that Fleet would give no trouble from the starting stalls. The bay half-sister to Pourparler and Display jumped smartly out of the gate and settled in quietly behind her stable-companion, Royal Saint. Half a dozen fillies were there with a chance at the Bushes. Edward Hide on the German filly Pia went in front but in The Dip Moore had persuaded Fleet to brave the gale and take the lead, keeping his filly going to hold off the strong challenge of St Pauli Girl.

George Moore was understandably over the moon and he announced proudly to the world: 'Well, I've managed to save the first two classics for England!' Certainly, as Piggott's successor, the Australian champion had been in an unenviable position, the obvious target of all the critics. In just a few weeks he had proved all the most extravagant claims to be true. He had completely justified the faith of Prince Aly and of Noel.

Legs, as every horseman knows, are there to be used, to provide impulsion, to direct lateral movement and to balance. Moore's horses, like Breasley's, were always perfectly balanced, poised to slip through openings the second they were presented. Moore's reactions were electric and he sat into his mount with a low stream-lined crouch which lessened wind resistance. Ironically it was Piggott on Royal Saint, whom the Australian master strategist chose to hide behind to break the strong wind in the early stages of the fillies' classic.

For too long since the retirement of Sir Gordon we have become accustomed to leading jockeys who have not learned to use their whips in the left hand as well as the right. Like the great riders of the thirties Moore, who never hit a horse hard, could, in a flash, pull his

---

ABOVE Sandy Barclay rides Lupe to victory in the 1970 Oaks
BELOW Owners Mr and Mrs Williams, with Altesse Royale, after her 1971 Oaks win

H

whip through from one hand to the other to balance or correct. He was an exceptional judge of pace, and he studied his horses. 'On Wednesday,' he said after the One Thousand, 'we were worried about Fleet. She was all worked up and Noel and I were afraid she might be too upset to do her best. But the moment I talked to her this morning I knew she'd be all right.'

Although the bookmakers tried to tempt betters to back him for the jockeys' championship, Moore announced that he had no intention of making a great effort to win it. 'I've had too much of it back home,' he said. 'Going here, there and everywhere. Then sometimes you have to disappoint people who want you to ride for them and that can be awkward.'

Over the years Noel enjoyed considerable success at Chester. The Roodeye is one of the most ancient courses – and the smallest – and records of racing there exist from 1540. It is shaped like a saucer set in a bend of the river Dee and is only just over a mile in circumference with a run-in of 230 yards, the shortest on any English track.

The Chester Vase is regarded as a significant Derby trial and numbers among its winners Derby victors such as Papyrus, Hyperion and Windsor Lad. Tulyar and Parthia, too, scored at Chester before going on to triumph at Epsom. The Cheshire Oaks has a similar reputation for indicating the winners of the classic fillies' race at Epsom showing, or perhaps teaching, classic animals to adapt themselves round turns.

Of all the wonderful races George Moore rode, one of the most memorable was that on Noel's Pink Gem in the Cheshire Oaks. It was his first visit to the course and, in a slow-run race, George had to keep Jim Joel's big, inexperienced chestnut filly in second place until the final turn when she was left in front. A furlong out however, the northern fans cheered 'Come on, Lester!' as the British champion jockey, riding locally-trained Ludham, swept past with a flourish. It looked as though the race was over. Pink Gem sprawled, but her jockey, now half a length behind, remained cool. Collecting and balancing his mount, George gentled her into her bridle again, so that she suddenly lengthened her stride and fought back in the last fifty yards to win by a head. Noel commented, 'That was a riding lesson. The filly has had only one previous race, she's green and was not suited to this sharp track.'

At the time it was a fantastic bonanza for Australian jockeys in Europe, with George Moore, Scobie Breasley and Bill Williamson, Ron Hutchinson, Russ Maddock, Des Lake and Bill Pyres all riding. But, despite his success, George was not happy. 'All the travelling over here is terrible,' he complained. 'In Australia we ride only two days a week.'

Noel had prepared Royal Palace for the Derby with his usual quiet skill and, as the big day drew near, it was clear that the colt's own laziness was the one factor that could bring about his downfall. Unlike many other trainers Noel never believed in sacrificing horses on the altar of his classic hopes. It is always necessary to have lead horses, that is to say animals who can gallop with the classic candidates, and for this purpose Noel had invested in Bunker, a fair four-year-old handicapper who had won well for Bernard van Cutsem and who was considered to be ideal for the job. Nevertheless in September Bunker, ridden by George Moore, won the Great Yorkshire Handicap, and it was clear that leading the Derby favourite in his work had certainly done him no harm at all.

The last serious work-out before the Derby was over eleven furlongs at Racecourse Side at Newmarket. The gallop took place on 31 May, exactly a week before the Derby. Royal Palace, now 2–1 favourite for the Epsom classic, ridden by Moore, was accompanied by the four-year-old Bunker and also Sucaryl and Astral Green, who set off in front and kept up a rousing gallop for a mile. As the leader faded Sucaryl, who was to prove himself a high-class horse in his own right, went on, closely followed by Royal Palace and Bunker. Inside the last furlong Moore asked for an effort and Jim Joel's colt accelerated in that thrilling way that proved him as the year's champion. But just as he had done when he passed Taj Dewan in the Guineas, Royal Palace considered that his job was now done. So, when at that crucial moment the lightly weighted Bunker delivered a perfectly timed challenge it needed all Moore's coaxing to keep the favourite going so that the bay and the brown passed the finish together. 'That was exactly what we bought Bunker for,' said Noel. 'I am well satisfied.'

Apart from the favourite, the field that Derby Day was not particularly impressive in the parade. None of the fancied runners gave any trouble in the stalls, but several who had no right to be in the line-up caused an uneccessary delay.

The gimmick of this Derby was El Mighty, a Lambourn-trained colt whose public form did not really justify his running in the classic, but who, on the strength of a much publicized dream by a Peterborough storekeeper, had been backed from 200–1 down to 25–1 in a crazy betting spree. Running in blinkers and ridden by Paul Cook, the chestnut came from last to first after they had gone a furlong and had left the top of the hill. Then Moore began to make up ground on the favourite. Moving smoothly down the hill, he was beautifully placed in fourth or fifth position at Tattenham Corner and took the lead much earlier than expected as they straightened out. Lester Piggott, riding little Ribocco, now drew level on the wide outside but, as Royal Palace met the rising ground, George came right away to win by two and a half lengths, with Scobie Breasely third on Dart Board two lengths away.

It was Noel's third Derby, and with the first three classics already under his belt, he had won £132,751 for his patrons – more than any other British trainer had ever before achieved in a whole season.

Moore was thrilled. 'This is better than any Melbourne Cup. Our head man told me that Sir Gordon Richards always said you must be in the first four at Tattenham Corner. Royal Palace pulled hard for the first furlong, but then he settled beautifully. I nudged him up to them at the top of the hill. I was going to let him flop down the hill, so I made him catch hold of his bit and that was really why we went to the front so soon. I knew that as soon as he met the rising ground he would be all right. Piggott got right up to me on the outside, but I hadn't done much by then. I was just waiting for the hill. If it had been another half mile, I'd have come even more easily.'

Looking back now, Noel tells me that he had been worried. 'George didn't give him the best of rides. The horse was all over the place. Fortunately he was a very good colt with a perfect temperament and the opposition was moderate. Still he won the Derby and he proved himself completely later on.' The plan for him was a rest after Epsom in preparation for an assault on the Triple Crown. The Great Voltigeur Stakes at York would be the preliminary to the St Leger.

Fleet failed to stay in the Oaks, finishing fourth behind Pia but, reverting to a mile at Royal Ascot, gave Moore his 2000th winner in the Coronation Stakes.

Everything continued to go well for Warren Place. Ribocco and Sucaryl paid tribute to Royal Palace by finishing first and second divided by only half a length in the Irish Sweeps Derby.

The fact that Sucaryl's first run of the season was in the Irish Sweeps Derby was not intentional. 'I'd declared the horse to run at Ascot,' says the Guv'nor. 'I was just walking down to the paddock when Tom Nickalls came up and said: "You're *not qualified* to run. Your colt has just not won enough money.'

So Noel, Julie and George Moore set off for the Curragh. In the waiting-room at Cambridge airport time went by and they were told that the plane was still not ready. There was a technical fault. 'I sent for the pilot,' says Noel, 'and he told me that they'd received a message that there was a bomb on board our plane. I told him to get cracking or we would be late. As we were taxi-ing away, a police car drove up but I told the pilot to kick on. As we took off, Moore asked the pilot what all the fuss was about. When he learned about the bomb scare he went as white as a sheet. "We must turn back," he said, and turned to Julie demanding in that Australian voice, "D'you want to die to-dye?"'

'I think that cost us the Sweeps Derby. He was in such a state that he shot out in front far too soon – three furlongs from home – but was still only beaten half a length.' Noel laughed. 'Still,' he said, 'the weights of the News of the World Handicap at Goodwood came out before the Sweeps Derby. If ever there was a racing certainty. . . .'

Fleet was now being aimed for the Eclipse Stakes at Ascot on 8 July. So too was another Murless horse who was destined to be a champion.

Today, when people rightly praise the magnificent bay stallion Bustino, a true classic horse who stands at the Royal Stud of Wolferton in Norfolk, and recall his tremendous battle with Grundy for the 1975 King George VI and Queen Elizabeth Stakes, referring to it as 'the race of the century', Noel laughs. 'I'll tell you this,' he says, 'Bustino's sire would have beaten them both comfortably. He was a very good racehorse indeed.' Busted, one of the most exciting stallions in Europe, has been standing for thirteen years at Snailwell Stud, Newmarket.

Stud manager Tony Earl says proudly, 'Busted has been fully

booked ever since he started and every year I have to turn away twenty or thirty people.' Yet it was not always like this.

The late Stanhope Joel was not averse to paying big prices for yearlings and, although by no means cheap in the fifties, the 1500 guineas paid with an eye for the stud by Dick Perryman for the filly by Vimy out of the Court Martial mare, Martial Loan, was decidedly low by his standards. It was, as might be expected from Dick, a shrewd purchase: Vimy's sire, Wild Risk, had already established himself as an outstanding sire of broodmares. Although Wild Risk was even smaller than Hyperion his son, Vimy, winner of the King George VI and Queen Elizabeth Stakes in 1955, was a big horse. On Dick Perryman's retirement the filly, Sans le Sous, was sent to Ireland to be trained by Brud Featherstonhaugh on the Curragh. Like many of her sire's stock she was tough and genuine, but not particularly fast. Still, she could gallop well enough to win a small race for Brud before being retired to the Joels' Snailwell Stud. Here, mated to Crepello, she foaled in 1963 a fine bay colt, which Stanhope Joel named Busted. He was sent as a yearling to Brud Featherstonhaugh.

Big and backward, the colt demanded time to mature and appeared only twice as a two-year-old in the very backend, first in the Beresford Stakes over a mile at the Curragh, and then, on the very last day of the season, in the seven-furlong Larkspur Stakes at Leopardstown. Busted was unfancied and did not impress in either events. He wintered well, grew still more and now began to show speed and class with a low devouring stride and after running second over one mile and a half at Naas, Busted put up his best performance as a three-year-old, winning the mile-and-a-quarter Gallinule Stakes at the Curragh by a head from Pieces of Eight. 'They rode him all wrong,' says Tony Earl. 'They even let him make all the running in the Irish Sweeps Derby, which was entirely against his nature.'

Now the master set to work. He entrusted the big colt to the hands of Bill Rickaby who, on the point of retirement, was now riding out for Noel. Acting on the trainer's instructions it was he who anchored Busted and taught him to settle. Part of the Murless secret is that he never liked his good horses to be fully extended at home. They had to work within themselves, gaining confidence and strength. So, when Busted was first asked to do the job for which he had been brought over and it was found that the four-year-old was going every bit as well as the best three-year-old in Europe, Noel decided that they should work together no more. So under the Guv'nor's careful tutelage Busted became a star in his own right and a fitting successor to his sire's memory.

On the Saturday before the Newmarket Spring Meeting (at which Noel was to win the two classics) Busted made his English début, ridden by Moore in the Coronation Stakes over a mile and a quarter at Sandown. His opponents included his conqueror at 'The Park', the redoubtable McGrath colt, Bluerullah. Moore settled the big colt happily in the large field, came fourth into the long, climbing straight, got a good run on the inner, took the lead at the distance and won very comfortably by three lengths from Haymaking, with Bluerullah third, a short head away.

A slight injury kept Busted off the racecourse for two months. But Noel had time to prepare him to the same course and distance for the historic Eclipse Stakes. Fleet was again partnered by George Moore, and Noel gave the ride on Busted in the £22,697 semi-classic to Bill Rickaby, who knew the colt so well. The veteran jockey made no mistake. He settled his mount towards the rear of the select field of nine runners which included Great Nephew, Fleet, Bluerullah, the Italian crack Appiani II and the Irish Sweeps Derby winner, Sodium. Once well into the straight the great stride lengthened and Busted swept past his rivals to win by two and a half lengths from Great Nephew in a very fast time.

Noel decided to try Busted for the King George VI and Queen Elizabeth Stakes at Ascot just a week later, though he would be taking no fewer than four Derby winners: Ribocco and Sodium (Irish), Necius (French) and Appiani II (Italian), as well as Bon Mot III, the first British-owned winner of the Prix de l'Arc de Triomphe and Salvo, fresh from his victory in Royal Ascot's Hardwicke Stakes.

Reunited with George Moore, Busted gave racing a day to remember. Once again he settled at the rear of his field and his jockey had such confidence in his colt's turn of foot that he broke his Ascot rules and did not move until well into the short straight. As soon as he was asked, Busted stormed through to take the lead a furlong out and won in the smoothest possible style from Salvo, who was a neck in front of Ribocco. The time was fast.

Noel then took Busted to Paris for the £8000 Prix Henri Foy on 3 September to prepare for the Arc de Triomphe. Parisian *turfistes* were most impressed by their first look at the magnificent Murless bay, who had beaten some of their best at Ascot and Sandown. Roger Poincelet made the running on Pot aux Roses while George Moore settled Busted behind the other eight runners. The order remained virtually unchanged until two furlongs from home when the English colt made a move. A hundred yards later he hit the front and, producing his now famous acceleration, came right away to win by four easy lengths in good time. On the same afternoon, Salvo, runner-up to Busted at Ascot, won the Grosser Preis of Baden-Baden, beating the German Derby winner Luciano.

After Busted returned to Newmarket, it was found that he had developed slight tendon trouble. He had run his last race and retired to stud unbeaten. Busted was honoured as 'horse of the year' and European champion of 1967. 'After his performances in 1968,' says Noel, 'I am convinced that Royal Palace should have been Horse of the Year instead of St Ivor.'

At the Snailwell Stud, Newmarket, Busted was an immediate success and his fertility percentage has never been below eighty per cent.

Noel's winnings had already easily passed his own British record, and our leading trainer and his Australian jockey kept up the success saga with winning expeditions to France. Noel broke through the £200,000 barrier when Sun Rock landed the Gordon Stakes at Goodwood, and he recalled that it was just ten years earlier that he had been the first British trainer to reach £100,000.

Royal Palace had the St Leger at his mercy. He would surely be the first British Triple Crown winner since Bahram won the Guineas, the Derby and the St Leger for the Aga Khan in 1935. The favourite was so well in himself and so full of beans one morning on Racecourse Side that he shied violently at a pneumatic drill working on the road and hit himself hard just above the joint. Noel says, 'I was worried about the suspensory trouble and, although I did my best to get him there (to Doncaster) you can't go against nature. He had a definite leg.'

Meanwhile the Queen's Hopeful Venture who had started the triumphant Moore-Murless partnership back at Newmarket's Craven Meeting, was going from strength to strength. He won

Chester's Grosvenor Stakes in a common canter by eight lengths and Noel says, 'If Royal Palace had not been so far in front of him at the time, I would certainly have wanted to run Hopeful Venture in the Derby. Instead we kept him for the King Edward VII Stakes at Royal Ascot where he was very unluckily beaten a short head as a result of stumbling on the final bend.' Hopeful Venture then won the mile-and-a-half Princess of Wales Stakes at the Newmarket July Meeting and the Oxfordshire Stakes at Newbury.

Noel now planned to go for the Prix Royal Oak – the French St Leger – in the middle of September, leaving our St Leger for Royal Palace. A fortnight before the St Leger, just ten days after he had rapped his joint, Royal Palace once again strode out well in a seven furlong half-speed gallop on The Limekilns at Newmarket. The pace was slightly increased and Royal Palace was allowed to go in front for the last two furlongs. The St Leger favourite moved well and trotted out sound. As a result Jim Joel's colt was brought back into the classic betting at 5–4 on by one firm of bookmakers but Noel, as scrupulously fair to the public as always, was still very cautious. He said, 'Time was getting short. Hopeful Venture would make a very adequate substitute if Royal Palace should not be ready for Doncaster.'

On 4 September, looking superbly fit, the Derby winner cantered on Newmarket Heath ridden by Noel's outstanding horseman head lad John 'Spider' Gibson, a quiet dedicated backroom boy who had ridden the colt in most of his homework. The odds shortened still further to 6–4 on. But, after the favourite's last full-scale work-out before the St Leger the following day the bookmakers knocked the colt out to 11–10 on. One firm even suspended betting on the race during an afternoon when nearly every other candidate for the Doncaster classic was said to have been backed.

The work-out was almost a repitition of the big bay's final gallop before the Derby. As in May he was not particularly impressive, but he pulled up perfectly sound, ridden by George Moore and partnered by Hopeful Venture (Bill Rickaby), Bunker (Willie Snaith), Sucaryl (Sandy Barclay) and Royal Falcon. Royal Palace was sent thirteen furlongs – further than he had hitherto raced. As Royal Falcon led the remainder in Indian file, the Derby winner was soon ten lengths behind. But he moved up at the mile post and finished on terms with his companions, just behind Royal Falcon and Sucaryl. Knowing how lazy he always was it was fairly obvious that he could have won at any stage. Noel announced: 'Royal Palace went well in his gallop and I am satisfied with his work.'

But when he worked the colt again on 9 September he finally and reluctantly scratched Royal Palace from the St Leger. 'His preparation was interrupted for ten days,' said Noel, 'and you've got to be 120 per cent fit for a classic. Although his leg has recovered well, he would probably break down if he were to get tired in the closing stages of the St Leger.'

Ribocco won the Doncaster classic with Royal Palace's understudy, Hopeful Venture, finishing one and a half lengths away second, just half a length in front of the Italian challenger, Ruysdael II, with Dart Board, trained by Sir Gordon Richards an unlucky fourth. The Derby and Irish Derby form had been so wonderfully regular in that vintage British season that George Moore, who had partnered Hopeful Venture, was fully justified in believing 'Royal Palace would certainly have won today. No risk. At his best he is five or six lengths in front of Hopeful Venture.'

Noel decided to saddle Sucaryl for the French St Leger the following Sunday, but Moore made too much use of Sucaryl and he finished third behind Samos III, beaten two and a quarter lengths.

But the Warren Place success story was not quite finished. Noel still had some formidable shots in his locker. On National Cancer Day at Ascot at the end of September he had two chances, with Sucaryl in the David Robinson Stakes and in the Michael Sobell Stakes with Fleet. Moore only had to remind Fleet over the last few yards to win by a comfortable neck from Resilience II.

It was a different story with Sucaryl who appeared badly placed, lying last of the five runners in Swinley Bottom. Suddenly, before any other jockey knew what was happening, George had slipped past them all and taken the lead before entering the straight. This brilliant, surprise manoeuvre, one of our last glimpses of the vintage Moore, gained Lady Sassoon's colt a decisive advantage and he held on well to win by one and a half lengths from Mariner.

Noel decided to stick to the plan of taking Hopeful Venture to France, so, at the beginning of October, they went for the Prix Henry Delamarre at Longchamp. 'It was the first time the Queen had ever had a runner in France, and I don't suppose many French reacegoers had ever seen the Royal colours, so it was something of an occasion.' It was indeed. Hopeful Venture, favourite at 7–4 and ridden by Moore, was first past the post in this event worth £11,000 to the winner. He won comfortably and the crowd went wild with excitement. As George rode his mount past the winning post they kept on cheering until he had unsaddled and walked up the stairs into the glass-fronted weighing room.

But Jack Leader had changed his mind about racing again in France and his filly, In Command, who had been disqualified in her previous French race, had finished second. Then it was announced that Brian Taylor, rider of the runner-up, had objected. A French commentator, dismayed at this unprecedented action by a British jockey to one of the Royal horses, said, 'The Stewards had no option but to hold an enquiry.' After examining the film of the race, the Stewards found that Hopeful Venture had crossed In Command. They awarded the race to Taylor and placed the Queen's colt second. But the Stewards demonstrated their feelings when they added that they absolved Moore from blame. They said he 'had done everything possible to avoid the incident'. Noel said, 'I personally thought they made the wrong decision.'

It was most unfortunate that this latest objection to a Royal horse should have happened in a foreign country. Hopeful Venture ran once more in France three weeks later on the eve of Moore's departure for Australia. The Prix Conseil Municipal has so often been a graveyard for good horses, and when it is soft the going at Longchamp is bottomless. 'In any case,' Noel said, 'Hopeful Venture had gone, he was over the top.' The same applied to Royal Palace when he turned out for the Champion Stakes, but this run proved once more Noel's skill in bringing the Derby winner back to soundness ready for the coming season.

So many other horses had figured in that truly remarkable year. For example, the Murless-bred St Chad, running in Gwen's colours, had established himself as a grand stallion prospect with sparkling victories including the Jersey Stakes at Royal Ascot, the Hungerford Stakes at Newbury and the Wills Mile at Goodwood. There was tremendous hope too, for his little sister Caergwrle, who won at Chester. Among the other promising two-year-olds was Lorenzaccio, a consistent winner of the July Stakes, who had been placed in both the Prix Robert Papin and the Prix Morny as well as the Champagne Stakes at Doncaster. Cranberry Sauce and St Padarn had won top class races.

By the end of 1967, thirty-four Warren Place horses had won sixty races worth £256,899 in England alone. Moore, who had left for Australia undecided about his return to England in 1968, did not come back and Noel confirmed at the end of November that Sandy Barclay would be promoted as first jockey to the stable in the following season. At the age of nineteen the young Scotsman was to be first jockey to the champion trainer. It looked like being another good year for The Master of Warren Place.

10

The Connaught Career
1968–1969

❋

For the racing world the winter of 1967 was one of discontent, blighted as it was by the outbreak of foot and mouth. Horses are not affected by this disease, but the movement of all animals is severely restricted. Sales and exports suffered, and for more than two months National Hunt fixtures were cancelled at the request of the Ministry of Agriculture. French and Irish race programmes were published in the daily papers and the BBC even televised racing from Saint-Cloud to satisfy the punters.

Nevertheless, the British racing scene was enlivened by an important event at Tattersalls' Newmarket December Sales. The purchasing power of the dollar was in the ascendancy on the British Turf, and it was to prove irresistible that December.

1967 had seen the death of Major Lionel Holliday, a great owner who, late in life, had been made a member of the Jockey Club. This crusty old man was unpopular with some because of his curtness and his insistence on having his own way in everything, but Lionel Holliday really loved and understood horses. On his death the Jockey Club made his son Brook a member. Certainly some outstanding horses have since carried the Holliday white and maroon silks but the old man's racing empire had one last triumph in his memory that October when the Holliday jockey Bill Williamson won the Observer Gold Cup by seven lengths on Vaguely Noble.

This race for two-year-olds is run over a mile at Doncaster in October, and was inaugurated by Phil Bull as the Timeform Gold Cup. After changes of sponsorship it has now become the William Hill Futurity. In 1967 the race was worth £17,000; this was a large sum for a British two-year-old contest which, although considerably less that the value of the French Grand Criterium run over the same distance at Longchamp, made it compare very favourably with that race as a classic trial.

Reviewing the 1968 opposition Noel recognized only too well the enormous potential of Vaguely Noble, in the Doncaster contest but unfortunately, Vaguely Noble had not been considered good enough or well enough grown as a yearling to be entered for any of the classics. When the large Holliday draft of horses in training was offered at the December Sales there was betting on the amount that Vaguely Noble would fetch and certain confidence that he would break the previous British auction record for a horse in training of 47,000 guineas. Favourite in the betting at 4–1 was a price between 85,000 and 89,000 guineas. This figure was soon left behind when the star of the Holliday stable, who had been closely inspected by innumerable experts, entered the ring looking magnificent. The sale climaxed a day of hectic selling dominated by the dollar and the franc in Tattersalls' ring. Bidding for Vaguely Noble opened at 80,000 guineas and rose quickly.

'He could still be cheap,' shouted the auctioneer Ken Watt at the packed ring as the bids rose above 130,000 guineas. French blood-stock agent Godolphin Darley, who had made the running, hesitated and in stepped the splendidly extrovert American dealer Albert Yank, conspicuous in a fluorescent ski-suit among the sheepskin uniformed crowd. Pandemonium broke out when the hammer fell at a new world record price paid for a horse in training of 136,000 guineas to Mr Yank, who was apparently acting on behalf of Hollywood plastic surgeon Dr Robert Franklin 'and his beautiful wife Wilma'. The successful agent announced proudly, 'Dr Franklin is a world-famous plastic surgeon who works in Hollywood making beautiful women more beautiful. He already has twelve horses and three broodmares, but this is his first ready-made racehorse.'

Although it is only comparatively recently that we have in Britain come to realize the true financial power of Kentucky, we had a warning when Dr Franklin, speaking from his Beverley Hills mansion, said, 'We were determined to have this horse. We would have gone to a million pounds if we had to. I told Mr Yank if anyone gave him a tussle the sky was the limit. We are delighted to have him.'

Yank was acting in conjunction with the Anglo-Irish Agency, who sent the colt to the Curragh to be trained by Paddy Prendergast. This was an admirable arrangement because Bill Williamson, who had done so much to help in the making of Vaguely Noble, had just signed up as first jockey to Prendergast. When, soon after the sale, Texas oil tycoon multi-millionaire Bunker Hunt bought a large share of the colt (knowing more about racing than the plastic surgeon) he quickly decided that if this colt was to justify his purchase price there was only one chance. He must win the world's greatest and richest race, the Arc de Triomphe. The whole gamble depended on this, and he decided to send Vaguely Noble to Chantilly to be trained by Etienne Pollet. It was a bitter blow for Prendergast and for his jockey.

Further opposition to Noel's big race plans in 1968 came from Ireland where the huge former international polo-player Raymond Guest was now the American ambassador. Raymond had imported a magnificent bay colt by Sir Gaylord call Sir Ivor who, in 1967, had won three of his four starts including the National Stakes at the Curragh and the Grand Criterium at Lonchamp, with Lester Piggott in the saddle. How he was ever beaten first time out in the Tyros' Stakes at the Curragh on 21 July it is hard to tell. Sir Ivor started at 20–1 and finished out of the first four on that occasion. Sir Ivor was favourite to win the 1968 classic races. It was easy to see why. Quite apart from his racecourse performances, he was a really high-class colt, combining power and grace of body and action with a lovely intelligent head. He had grown during the winter and now stood 16 hands 2 inches.

Apart from his own Warren Place prospects, Noel recognized in Petingo one other potential classic winner in England. Lester Piggott was in an enviable position; he could choose between Sir Ivor and this top English colt, on whom he had won the Gimcrack Stakes at York and the Middle Park Stakes at Newmarket for his father-in-law, Sam Armstrong. Petingo, a brilliantly fast, rich bay son of Petition, with a distinctive white face and hind socks, now stood 15 hands 3½ inches. He was rated as the top British two-year-old of 1967, with 9 stone 7 pounds, just one pound above Vaguely Noble. Sir Ivor, on the other hand, had always been earmarked for Epsom, and when on 17 March Lester announced that he would ride Sir Ivor in the classic the Guest colt was already 5–2 for the Guineas and 5–1 for the Derby. He was 6–4 for the first classic after he had won Ascot's Two Thousand Guineas Trial by half a length in a time nearly half a second faster than the average for the track despite the earliness of the season. It was only 5 April.

So in 1968, the year which came to be known as 'the year of Sir Ivor', that was the line-up. Whatever Sir Ivor's successes it was still another triumphant year for Noel, who became champion trainer once again. Thirty of his horses won forty-seven races worth £141,508 and his jockey, Sandy Barclay, finished in second place behind Lester Piggott with 116 winners. Noel's stars of that season were the four-year-olds Royal Palace and Hopeful Venture, the three-year-olds Connaught, Lorenzaccio and Caergwrle and the two-year-old Welsh Pageant. The new trainer-jockey partnership of Murless and Barclay got off to a good start at Kempton on Easter Monday, where their double included the victory of Caergwrle in the One Thousand Guineas Trial. This chestnut was bred by Noel and by Gwen, in whose colours she ran. Gwen had named her after a village on the Welsh border near Chester; the chestnut filly's dam, whom the Murlesses also bred, was called Caerphilly. Caergwrle is pronounced 'Caer-girlie' and, as a Scot, Gwen says: 'Well, "girlie" is Scottish for filly, isn't it?'

When Newmarket's Craven Meeting started the following day, Petingo easily won the Craven Stakes ridden by his new jockey, Joe Mercer. Noel's Lorenzaccio, giving fourteen pounds to the winner, was beaten only a neck in the Free Handicap. And the spring sun was obviously shining for Warren Place when Sandy Barclay won the Wood Ditton Stakes on Lady Sassoon's Sugar Apple, and the Nell Gwyn Stakes on the same owner's Abbie West.

In some quarters·Sandy Barclay was already being compared unfavourably with his predecessor George Moore. Criticism had arisen from his handling of Connaught in the Two Thousand Guineas the previous day, when Sir Ivor had won by one and half lengths from Petingo, with the big bay Murless colt way down the course. It was said that Barclay was not man enough to handle a classic animal of this type. But the nineteen-year-old Scot silenced all the critics on 2 May by winning the One Thousand Guineas on Caergwrle. Barclay's handling of this superbly fit, exuberant favourite completely justified the faith of his employer.

'Tweedledum and Tweedledee' – Noel and Sir Gordon Richards deep in conversation at the Houghton yearling sales

Connaught was another good horse and Noel trained the massive bay through a series of dramas to win seven top-class races at three, four and five years and earn his owner-breeder Mr Jim Joel nearly £100,000 in stakes. 'Connaught was a very good racehorse indeed,' he said, 'who would have won eight out of ten Derbys.' Noel naturally regrets that this favourite 'character' was foaled in the same year as Sir Ivor. 'Connaught was a wonderful mile and a quarter horse,' he says. 'He really didn't get further. But, yes, he'd have lasted home at Epsom in any normal year.' One would have expected the sons of Noel's second Derby winner St Paddy to be big. Connaught over-did it. 'He's always been tremendous,' Noel continued. 'In the stalls he touched both sides and each end. Barclay couldn't get his legs down!' This caused the first of a series of dramas which became a part of Connaught's life. The huge colt – 'he stands over 16 hands 3 inches and is so broad with it' – had the power of a bull but had also shown at home that he possessed the speed of a gazelle. On 22 August 1967 Noel had taken him to York where Connaught was installed 5–1 favourite for the six-furlong Convivial Stakes. 'He was a certainty,' says Noel. 'He only had to go down and come back. But George Moore couldn't get him into the stalls. The horse would never go in if there was anybody behind him. He was withdrawn.'

In 1967 British stalls were then still in their infancy and the handlers were not as efficient as they are today. In order to give Connaught a run before the end of that season, Noel took the colt to Doncaster, where there were no stalls, for the Observer Gold Cup. Once again Connaught was made favourite. It was his first race and although still green and very backward, he ran well to finish fifth in the race which Vaguely Noble dominated, just half a length behind his more experienced stable-companion, Lorenzaccio.

Connaught thrived during the winter and on 20 April 1968 went to Newbury for the Greenham Stakes, the seven-furlong event which has long been regarded as a trial for the Two Thousand Guineas but yet has seldom produced the true solution to the first classic. He was backed down to 9–2 but once again was foiled by the

---

ABOVE Geoff Lewis on Owen Dudley winning the 1973 Wood Ditton Stakes at Newmarket

BELOW Noel with Mr Arpad Hesch (centre) and Mr Peter Burrell (right)

J

stalls and had to be withdrawn. Noel says, 'I took him home and got permission to use the stalls on the racecourse at Newmarket. I would put him in the stalls, jump him off, let him gallop for about a furlong and a half, pull up, go back and do it again. We would do this quite a few times and he became good at it. So good that in the Two Thousand Guineas he went straight into the stalls, jumped off, galloped about a furlong and a half and tried to pull up! He finished last but one behind Sir Ivor. I was so furious with him that I said I'd send him down to the vet's, have him castrated and send him jumping. However, I relented and decided to give him another chance in the Chester Vase over one and a half miles five days later. He ran a marvellous race and looked like winning when he took a lead half a mile from home, but he came under pressure a furlong out and was beaten half a length by Jakey Astor's Remand. With hindsight I suppose I should have realized then that he didn't really stay more than a mile and a quarter in top company.'

Nevertheless this performance earned Connaught a run in the Derby at Epsom, where he started third favourite behind Sir Ivor and Remand. Though sweating a little, he went straight into the stalls and the other runners followed quickly. At the top of the hill Benroy led from Connaught, Laureate, Society, Atopolis, Remand, Mount Athos and Sir Ivor. Halfway down the hill Barclay sent Connaught into the lead and, as the big horse rounded Tattenham Corner superbly balanced, made his best way home. Inside the final furlong he could not resist the powerful challenge of Sir Ivor and was beaten one and half lengths by the American champion. Mount Athos was two and half lengths away third and Remand fourth. Noel could see how much the big, backward bay had improved since Chester and was still improving.

Noel normally refused to take Epsom three-year-olds to Royal Ascot on the grounds that the big meeting usually comes too soon after an inevitably hard race. 'That year was an exception,' he says. 'There was a three weeks' gap between the meetings. So I went for the King Edward VII Stakes and Connaught won very easily in a fast time.' In fact Connaught won by twelve lengths from Ribero, who was shortly to win the Irish Sweeps Derby and then the St Leger. The future Washington International hero Karabas, trained by Bernard van Cutsem, was four lengths away third. Barclay became top jockey of Royal Ascot with five winners.

On 1 August Goodwood erupted when Connaught, hot favourite for the Gordon Stakes, got loose and had to miss the race, and the Derby third place Mount Athos was rewarded with the £4093 prize. John Dunlop, his trainer, said, 'We weren't going to run because of Connaught, but the Duke of Norfolk told me, "You must never dodge one horse. Anything can happen."' Even the Duke couldn't have anticipated the accident which occurred as the chief Murless work-rider, Charlie Dyson, set off with Connaught on the one and a half mile trek from the racecourse stables to the paddock. 'He was stung by something,' says Noel. When Dyson, who had been kicked by the agonized colt, staggered back to the stables to report that Connaught had broken loose and galloped into the woods, he was sent to hospital; the horse, when caught, was clearly in no state to race. Noel reported that after his headlong trip through Birdless Grove he was covered with nettle stings and scratches.

Next came the Great Voltigeur Stakes of one and half miles at York's Festival Meeting. Once again Connaught, starting at 3–1 on, came in for his share of incident. After Barclay had taken the lead at the distance, Piggott on Riboccare challenged and hampered the favourite so badly before getting home by a neck, that a Stewards' enquiry followed immediately and the race was deservedly awarded to Connaught. Now Connaught was odds-on favourite for the St Leger. But it rained all night and all morning and the Guv'nor knew that his chance had gone. During the early stages Barclay held him up in an effort to conserve his speed. He lay third coming into the straight but, when asked for an effort three furlongs from home, could produce nothing and finished fifth behind Ribero. Noel remembers, 'Connaught ran well enough but, of course, he just didn't stay that trip.'

1969 started well for Connaught. In the previous year's Two Thousand Guineas Jimmy Reppin, subsequent winner of the Hungerford Stakes and Wills Mile, had finished third, four lengths behind Sir Ivor. Moreover he had already won the Yorkshire Stakes at Doncaster in March before meeting Connaught at level weights in Sandown's one and a quarter mile Coronation Stakes on 26 April. The Warren Place colt, running for the first time as a four-year-old, won by an astonishing six lengths. Lack of stamina caused him to finish a close third to the Duke of Devonshire's splendid mare, Park Top in a very fast-run Coronation Cup over the one and a half mile

Derby course. He had, incidentally, maintained the drama by dropping his jockey before the start. As in the previous year's Derby, Piggott collared Barclay inside the final furlong.

The only occasion on which Noel was called before the Jockey Club occurred during this stage in his career – he was reported for opening the trial ground on The Limekilns during high summer to work Connaught. He explains, 'Connaught was a stuffy horse and I always liked to send him along for a sharp four furlongs to clean him out on the day before I was going to give him a mile or a mile and a quarter gallop. On this particular Friday The Limekilns were supposed to be closed. Humphrey Cottrell saw me using the trial grounds and reported me to the Jockey Club. I received a summons to attend to answer for my sins. So I told them that I would attend only if both Cottrell and their Newmarket agent Fellows were present. I was duly ushered in and there they were all sitting there, including those two. General Sir George Burns asked me what I had to say about it. I said, "Am I to understand, sir, that somebody is trying to teach me how to train racehorses?" That was the end of that. Although I have not on all occasions seen eye to eye with the Jockey Club, I have always thought that they were doing what they considered was best for the sport, and I have always been a great upholder of it. I would hate to see professional Stewards coming in. I've always found the Jockey Club to be very fair people.'

On to Royal Ascot, where Connaught ran 'a blinder' in the Prince of Wales Stakes, making all the running to beat the subsequent Eclipse winner Wolver Hollow by five lengths and break the Ascot one and quarter mile record by 3·95 seconds.

'After this Connaught, along with a number of my other horses, suffered from influenza,' says Noel. 'I gave him three runs at the backend, and, although he was a long way below par, he still finished third in the Scarborough and second in the Queen Elizabeth II Stakes.' In 1970 Noel gave Connaught three races as a five-year-old and he won them all. Fully recovered from his 'flu, but bigger than ever, he was given time to come to hand and reappeared at Sandown on 26 May to win the one and a quarter mile Westbury Stakes very smoothly as a nice curtain-raiser for another crack at the Prince of Wales Stakes.

On Ascot's opening day, Paul Mellon's two-year-old Mill Reef won the Coventry Stakes and Connaught, despite spreading a plate, hurtled home by four lengths to knock a third of a second off his own course record. He was now aimed for the world's most famous mile-and-a-quarter contest, the historic Eclipse Stakes at Sandown.

The bookmakers made the Hardwicke winner, Karabas, favourite at odds-on. As though to give the lie to this insult the gentle giant, squeezed once more into his stall, terrified his supporters by stumbling badly as he left it, but still made all the running to win by two and a half lengths and break the track record by half a second. Noel says, 'Mr Joel came into the unsaddling enclosure with a hand over his heart and his face wreathed in smiles. "That's enough," he told me. "I can't stand any more"!'

So Connaught was retired to the Woodditton Stud, still in the care of his trainer. 'He was one of the soundest racehorses I've ever known. That huge frame was carried on firm ground by legs of iron, which never knew a bandage in his life. Of course, he had a superlative action. He's always been a terrific old character. Although he wouldn't allow a vet in the yard, he's just like a big shaggy dog. You feel you should bring him into the house. I love him. He's not doing too badly as a stallion, is he?'

Connaught apart, the real star of Noel's 1967 and 1968 was Royal Palace and the Guv'nor's handling of Mr Joel's Derby winner as a four-year-old was quite masterly. Royal Palace had wintered well, and the improvement was obvious to all when Sandy Barclay rode him in public for the first time, landing the odds comfortably in the one and a quarter mile Coronation Stakes at Sandown on 27 April. In order to ensure a good gallop in the small field, Noel ran Royal Falcon ridden by Bill Rickaby in the Joel second colours as a pacemaker. Only three runners turned out against Royal Palace when he returned to Epsom to win the Coronation Cup over the Derby course in the style of a true champion. But Dan Kano, who had made all the running to win the previous year's Irish St Leger, now ridden by Lester Piggott fresh from Sir Ivor's Derby triumph, played into the favourite's hands by leading the field at a common canter in the early stages. From a seemingly hopeless position, shut in on the rails, Sandy broke out two furlongs from home and Royal Palace reproduced the brilliant speed that had won him the Two Thousand Guineas. Racing clear, he won going away by two lengths from Bamboozle with Dan Kano a neck away third.

The next outing on the champion's schedule was Royal Ascot's

133

new one and a quarter mile Prince of Wales Stakes. It was an ideal
curtain-raiser for the Eclipse, and as Noel said, 'Royal Palace needed
plenty of racing.' Starting at 4–1 on, the champion had no difficulty
in earning another £4630.

That summer was packed with drama which started at Sandown
on 5 July. Lester Piggott has gone on record as saying that Sir Ivor
did not really stay more than one and a quarter miles in a true-run
race. This fact accounted for his sensational defeat in the Irish
Sweeps Derby by Ribero, whom Connaught had beaten twelve
lengths at Ascot. Since the former Irish champion jockey, Liam
Ward, was engaged to ride all the O'Brien runners in his native
country, Piggott had partnered Ribero for Charles Engelhard and
beaten his own favourite horse to win the classic.

Raymond Guest, undeterred by Sir Ivor's defeat in the Irish
Derby, announced that he would run Sir Ivor in the Eclipse. Now
reunited with Piggott, and running at what we realize today was his
best distance, the American colt was to take on Royal Palace. Sir
Ivor's trainer said before the race, 'My colt is tremendously well, so
we have decided to let him take his chance. There are so few
one-and-a-quarter-mile races.'

The encounter in the traditional semi-classic race was strengthened by the presence of two French colts, Franc Castel and Taj
Dewan, who had been so narrowly beaten by Royal Palace in the
Two Thousand Guineas and was now ridden by the splendid
French champion, Yves Saint-Martin. Noel had decided not to run
Lorenzaccio, but the Lincoln winner, Frankincense, was also in the
field. The weight-for-age scale at that time in July has always
favoured the three-year-old. Since 1903 the Eclipse had not produced such a fascinating clash as this battle between two Derby
winners and a crack French colt. Then Rock Sand, winner of that
year's Two Thousand Guineas and Derby and due to complete the
Triple Crown, was opposed by Ard Patrick, winner of the previous
year's Derby and the filly Sceptre, who had taken all the other four
classics in 1902. On that occasion the four-year-olds prevailed.
Although carrying 10 stone 4 pounds Ard Patrick, ridden by
American 'Skeets' Martin, beat Sceptre by a neck with Rock Sand
three lengths away third.

It was reported that Royal Palace had been going particularly
well in his work at home and had never looked better, but he was

easy to back at 9–4, while Sir Ivor was 5–4 on favourite and Taj Dewan was at 7–2. It was a historic contest run at a cracking pace as the time two minutes 7·5 seconds (6·5 seconds under average) bore witness. Taj Dewan followed his compatriot, Franc Castel, round the bend and took the lead entering the stiff Sandown straight. A quarter of a mile out Sandy – just twenty years old and over-enthusiastic – kicked and Royal Palace sprawled. But he recovered his balance and battled on to win by a whisker. Afterwards Barclay admitted, 'It was my fault that Royal Palace didn't win more easily. I asked him to go soon and unbalanced him. I had to get him balanced again before I could go after Taj Dewan.'

In racing the French can seldom be congratulated on being the world's best losers. This occasion was no exception. They found it apparently almost impossible to believe the photographic evidence of their own eyes. Sir Ivor finished three-quarters of a length away in third place, and Lester said that the Epsom Derby winner was never striding out on the firm ground – an excuse which Noel dismissed. 'The going was just the same for all of us,' he says. 'Royal Palace disliked it just as much as Sir Ivor.'

Noel had in mind one more race for this gallant colt, the 1968 King George VI and Queen Elizabeth Stakes at Ascot – the supreme test. Royal Palace had beaten the current Derby winner over that colt's best distance. Now he was tackling not only the Frenchmen Felicio II and Topyo, winner of the previous year's Arc de Triomphe, as well as Carlos Primero from Italy, but also Ribero, who had defeated Sir Ivor at the Curragh. The start for the £24,020 race was delayed for more than ten minutes after Lester, with his ultra-short stirrup leathers, had been dislodged by Ribero on the way to the start. Nevertheless he took the lead in Swinley Bottom and galloped on strongly into the straight in front of the favourite. Sandy picked Royal Palace up and the colt responded immediately, lengthening his stride in the way he had come to know so well. He was already being cheered home when 150 yards out he faltered. The champion had broken down. Where most jockeys would have lost their heads, the young Scotsman remained cool. Even though the French challengers, with the whips of Poincelet and Pyers cracking, came at him, he never went for his stick, but rode his mount out with hands and heels. Royal Palace's sheer guts and will to win enabled him to last home by half a length for his last great

135

victory. As he limped into the winner's enclosure, there were few dry eyes at Ascot. It was the performance of a true champion. Noel says that John Hancock the judge told him that fifty yards from the post the French horse was in front.

Royal Palace retired to stud as the biggest English and Irish stakes winner up to that time with earnings of £164,000. His successes as a stallion include the Royal filly Dunfermline who won the Jubilee Oaks and St Leger for the Queen. Noel says today, 'He was a very good horse indeed. He had the two great essentials, speed and courage.'

11

Made all the Running
1968–1971

❀

What a wonderful July it was for Noel. Hopeful Venture, the Queen's runner-up in the St Leger, had remained in training. He had had his first race of 1968 in the one mile five furlong Ormonde Stakes at Chester, in which he was taking on Park Top, who already had the benefit of a race. There were few better training performances that season than that of Noel, producing the Queen's colt fit not only to win first time out, but also to make all his own running. As nothing else would go on Barclay sensibly took the lead from the start. At halfway Russ Maddock on Park Top went into second place and raced alongside Hopeful Venture coming into the final turn. Close company was just what the big bay wanted, and the Royal colt galloped right away from the filly to win by five lengths. It was Barclay's second winner for the Queen and it was not his last. On 21 June he returned to Royal Ascot where, in 1967, he had won the King Edward VII Stakes. This time he was going for the Hardwicke Stakes over one and a half miles, worth that year £8007. After Hopeful Venture had taken the lead half a mile from home and galloped on strongly to become the first Royal winner at the meeting for seven years, Noel announced that the four-year-old bay's next race would be in France. On 7 July he would take on Vaguely Noble in the £51,000 Grand Prix de Saint-Cloud. Victory in the Hardwicke Stakes ensured that Noel was top trainer at the Royal meeting and that Sandy Barclay, who had never ridden a winner at the meeting before, finished up as top jockey with his five successes.

Vaguely Noble had looked worth every penny of his 136,000 guinea purchase price when he had annihilated the opposition in the one and a half mile Prix du Lys at Chantilly the previous Sunday.

He would certainly be Noel's main threat in the Saint-Cloud. Hopeful Venture was well named and the 1968 Grand Prix de Saint-Cloud was a thrilling race. For Noel it remains a wonderful memory. He had already enjoyed two winners in France that season. This one crowned one of the greatest weekends in the history of British racing. Only twenty-four hours earlier he and Sandy had won that dramatic Eclipse Stakes at Sandown with Royal Palace, routing the French and the Americans, and now they were aiming at a £73,000 double.

They were so nearly too late. The aircraft carrying the Queen's racing manager Richard Shelley, Noel, Gwen and Sandy as well as Peter Burrell, Director of the National Stud which had bred Hopeful Venture, was held up for Customs clearance at Cambridge and then, after landing in Paris, they had difficulty getting through the Sunday traffic on the way to the course. By the time Sandy had changed and Noel had saddled the Royal colt an enormous crowd was thronging the enclosures as the twenty runners paraded in damp, thundery heat. Vaguely Noble, the 2–1 favourite, sweated up badly. He had not yet been reunited with his old partner Bill Williamson and was ridden by the unpredictable Jean Deforge. Hopeful Venture was hard and fit in his bay coat but was an outsider at more than 12–1, in spite of a large British gathering.

The going was perfect as Admiral's Boy, pacemaker to the favourite, set off in front with Hopeful Venture close up and Vaguely Noble well in the rear. When at halfway Admiral's Boy still led, Barclay was already niggling at Hopeful Venture in sixth position and Deforge, although lying out of his ground, was gradually moving up on Vaguely Noble. Before the long final turn, Freddie Head shot Minamoto into the lead followed by Yves Saint-Martin on Pola Bella, heroine of the French One Thousand Guineas. A furlong from home, these two were fighting out the finish with Hopeful Venture four lengths behind and Vaguely Noble coming late on the scene. It looked all over before Barclay, incredibly, galvanized the Royal colt and, forcing him between the leaders, won by a neck from Minamoto with Vaguely Noble two lengths away third and Pola Bella fourth. Sensational scenes followed as the French cheered the Queen's first winner in their country. Noel was thrilled. He says, 'The race didn't matter. It was so wonderful for the Queen.' And Marcel Boussac ordered an official to send the patrol film to take back for the winning owner.

Further triumph followed in the Irish Oaks. Under its new name of the Irish Guinness Oaks the race had not yet been won by an English filly. In 1968, thanks to the national brewers of stout, the contest was worth £20,000 and Glad One, who had finished runner-up to La Lagune in the Oaks at Epsom, was firm favourite to keep that prize in Ireland. However, just as three weeks earlier the Curragh's one and a half miles had exploded the stamina pretensions of America's Sir Ivor in the Irish Sweeps Derby, so many others thought that she might be found wanting on the world's stiffest classic circuit. Noel challenged with Celina, who had apparently been an unlucky third in the Riddlesdale Stakes at Royal Ascot. Sandy Barclay's previous Curragh experience was a winner on his only ride, Night Star in the 1966 Irish Lincoln. His limited experience of the course never showed as he waited in front with a cool assurance of George Moore and came right away in the straight to win by five lengths. That classic and Royal Palace's triumph in the King George VI and Queen Elizabeth Stakes a week later carried Noel's European winnings that season to £200,000.

Towards the end of 1968 Vaguely Noble, reunited with Williamson, duly won the race for which he had been bought by the Americans, the Prix de l'Arc de Triomphe. In so doing he comfortably defeated Sir Ivor, who then proceeded to win the Champion Stakes at Newmarket and rounded off his career by taking the Washington International in his native country! Both these horses are now leading international stallions in Kentucky.

Their success speaks for the outstanding skill of Noel, who had produced Hopeful Venture and Royal Palace to beat both of them in top Group I races, when the foreign horses were strongly fancied to win. The Queen's Stud Manager Michael Oswald told me, 'The Queen's twenty-three mares must be the best collection of broodmares in the country, rivalled only by those of Mr Jim Joel. They are all top quality flat race type mares, who are either winners of Group I or Listed races or dams, daughters or half-sisters of such winners.'

As a sire, Tudor Minstrel was never as good as might have been expected and he was exported to America in 1959. The best of his produce was probably Tudor Melody, bred in 1956 by Mrs Jane Levins Moore and sold for only 610 guineas as a yearling. Trained by young Dick Peacock at Middleham, he won five races as a two-year-old, including the Chesham Stakes at Royal Ascot and the Prince of Wales Stakes, and was placed top of the Free Handicap. He was then exported to America where he raced for two seasons, winning twice. He returned to England and went to stud in 1961. He did extremely well there and produced many winners, including the French-trained Kashmir II, who won the Two Thousand Guineas in 1966. He died at the National Stud in 1978.

Welsh Pageant bears a distinct family resemblance to Tudor Melody. When I visited him at Woodditton he, Connaught and Owen Dudley were in their 'summer quarters', turned out in lovely paddocks a short way from Noel's house and the main stud buildings. A dark bay, whose high withers make him measure taller than he looks, Welsh Pageant has a perfect temperament. Woodditton's Stud Groom, Mr Salzmann says, 'He's very quiet and sensible – super to handle. One of the few stallions you can always walk behind in his box without a worry or care.'

Welsh Pageant made his bow in 1968. A little slow coming to hand, the colt had his first run in the Portsmouth Road Plate at Sandown on 4 June. It seems such a short time ago and yet British racing then was still in such a sorry state that this five-furlong event in high summer at one of our major metropolitan courses was worth just £414 to the winner. It was won by Jukebox from Laser Light, with Tower Walk fourth and Welsh Pageant fifth. After finishing second to Burglar in the July Stakes at Newmarket, Welsh Pageant turned out for the six-furlong Newham Stakes on the opening day of the Goodwood Festival Meeting and made all the running to win by one and half lengths. Believe it or not, that victory earned just £866 for his owner-breeder, Mr Joel. Finally on 15 August he made all again to win Nottingham's House Ale Stakes for Noel over the same distance 'hard held'. At the end of the season Welsh Pageant received 8 stone 10 pounds in the Free Handicap – 11 pounds behind the top-rated two-year-old, the ill-fated Ribofilio.

Noel reckoned this a fair weight. So fair in fact that he decided to give the colt his first run of 1969 in the Tote-sponsored seven furlong Free Handicap at Newmarket's Craven Meeting on 16 April. He was right. Welsh Pageant jumped off straight into his stride, made all and won so confortably that he became a certain starter for the Two Thousand Guineas. He had started at 5–2 and was the first favourite to win the Free Handicap for thirty years. He carried second top weight and his victims included Hotfoot, Tudor Music and Balidar. As he dismounted, Sandy Barclay assured Noel, 'Welsh Pageant will get the extra furlong all right in the Guineas. Making all his own running, he was idling into the Dip, but if anything had come to him he would have raced away.'

Two Thousand Guineas day in 1969 must always remain one of the blackest days in Turf history. It began badly when, on the eve of the first classic, Noel broke his shoulder in a fall from his hack on Newmarket Heath. Before the Two Thousand Guineas, book-makers fielded strongly against the red-hot winter classic favourite, Ribofilio, who was sweating slightly in the parade. He cantered down 'like a dead duck', according to his jockey Lester Piggott, was never going at any stage, was pulled up before the winning post and finished in a distressed condition. Much later Lester was convinced 'Ribofilio was "done". But they found no trace of dope, did they?' The guineas was won well by Right Tack, a good tough horse who was to complete a classic double by taking the Irish Guineas at the Curragh. Runner-up was Tower Walk, who beat Welsh Pageant for second place by only a head. So Mr Joel's colt had run his usual sterling race and it was not surprising to find him starting odds-on favourite for Epsom's St James' Stakes run over 1 mile and 110 yards, half an hour after Blakeney had won the Derby. This time Barclay rode him from behind, but took the lead a quarter of a mile out and landed the odds nicely.

For the Hungerford Stakes at Newbury on 15 August, Welsh Pageant was easy to back at 7–1, so hot a favourite was Jimmy Reppin, the four-year-old winner of the Sussex Stakes. But as they entered the final furlong, a tremendous battle ensued and it was only right on the line that the older horse regained the advantage to win a most thrilling race by a head.

At Newcastle on 30 August it was Welsh Pageant's turn to start at odds-on despite the fact that he was easily top weight with 9 stone 7 pounds in the one mile Northern Goldsmiths' Handicap. He ran a magnificent race to win by three-quarters of a length from Prince de Galles, to whom he was given 17 pounds – the horse who was to pull off a tremendous gamble in the first of his two Cambridge-shires five weeks later.

In 1969 Warren Place had suffered its share of the Miami 'flu which swept the country, ruining plans and decimating fields at the height of the season. It was the year Blakeney became the first Derby winner bred, owned and trained by Arthur Budgett at Whatcombe. However, not even Budgett or any other racehorse trainer in history could have handled the filly Lupe as brilliantly as the Guv'nor.

Noel was well prepared for this all-quality, all-action bay filly. Although her sire had won the Ebor with 9 stone, and her dam Alcoa (by Alycidon) was an out-and-out stayer, runner-up in the 1961 Cesarewitch, their most attractive daughter possessed a great turn of foot.

By the Doncaster St Leger meeting of 1969 Noel, whose stable had been so badly hit by the cough, was coming right back to form: his four two-year-old runners won; Stanhope Joel's Saintly Song won the Champagne Stakes; Mrs Ogden Phipps' American-bred Newmarket winner Politico took the Prince of Wales Nursery; and Lady Sassoon's A-Bye gave Barclay an easy victory in the Princess Mary Nursery.

Although she was appearing in public for the first time Lupe was installed favourite at 9–4 in the six-furlong Devonshire Stakes for maiden two-year-old fillies. From a bad draw she was always close up, and when Sandy asked her for an effort inside the final furlong she responded well, took the lead and won by one and a half lengths. It was an admirable initiation and all that a staying-bred classic filly required in her first season. The timing of Lupe's next race was perfection, proving once again the truth of Atty Persse's dictum, 'The word "trainer" means a man who can train his horse at home to produce its best form first time out on a racecourse.' So the classic filly, unbeaten of course, but with the experience of just one outing, reappeared after eight months at home in the Cheshire Oaks which was run over an extended one and a half miles on 6 May – Cup Day at Chester's Festival Meeting which, in 1970, was blessed with superb weather and record crowds.

Sandy Barclay had been rightly criticized for trying to imitate Lester Piggott, riding with ultra-short stirrup leathers, but now twenty-one-year-old Barclay appeared to have learned his lesson; he kept Lupe tucked in on the rails behind Piggott on Pretty Puffin and allowed the champion jockey to dictate the pace for ten of the dozen furlongs. Then, just as it seemed he might be shut in on the final bend, he slipped Lupe through on the outside to win on a tight rein by a length. Noel says, 'She wasn't even extended. And, as she hadn't got her summer coat yet, she was sure to improve.' He was particularly pleased that his young stable-jockey had rediscovered his best form now that he had let his leathers down. 'You can't ride with your knees strapped under your chin,' said Noel.

'When Lupe returned from Chester,' says her trainer, 'she just didn't thrive. In fact she did so badly that I only galloped her once between Chester and Epsom – just six furlongs alone around New Ground. However she came back to herself in time for Epsom.'

Although Nijinsky won the Derby, it was Noel who won the other two Group I races at the Epsom Summer Meeting. On the Saturday came the Oaks, worth that year £31,320 to the winner and Lupe had looked sensational, starting favourite at 100–30. Barclay made his move down the hill and took the lead soon after rounding Tattenham Corner and came right away in the straight to win Noel's third Oaks by four impressive lengths from State Pension.

The Holliday filly, Highest Hopes, trained by Dick Hern, who had inexplicably and ignominiously tailed off in the One Thousand Guineas, won by Humble Duty, had then recovered her form to finish second in the French Oaks at Chantilly and to win the Prix Eugene Adam at Saint-Cloud. So later that summer she provided really tough opposition in the one-and-a-half-mile Yorkshire Oaks on 18 August. Forced to make his own running in the three-horse field, Barclay was headed by Joe Mercer's mount a furlong out, but Lupe quickened like a true classic filly and won by two lengths.

Four-year-old fillies are apt to be temperamental and constitute the most treacherous hazards for a racehorse trainer. Many shun the challenge. But Noel, who had already proved that he was more than equal to it, as we had seen with Petite Etoile and Aunt Edith, continued to keep Lupe in training as a four-year-old. The decision was fully justified. She established herself as a true champion by winning her only two races in 1971.

As it happens, this was not as planned. Her trainer smiles as he recalls, 'The idea was to send Lupe to stud at the end of her three-year-old season. But she injured her hock so badly at the start of the Prix Vermeille at Longchamp that she had to stay in her box for three months. So I kept her in training.'

He and Gwen look back with pride on that 1970 Epsom which they virtually 'farmed' for Stanhope Joel – the St James' Stakes with

Saintly Song, the Coronation Cup with Caliban and the Oaks with Lupe. All that followed by a fantastic Ascot and five winners – the Queen Anne with Welsh Pageant, the Prince of Wales with Connaught, the St James' Palace with Saintly Song, the Bessborough with Mr Joel's Prince Consort and finally the Ribblesdale with Parmelia for Lord Howard de Walden.

1970 will be remembered as the year when Nijinsky won the Triple Crown. But it also produced a true champion miler in Welsh Pageant who reappeared after his winter's rest in the seven-furlong Victoria Cup carrying 9 stone 6 pounds, to be installed joint favourite at 4–1. He duly obliged, making all the running to win by three-quarters of a length from Crooner. Welsh Pageant then went on to Newbury for the one-mile Group Two Lockinge Stakes, and once again he made all the running winning by three lengths, surprising Realm, Crooner, Shiny Tenth and Divine Gift.

In the Queen Anne Stakes, Welsh Pageant, under top weight of 9 stone 5 pounds won by five lengths in a new record time, and at the end of September he won the Queen Elizabeth II Stakes.

Towards the end of 1970, champion trainer for the eighth time with fifty-seven races won to the value of £220,475, Noel once again had decided to change his jockey: 'As I knew, it was not in Lester's interests to be tied down to one stable. But it had been a tremendous blow losing him and now Sandy Barclay appeared just not to have the mentality to make the grade. Perhaps I was a bit hard on him, but he was always turning up late for work and sometimes not coming at all. Then, when he rode a very bad race on Parmelia, I got bloody annoyed and sacked him.'

The Guv'nor had planned a farewell for Sandy Barclay in the final Newmarket meeting on 29 October. Unfortunately it was spoiled by a misunderstanding. 'I had fixed up for Sandy to ride Relate so that he could finish off with a winner for me,' Noel said, 'but at the last moment he asked if Lewis could take his place so that he could ride for Arthur Budgett. Unhappily, another jockey had already been declared for the Budgett horse, Alderney, so that Barclay was grounded.' This was the last day of a wonderful season. It provided a double for Noel with Hill Run and Relate and a four-timer for his new jockey – the bustling, popular Epsom rider Geoff Lewis, who

Julie Murless with Adam's Walk at Newmarket

rode Lorenzaccio, and upset the entire racing world by defeating the Irish-trained Triple Crown winner Nijinsky in the £25,079 Champion Stakes at Newmarket. Nijinsky, ridden by Lester was, of course, a very hot favourite at 11–4 on. Lorenzaccio was almost unconsidered at 100–7, but Geoff Lewis made all the running and got to work on his horse down the hill to win by one and a half lengths. Despite his somewhat unsightly forelegs, chestnut Lorenzaccio was as sound as a bell. In his four racing seasons he had run twenty-three times, winning seven races and had only twice finished out of the first four – yet another example of Noel's brilliance.

The change of jockey made no difference to Welsh Pageant, who maintained his form to the end. Returning to Newbury in June 1971 he made nearly all the running to win the Group II Lockinge Stakes for the second successive year and confirmed his superiority over Joshua in the seven-furlong Group III Hungerford Stakes on the same course in August, when he took the lead from the off and never looked like relinquishing his grip. Noel ran him twice over one-and-a-quarter miles in top-class company, and the brave five-year-old never failed him. In the Eclipse Stakes at Sandown, Lester rode him to take on mighty Mill Reef and the French Caro. Although badly hampered two furlongs out and forced to switch, he still rallied and ran on to take third place.

Lewis had the mount again in Welsh Pageant's final race, the Champion Stakes at Newmarket. This was the occasion when Brigadier Gerard so nearly tasted defeat for the first time. John Hislop's colt was absolutely all out to hold Irish challenger Rarity by a short head. The famous Joel 'black, red cap' colours on Welsh Pageant were only two and a half lengths away in third place. This splendid horse has not failed since he went to stud in 1972. In nearly five seasons of runners he has sired the winners of well over a hundred races including Gwent, Man of Harlech, Orchestration, Royal Plume, Welsh Chanter, Fluellen, Avgerinos and the Champion Stakes heroine Swiss Maid, as well as good winners abroad like French Pageant.

ABOVE Mysterious is led into the winner's enclosure by owner George Pope Jr after winning the 1973 Oaks

BELOW Goodwood 1976 – Lester Piggott and J. O. Tobin take the Richmond Stakes

Also in 1971, her final racing year, Lupe met Gerry Oldham's Stintino, trained by François Boutin at Chantilly, and rated one of the best four-year-olds in Europe. Winner of the previous year's Prix de Guiche, Prix Lupin and Prix Chantilly, he had finished third in the Derby and was strongly fancied at 11–8 on to win the Coronation Cup over the same course and distance. Ironically Sandy Barclay, now riding for Boutin, was on the French favourite, while his 1970 classic filly was partnered by Geoff Lewis, his successor at Warren Place. Taking the lead three furlongs out, Lupe ran on with tremendous courage to hold Stintino's late challenge by a neck. This was another superb training feat, because, whereas Stintino had run twice already, Lupe faced the great test without the benefit of a previous outing. Geoff Lewis gave Lupe her last triumphant run when she landed the odds in the one and a half mile Princess of Wales' Stakes at Newmarket's July Meeting, taking the lead before The Bushes and running on strongly to win by two lengths going away from Sacramento Song. Lupe's career will always remain a lesson in racehorse training at its finest, confirming Noel's touch of true genius.

1971 will be remembered as an excellent Murless year with George Pope's horses, many of them by his own stallion Hillary, running particularly well and the Hue-Williams' filly, Altesse Royale, winning three more classic victories for Noel. This may have been the year of Mill Reef and Brigadier Gerard, but it was Noel who won the fillies' races – the One Thousand Guineas, the Oaks and the Irish Guinness Oaks with Altesse Royale, as well as the Coronation Cup with Lupe. Lewis rode the last three races, but in the One Thousand he chose to ride Magic Flute for Lord Howard de Walden. As a result the ride on Altesse Royale was given to Yves Saint-Martin who, as Noel says, is a true artist and rides every course all over the world with complete brilliance. At Newmarket he jumped off in front, made all the running and kept the 25–1 outsider going so well that he got home by one and a half lengths from Lester on Super Honey.

12
The Final Years at
Warren Place 1971–1976

✳

Noel feels very strongly about the economics of racing today. 'The stake money that we are running for now, apart from the big races and a few handicaps, is just chicken feed. The Government take, I believe, well over £100 million out of betting tax. What I would like to see is the Levy Board done away with and probably £20 million or so from the betting money channelled back into racing. I can see that amount of money coming back into the sport to raise the standard of our stake money.'

So many men of the Guv'nor's vintage are set in their ideas and stick firmly to tradition but not Noel. In 1965, when it was finally decided that starting-stalls should be introduced, Noel was the prime supporter among the professionals. He supervised all the trials, using his own lads as a team. And it was that team with the Guv'nor and his old friend, Alec Marsh, by now Senior Starter, which operated the gates on that historic first stalls-start in the Chesterfield Stakes at Newmarket on 8 July.

Noel remembers, 'I had Bracey Bridge running at the Curragh in the Irish Oaks which was being broadcast. So we took our transistors down to the start at Newmarket. We couldn't wait to get those two-year-olds into the stalls before the "off" in Ireland. However, we managed it just in time and heard that Bracey Bridge finished third.'

The stalls were formally introduced to British racing in 1967. Noel continues, 'I suppose they have taken some of the colour away from racing and I thought originally that they would also take away a lot of the skill of jockeyship. Now I don't know that they have done so. The best jockey is first out of the stalls as a rule, just as he was first away from the barrier. But perhaps they have removed some of the fun. It makes me think of a meeting at Leicester when there was a big field of two-year-olds. Gordon was riding the hot favourite and as they were coming up into line Gordon had not got in. He shouted, "No, sir, no sir!" and so the starter, old Captain Allison, stopped them and told them to go back and come up again. Harry Wragg (on horse) was almost hidden right under the starter's box. He didn't go back and as they were coming in the second time, the starter shouted, "Are you all right, Richards?" "Yes," shouted Harry Wragg and jumped off about four lengths in front of the others and there he stayed! That was racing . . .'

By the end of 1968 Sir Cecil Boyd-Rochfort had retired and Henry Cecil, with Julie always at his side, started training on his own with stables in Newmarket's Hamilton Road near the Rowley Mile racecourse. At Warren Place a routine had by now been firmly established. Most of the foals would probably be taken up to Yorkshire. 'I do like to get then on to the limestone land. They grow good bone up at The Cliff, good feet and legs. It makes a lot of difference when you come to train them.'

Then the foals were all weaned up there. 'We put the mares where they couldn't hear the foals and the foals where they couldn't hear the mares,' says the Guv'nor. 'It was done in batches. We left the foals in the paddocks where they have been all along and took the mares away. Then the foals didn't worry because they were in their own familiar surroundings.' Later, as yearlings, they would come down to be broken at Beech House and learn the first lessons of life before finally, in early December, arriving at Warren Place where they learned the order and discipline of a racing stable in the most protected and luxurious conditions.

Both Noel and Gwen assert that the happiest part of their life is being up in Yorkshire among the young animals. 'We love it. It is often difficult to judge foals in the early stages because they will alter so much. You will see foals born with all sorts of crooked legs or down on their pasterns, but it is amazing how they will alter in just a few weeks. You should see plenty of strength across the back and loins, with nicely rounded quarters, a good width between the eyes, and a nice bright eye. A proper clean-cut head.'

At all stages in their lives the Murless horses are fed on nothing but the very finest basic food. 'Oats and hay, goot hot mashes with linseed,' says the Guv'nor. The painstaking Murless pattern which

148

had always proved so satisfactory with the likes of Caergwrle was to reach perfection with Mysterious.

Though George and Patsy Pope were such a long way away in California it was a great thrill to breed from Crepello for friends, particularly when they sent over a really good winning mare like Hill Shade. By their own horse Hillary, she had won excellent races at one mile to one and a quarter miles. She was a maiden when she went to Crepello. So the birth of her first foal Mysterious at The Cliff Stud in 1970 was quite an event. This most attractive chestnut filly came into training just before Christmas at Warren Place. Noel gave her just one run in July, by which time he knew that she was well above the average. She had shown him enough at home to run in one of the season's top two-year-old races first time out. The touts at Newmarket obviously knew how good she was too, and Mysterious started co-favourite for the 1972 Cherry Hinton Stakes at the Newmarket July Meeting. She made all, despite running green, and was always going like a winner. It was obvious that she would be much better for experience but still Noel put her by for the following year.

Mysterious was unquestionably the best filly of 1973. Noel campaigned her accordingly, winning first the Fred Darling Stakes at Newbury on 13 April and then going for the One Thousand Guineas at Newmarket on 3 May. There she had to take on the unbeaten filly, Jacinth. But it was all too easy. After challenging going into The Dip, she was soon on top and stayed on strongly up the hill to win by three lengths. Mysterious also won the Oaks at Epsom very easily indeed by four lengths from Where You Lead, and then took the Yorkshire Oaks most impressively from the French Oaks third, Virunga.

That same season, Louis Freedman's Attica Meli had trained on really well to win not only the Geoffrey Freer Stakes at Newbury but also the Doncaster Cup.

Though he continued to do very well over the next two seasons with many more good horses of the calibre of Sir Reginald MacDonald-Buchanan's Stirling Castle, Louis Freedman's Owen Dudley and Lieutenant-Colonel Sir John Hornung's Sauceboat. Noel had definitely made up his mind to retire at the end of 1976 and accordingly he had made arrangements to sell Warren Place to Henry Cecil.

149

Before the Laurent Perrier Champagne Stakes at Doncaster, Noel galloped Tobin over seven furlongs to make sure that he would get the distance. That old Murless instinct prompted him to put the very best of the older horses into the gallop and once again the Guv'nor was right. 'When you've been watching your horses for a long time, you've a pretty fair idea of how good they are. It's the way a horse moves, the way he moves up to his lead horse.' In this case Tobin moved up to his lead horse, giving weight to a top-class handicapper with consummate ease, and drew easily away from him prompting his trainer to say: 'He was very, very good. Brilliant. He would have won the Derby of 1977 if Lester had ridden him, though I don't know whether Lester would have been able to take the ride. As it was, Lester won the race very narrowly on The Minstrel, and though Tobin did not get a mile and a half he would have got the Epsom distance if he had been ridden by Lester. Yes, I'm convinced he would have won the Derby, but by then I had already decided to give up.'

George Pope, the supreme American horsemaster, horseman and breeder, realized that the Guv'nor's tremendous strength of character would assert itself in the taking of this decision. Only those who had been round evening stables with him or stood with him on the gallops as he barked orders like a true leader, could appreciate the absolute determination and authority of this seemingly quiet man. Noel says, 'George told me that if I could not continue to train J. O. Tobin he would not send him to any other trainer in England but would send him back to America. I retired and this he did. When Tobin returned to the States he was proved good enough to beat the very finest in the world – he actually defeated the American Champion Seattle Slew. But J. O. Tobin was very highly strung and they drove him up the wall there. They do in a lot of horses in America – far more than we do here. I didn't have many American horses, unlike most of the trainers today. I had one or two for Mrs Ogden Phipps. I liked sticking to the breeds of horses and the people that I knew.'

Noel's very last three winners were Mr Jim Joel's Elizabethan, ridden by Lester Piggott at Sandown, Gwen's own Ferrybridge at Haydock and finally, on 2 November 1976, Lieutenant-Colonel Sir John Hornung's Timothy Green in the Ticehurst Stakes at Lingfield with Lester Piggott once more in the saddle. An era had come to an end.

Unlike Etienne Pollet who had stayed on for another year to train Gyr for his Derby, the Guv'nor had resisted what must have been a fantastic temptation to stay on to saddle J. O. Tobin for the 1977 Derby. His decision had been made and the same quiet determination that has characterized his life now helped him carry out his plan of retirement. Unobtrusively, just as he had moved first to the 'Ritz' at Hambleton, then to Middleham, then back to Hambleton House, to Beckhampton and, in twenty-four hours, to Warren Place, so with Gwen, Noel faded quietly out of the picture, leaving his beloved Warren Place to his daughter and her husband, and slipped down the road to the Woodditton Stud with his stallions, brood-mares, foals and, inevitably, his dogs.

In the Jubilee Honours of 1977 Noel Murless was knighted by the Queen, whom he had served so well and for whom, with her knowledgeable love of racing, he had provided so much enjoyment with his skilful handling of such royal horses as Carrozza and Hopeful Venture. From that humble start with one winner of a contest worth £103 in 1935 the Guv'nor had won 1431 races worth £2,646,766 in over forty years of dedication to his career.

Sir Gordon, one of Noel's four champion jockeys, said, 'He understood his horses. He only had to open the box door at night to know whether they were right or wrong. He would be out with the string in the morning and he'd glance down them. He could pick out one with a dull eye. He just had it, that gift, and that was the great thing.'

Humour and strength, dignity and compassion are combined in the man, who will always remain for me the greatest trainer of all time. Lester Piggott thinks of him as 'One of the really great trainers. A marvellous horseman with understanding and patience, who never hurried his horses and always had them relaxed. Out-standing among the many grand horses I rode for him were Cre-pello, Petite Etoile, Sir Paddy, J. O. Tobin and Pinturischio.' And he added, 'Petite Etoile was terrific.'

When the time does come to compose a fitting epitaph for the Guv'nor I can think of none better than 'Sir Noel Murless, trainer of racehorses. He loved his horses and they loved him. Here was a man who really could talk to his animals.'

The Racing Record

	OWNER	HORSE
1935		
Sep 2	Mr J. T. Roger's	RUBIN WOOD
1936		
Jun 27	Mrs R. Taylor's	OUTLAW
1937		
Jul 1	Miss H. Cooper's	SECOND POP
Aug 28	Miss H. Cooper's	LORENZO
Oct 2	Mr A. E. Lowther's	SEA FEVER
Nov 12	Mrs A. E. Lowther's	SEA FEVER
1938		
May 13	Mr A. E. Lowther's	SEA FEVER
Jun 25	Miss H. Cooper's	SECOND POP
Jun 30	Mr E. M. Sykes's	MASTER BIMBO
Jul 20	Mr E. M. Sykes's	SECOND POP
Jul 29	Mr E. M. Sykes's	SECOND POP
Aug 5	Mr A. E. Lowther's	CARTOWN
Oct 19	Mr A. E. Lowther's	CLAQUE
1939		
Apr 8	Miss G. Carlow's	LIMACE
Jun 1	Mr A. E. Lowther's	SEA FEVER
Jun 5	Mr I. Adlestone's	HARLAND
Jun 27	Mr E. M. Sykes's	SECOND POP
Jun 28	Mr E. M. Sykes's	MASTER BIMBO
Jul 8	Mr A. E. Lowther's	SEA FEVER

COURSE	JOCKEY	PRIZE
Lee Plate, Lanark	*C. Smirke*	103
	Races Won 1 Winning Stakes £103	
Montrose Handicap, Ayr	*J. Caldwell*	196
	Races Won 1 Winning Stakes £196	
Curnruw S. Plate, Carlisle	*D. McGuigan*	133
Campsie Plate, Hamilton Park	*W. Stephenson*	103
Topcliffe Nursery Handicap, Thirsk	*W. Carr*	166
Downe Nursery Handicap Plate, Liverpool	*W. Carr*	166
	Races Won 4 Winning Stakes £568	
Cecil Frail Handicap, Haydock Park	*W. Carr*	334
Saturday Handicap, Haydock Park	*W. Nevett*	143
Carlisle Bell Handicap, Carlisle	*W. Christie*	166
Grasmere Plate, Liverpool	*W. Carr*	192
Catterick Handicap, Catterick	*W. Carr*	166
Begby Handicap, Thirsk	*W. Carr*	167
Scurry Welter Handicap, Newcastle	*T. Weston*	142
	Races Won 7 Winning Stakes £1310	
Wolviston Handicap, Plate, Stockton	*W. Carr*	166
Mark Price Handicap Plate, Manchester	*W. Carr*	206
Montrose Handicap, Ayr	*W. Nevett*	147
Holm Hill Handicap Plate, Carlisle	*K. Mullins*	124
Cumberland Plate, Carlisle	*K. Mullins*	728
Durham Plate, Stockton	*W. Carr*	417

	OWNER	HORSE
Jul 14	Sir Alfred McAlpine's	CLAQUE
Jul 19	Sir Alfred McAlpine's	HOBSON'S CHOICE
Aug 4	Sir Alfred McAlpine's	CRYSTAL PALACE
Sep 1	Sir Alfred McAlpine's	CRYSTAL PALACE

1940

Jun 5	Mr E. M. Syke's	MASTER BIMBO

1941

1942

1943

Jun 26	Mrs G. B. Portman's	SEJANUS
Aug 28	Mrs G. B. Portman's	SEJANUS

1944

Apr 22	Captain A. Johnstone's	MASHALLAH
Jul 22	Mrs G. B. Portman's	SEJANUS
Aug 12	Mr C. Cullimore's	SHEPERDINE
Sep 16	Mrs G. B. Portman's	SEJANUS
Sep 23	Mr R. White's	APROLON

1945

Apr 7	Major H. Quennell's	LADY NIKOTINE
Jul 21	Major H. E. Keylock's	RESTIVE
Aug 4	Sir Loftus Bate's	ARMISTICE
Aug 18	Mr H. Howitt's	BLACK MOON
Sep 1	Mr R. White's	APROLON

COURSE	JOCKEY	PRIZE
Markland Handicap Plate, Hamilton Park	*W. Carr*	103
Grasmere Plate, Liverpool	*T. Weston*	192
Kilburn Plate, Thirsk	*W. Nevett*	167
Loom Handicap Plate, Manchester	*G. Richards*	167

Races Won 10   Winning Stakes £2417

Beverley Handicap Plate, Beverley	*J. Taylor*	206

Races Won 1   Winning Stakes £206

Brecongill Plate, Stockton	*A. Carson*	117
August Handicap, Pontefract	*J. Taylor*	394

Races Won 2   Winning Stakes £511

Pontefract Handicap, Pontefract	*J. Taylor*	303
Ashgill Handicap, Stockton	*W. Nevett*	390
Blakiston Stakes, Stockton	*W. Bullock*	312
Glaisdale Handicap, Stockton	*J. Taylor*	306
Castle Plate, Pontefract	*J. Taylor*	331

Races Won 5   Winning Stakes £1642

Carlton Stakes, Stockton	*J. Taylor*	288
Hambleton Plate, Catterick	*J. Taylor*	167
Leven Handicap, Stockton	*D. Taylor*	271
Caistor Handicap, Catterick	*M. Butterwick*	167
Rosedale Handicap, Stockton	*J. Taylor*	389

	OWNER	HORSE
Sep 4	Mr R. White's	DRUMMOND
Sep 15	Mrs G. B. Portman's	SEJANUS
Sep 22	Mr R. White's	APROLON
Oct 3	Mrs G. B. Portman's	SEJANUS

1946

	OWNER	HORSE
Apr 5	Mrs L. W. Smith's	MINSTER
Apr 27	Mr C. Cullimore's	SHEPERDINE
May 3	Major W. Newland-Hillas's	THE JUDGE
May 21	Mr C. Cullimore's	SHEPERDINE
May 23	Mrs L. W. Smith's	MINSTER
Jun 5	Major W. Newland-Hillas's	THE JUDGE
Jun 10	Major W. Newland-Hillas's	OROS
Jun 10	Major H. E. Keylock's	RESTIVE
Jun 15	Mr R. White's	JULIUS
Jun 27	Mrs K. Kelly's	NICCOLA
Jun 28	Mrs G. B. Portman's	SEJANUS
Jun 29	Mr R. White's	APROLON
Jul 6	Mr R. White's	CLOSEBURN
Jul 6	Mr R. White's	JULIUS
Jul 8	Mr H. Hewitt's	BLACK MOON
Jul 13	Mr R. White's	CLOSEBURN
Jul 24	Mr R. White's	CLOSEBURN
Aug 10	Mrs K. Kelly's	NICCOLO
Aug 16	Mr R. White's	CLOSEBURN
Aug 17	Mr W. L. Christie's	STARSTONE
Aug 22	Mrs E. A. Pilcher's	DELVILLE WOOD
Aug 31	Mr H. Hewitt's	BLACK MOON
Sep 10	Mrs E. A. Pilcher's	DELVILLE WOOD
Sep 12	Major W. Newland-Hillas's	OROS
Sep 12	Mr W. J. Kelly's	LADY DANDY
Sep 20	Captain S. Riley Lord's	SAN FAIRY ANNE
Sep 23	Colonel B. Hornung's	BUXTED
Sep 28	Mr W. L. Christie's	STARSTONE
Oct 9	Captain A. S. Wills's	PREFABRICATED
Oct 10	Mr R. White's	APROLON
Oct 15	Mr R. White's	JULIUS
Oct 16	Mrs G. B. Portman's	SEJANUS

COURSE	JOCKEY	PRIZE
Clifton Welter Handicap, York	*J. Taylor*	477
Eston Handicap, Redcar	*J. Taylor*	305
Stewards's Handicap, Stockton	*J. Taylor*	1000
Stansfield Handicap, Newmarket	*J. Taylor*	365

Races Won 9 Winning Stakes 3429

Earl of Sefton's Plate, Liverpool	*A. Carson*	690
Manor House Handicap, Catterick	*J. Taylor*	345
Gormire Handicap, Thirsk	*A. Carson*	207
Flying Dutchman Handicap, York	*J. Taylor*	666
Sledmere Handicap, York	*A. Carson*	715
Carew Handicap, Epsom	*A. Carson*	412
Langbarugh Plate, Redcar	*J. Taylor*	276
Zetland Handicap, Redcar	*P. Evans*	328
Lytham Stakes, Manchester	*J. Taylor*	858
Royal Liver Stakes Handicap, Liverpool	*A. Carson*	820
Falmouth Handicap, Doncaster	*H. Wragg*	345
Harewood Handicap, Doncaster	*J. Taylor*	690
Carr's Stakes, Stockton	*J. Taylor*	281
Tibbersley Stakes, Stockton	*J. Taylor*	345
Bramcote Handicap, Nottingham	*A. Carson*	138
Royton Stakes, Manchester	*J. Taylor*	279
Blankney Stakes, Lincoln	*J. Taylor*	430
Farndale Handicap, Redcar	*A. Carson*	207
Hardwicke Stakes, Stockton	*J. Taylor*	426
Crathorne Handicap, Stockton	*A. Carson*	276
Alnwick Handicap, Newcastle	*W. Nevett*	414
Canal Handicap, Liverpool	*C. Elliott*	207
Great Yorkshire Handicap, Doncaster	*G. Richards*	824
Rous Stakes, Doncaster	*H. Wragg*	502
Princess Mary Nursery, Doncaster	*A. Carson*	884
Land of Burns Nursery Handicap, Ayr	*A. Carson*	581
Garrion Plate, Lanark	*A. Carson*	207
Brandling Handicap, Newcastle	*W. Nevett*	207
Lendal Stakes, York	*W. Nevett*	434
Little-Go Handicap, York	*H. Wragg*	788
Clearwell Stakes, Newmarket	*G. Richards*	655
Heath Handicap, Newmarket	*H. Wragg*	406

	OWNER	HORSE
Oct 26	Mr W. L. Christie's	STARSTONE
Nov 16	Mr R. White's	APROLON

1947

Apr 26	Mrs L. W. Smith's	MINSTER
Apr 30	Mr H. Howitt's	BLACK MOON
May 15	Mr R. White's	CLOSEBURN
May 20	Mr F. D. Wadia's	IRAN SHAH
May 20	Mr A. E. Cooley's	SWIFT CARD
May 21	Mr R. White's	CLOSEBURN
May 26	Mr H. Howitt's	BLACK MOON
Jun 19	Major W. N. Hillas's	OROS
Jun 21	Mr R. White's	NEW WELLS
Jun 24	Mr C. Cullimore's	BEACON BRIGHT
Jun 25	Lt Col R. Taylor's	FORT WILLIAM
Jun 26	Capt A. S. Wills's	GOLD MIST
Jun 27	Col B. Hornung's	BUCKTHORN
Jun 27	Major W. N. Hillas's	YOUNG JUDGE
Jul 4	Major W. N. Hillas's	OROS
Jul 23	Mr W. L. Christie's	STARSTONE
Jul 29	Mr R. White's	CLOSEBURN
Aug 2	Major W. N. Hillas's	COLLEGE BOY
Aug 2	Mr F. D. Wadia's	CHATEAU ROUSSEL
Aug 4	Mrs J. Dixon's	TAJ BANOO
Aug 9	Col B. Hornung's	BUCKTHORN
Aug 11	Mr J. R. Follett's	RAMPONNEAU
Aug 21	Capt S. Riley Lord's	SAN FAIRY ANNE
Aug 23	Mr R. White's	NEW WELLS
Aug 25	Col B. Hornung's	BUCKTHORN
Aug 27	Capt A. S. Wills's	PLASTIC
Aug 27	Col B. Hornung's	BUCKTHORN
Sep 12	Mr W. L. Christie's	STARSTONE
Sep 17	Lady Portman's	SEJANUS
Oct 2	Capt A. S. Wills's	GOLD MIST
Oct 17	Mr R. White's	CLOSEBURN
Oct 31	Mr J. R. Follett's	RAMPONNEAU

COURSE	JOCKEY	PRIZE
Clayton Handicap, Doncaster	*W. Nevett*	207
Farewell Handicap, Manchester	*H. Wragg*	276

Races Won 34   Winning Stakes £15,326

Thirsk Handicap, Thirsk	*A. Carson*	345
Stewards' Handicap, Ayr	*W. Nevett*	207
Wilburton Handicap, Newmarket	*J. Taylor*	950
Glasgow Maiden Stakes, York	*G. Brierley*	339
Tadcaster Stakes, York	*J. Sword*	351
Hambleton Stakes, York	*J. Taylor*	903
Redcar Handicap, Redcar	*W. Nevett*	690
Britannia Stakes, Ascot	*G. Richards*	1864
Rose Hill Stakes, Doncaster	*W. Rickaby*	645
Blagdon Stakes, Newcastle (W.O.)	*E. French*	232
Gibside Plate, Newcastle	*A. Carson*	276
Seaton Delaval Plate, Newcastle	*W. Carr*	414
Wellington Handicap, Sandown Park.	*G. Richards*	818
Scarborough Maiden Plate, Redcar	*W. Rickaby*	207
Milton Handicap, Newmarket	*G. Richards*	1010
Lincoln Summer Cup, Lincoln	*W. Rickaby*	1058
Stewards' Cup, Goodwood	*G. Richards*	1622
Croxteth Plate, Liverpool	*W. Rickaby*	345
Riverside Handicap, Liverpool	*W. Rickaby*	523
Anchor Plate, Liverpool	*W. Nevett*	276
Cheviot Plate, Newcastle	*W. Carr*	971
Midland St. Leger Trial Stakes B'm.	*D. Smith*	1060
Whepstead Handicap, Newmarket	*D. Smith*	669
Wynyard Stakes, Stockton	*W. Rickaby*	491
Gt. Midland Breeders' Pte., Nottm.	*G. Richards*	890
Severus Stakes, York	*W. Rickaby*	363
Duke of York Stakes, York	*W. Carr*	691
Town Moor Handicap, Doncaster	*G. Richards*	857
Great Tom Handicap, Lincoln	*W. Carr*	690
Bentinck Fund Nursery, Newmarket	*G. Richards*	688
Challenge Stakes, Newmarket	*G. Richards*	599
Final Handicap Stakes, Newmarket	*G. Richards*	1592

Races won 32   Winning Stakes £22,636

OWNER	HORSE

1948

Apr 10	Sir Percy Loraine's	QUEENPOT
Apr 14	Mr J. A. Dewar's	ARC-EN-CIEL
Apr 15	Col B. Hornung's	LADY VELOCITY
Apr 23	Mrs R. Macdonald-Buchanan's	ROARING FORTIES
Apr 24	Mrs R. Macdonald-Buchanan's	CADWALLADER
Apr 30	Sir Percy Loraine's	QUEENPOT
Apr 30	Mrs R. Macdonald-Buchanan's	STOCKADE
May 11	Mr F. Darling's	GOBLET
May 13	Mrs R. Macdonald-Buchanan's	ABERNANT
May 20	Mrs R. Macdonald-Buchanan's	GLENDOWER
May 21	Mr R. White's	CLOSEBURN
May 27	Mrs R. Macdonald-Buchanan's	STOCKADE
May 27	Maj R. Macdonald-Buchanan's	ROYAL FOREST
Jun 11	Mr F. Darling's	FEU FOLLET
Jun 15	Maj R. Macdonald-Buchanan's	ROYAL FOREST
Jun 16	Maj W. Newland-Hillas's	OROS
Jun 18	Maj R. Macdonald-Buchanan's	ABERNANT
Jun 28	Mr J. A. Dewar's	PERSIAN REBEL
Jun 28	Mr J. A. Dewar's	TEMBU
Jun 29	Maj W. Newland-Hillas's	OROS
Jul 7	Mr J. A. Dewar's	ARC-EN-CIEL
Jul 8	Mrs R. Macdonald-Buchanan's	STOCKADE
Jul 8	Sir Percy Loraine's	WAT TYLER
Jul 8	Mrs R. Macdonald-Buchanan's	FRANCHISE
Jul 9	Mr J. A. Dewar's	FAUX TIRAGE
Jul 10	Mrs R. Macdonald-Buchanan's	GLENDOWER
Jul 14	Mr F. Darling's	GOBLET
Jul 17	Maj R. Macdonald-Buchanan's	ABERNANT
Jul 28	Lt Col Giles Loder's	THE COBBLER
Jul 29	Sir Percy Loraine's	WAT TYLER
Jul 30	Mr F. Darling's	GOBLET
Jul 31	Mr J. A. Dewar's	TEMBU
Aug 2	Lady Portman's	SEJANUS
Aug 2	Mr J. A. Dewar's	PERSIAN REBEL
Aug 5	Col B. Hornung's	GREENBRIDGE
Aug 11	His Majesty's	GIGANTIC
Aug 11	His Majesty's	ROYAL BLUE
Aug 12	Mr J. A. Dewar's	SUNKISSED
Aug 16	Sir Percy Loraine's	WAT TYLER

162

COURSE	JOCKEY	PRIZE
Katheryn Howard Stakes, Hurst Park.	G. Richards	1946
Pulteney M. Plate, Bath	G. Richards	138
Marshfield Stakes, Bath	G. Richards	370
Tudor Maiden Stakes, Sandown	G. Richards	1005
Marcus Beresford Maiden Stakes, Sandown	G. Richards	622
One Thousand Gns., Newmarket	G. Richards	12,433
Brinkley Handicap, Newmarket	G. Richards	650
Haverhill Stakes, Newmarket	G. Richards	823
Bedford Stakes, Newmarket	G. Richards	518
Empire Handicap, Bath	G. Richards	414
Salford Borough Handicap, Manchester	G. Richards	846
Wiltshire Handicap, Salisbury	G. Richards	355
Fullerton Stakes, Salisbury	G. Richards	256
Englefield Maiden Plate, Windsor	C. Smirke	138
Coventry Stakes, Ascot	G. Richards	2731
Rous Memorial Stakes, Ascot	C. Smirke	1196
Chesham Stakes, Ascot	C. Smirke	2616
Mabon Maiden Plate, Chepstow	G. Richards	138
Wye Maiden. Plate, Chepstow	G. Richards	138
Bottisham Stakes, Newmarket	G. Richards	774
Weyhill Stakes, Salisbury	G. Richards	334
Southern Handicap, Salisbury	G. Richards	314
Champagne Stakes, Salisbury	G. Richards	749
Tisbury Maiden Stakes, Salisbury	G. Richards	338
Granville Stakes, Ascot	G. Richards	921
Sandringham Stakes, Ascot	G. Richards	595
Falmouth Stakes, Newmarket	G. Richards	2193
Nat. Breeder's Produce Stk., Sandown	G. Richards	5797
Halnaker Stakes, Goodwood	G. Richards	609
Rous Memorial Stakes, Goodwood	G. Richards	995
Nassau Stakes, Goodwood	G. Richards	1242
Chepstow Stakes, Chepstow	G. Richards	277
Queenborough Handicap, Chepstow	G. Richards	207
August Plate, Chepstow	G. Richards	207
Falmer Plate, Brighton	G. Richards	345
Fernley Maiden Plate, Bath	G. Richards	138
Bathampton Plate, Bath	G. Richards	138
Fillies' Maiden Plate, Bath	G. Richards	138
Burton Stakes, Birmingham	G. Richards	557

	OWNER	HORSE
Aug 20	Mr J. A. Dewar's	PERSIAN REBEL
Aug 26	His Majesty's	BERRYLANDS
Aug 26	Mr J. A. Dewar's	ARC-EN-CIEL
Aug 26	Lt Col Giles Loder's	COALITION
Aug 28	Mr J. A. Dewar's	TEMBU
Aug 31	Lt Col Giles Loder's	BIG ROMANCE
Sep 1	Capt A. S. Wills's	PERNICKITY
Sep 2	Mr J. A. Dewar's	RAY
Sep 2	Mr J. A. Dewar's	SUNKISSED
Sep 2	Col B. Hornung's	GREENBRIDGE
Sep 6	Capt A. S. Wills's	WHINBROOM
Sep 8	Maj R. Macdonald-Buchanan's	ABERNANT
Sep 10	Capt A. S. Wills's	GOLD MIST
Sep 15	Mr J. A. Dewar's	WOODRUFFE
Sep 15	Col B. Hornung's	ORANGE QUILL
Sep 18	His Majesty's	GIGANTIC
Oct 1	Mr J. A. Dewar's	FAUX TIRAGE
Oct 8	His Majesty's	BERRYLANDS
Oct 10	Lt Col Giles Loder's	COALITION
Oct 12	Maj R. Macdonald-Buchanan's	ABERNANT
Oct 15	Lt Col Giles Loder's	THE COBBLER
Oct 28	Maj R. Macdonald-Buchanan's	ROYAL FOREST
Nov 5	Lt Col Giles Loder's	BIG ROMANCE
Nov 6	Capt A. S., Wills's	PERNICKITY

1949

	OWNER	HORSE
Apr 6	Maj R. Macdonald-Buchanan's	BRECON BEACONS
Apr 6	Maj R. Macdonald-Buchanan's	ABERNANT
Apr 13	Mr J. A. Dewar's	WELSH MINSTREL
Apr 14	Mr J. A. Dewar's	FAUX TIRAGE
Apr 14	Lord Feversham's	FAIR TASK
Apr 22	Mr G. R. H. Smith's	RIDGE WOOD
Apr 23	Mr J. A. Dewar's	WELSH MINSTREL
Apr 23	Lord Feversham's	KRAKATAO
Apr 28	Lt Col Giles Loder's	THE COBBLER
May 4	Maj R. Macdonald-Buchanan's	ROYAL FOREST
May 10	Sir Percy Loraine's	WAT TYLER
May 10	Lord Feversham's	KRAKATAO

Appendix

COURSE	JOCKEY	PRIZE
Taplow Stakes, Windsor	G. Richards	366
Bullford Maiden Stakes, Salisbury	G. Richards	344
Whitchurch Stakes, Salisbury	G. Richards	338
Upavon Maiden Stakes, Salisbury	G. Richards	310
Saddlescombe Stakes, Brighton	G. Richards	417
Downs Plate, Lewes	G. Richards	207
Monument Maiden Plate, Bath	G. Richards	207
New Course Handicap, Bath	G. Richards	483
High Hill Nursery Handicap, Bath	G. Richards	276
September Maiden Plate, Bath	G. Richards	138
Shirenewton Maiden Plate, Chepstow	G. Richards	138
Champagne Stakes, Doncaster	G. Richards	3434
Portland Handicap, Doncaster	G. Richards	2684
Dome Handicap, Brighton	G. Richards	418
Dyke Maiden Plate, Brighton	G. Richards	276
Imperial Stakes, Kempton Park	G. Richards	2335
Rous Memorial Stakes, Newmarket	G. Richards	1109
Duke of Edinburgh Stakes, Ascot	G. Richards	1540
St Andrew's Maiden Plate, Chepstow	G. Richards	138
Middle Park Stakes, Newmarket	G. Richards	3883
Challenge Stakes, Newmarket	G. Richards	608
Dewhurst Stakes, Newmarket	G. Richards	2497
Riverside Nursery Stakes, Windsor	G. Richards	325
Winkfield Stakes, Windsor	G. Richards	374

Races Won 64   Winning Stakes £67,046

Pulteney Maiden Plate, Bath	G. Richards	138
Somerset Stakes, Bath	G. Richards	573
April Maiden Stakes, Salisbury	G. Richards	456
Melbury Stakes, Salisbury	G. Richards	628
Stonehenge Maiden Stakes, Salisbury	G. Richards	310
Tudor Maiden Stakes, Sandown	G. Richards	899
Cobham Stakes, Sandown	G. Richards	613
Marcus Beresford Stakes, Sandown	G. Richards	687
Ely Stakes, Newmarket	G. Richards	320
Sandown Park Trial Stakes	G. Richards	1154
Wilburton Handicap, Newmarket	G. Richards	685
Whepstead Maiden Stakes, Newmarket	G. Richards	512

	OWNER	HORSE
May 11	Mr J. A. Dewar's	FAUX TIRAGE
May 11	Maj R. Macdonald-Buchanan's	BRECON BEACONS
May 12	Mrs R. Macdonald-Buchanan's	GLENDOWER
May 12	Mr R. White's	BYLAND
May 18	His Majesty's	BERRYLANDS
May 18	Lord Feversham's	FAIR TASK
May 19	Mr J. A. Dewar's	SEROCCO
May 19	Mr J. A. Dewar's	FOREST ROW
May 19	Capt A. S. Wills's	GOLD MIST
May 23	Mr J. A. Dewar's	ARC-EN-CIEL
May 23	Mr J. A. Dewar's	PERSIAN MAID
May 24	Maj R. Macdonald-Buchanan's	BRECON BEACONS
Jun 6	Mr G. R. H. Smith's	RIDGE WOOD
Jun 9	Mr J. A. Dewar's	PERSIAN MAID
Jun 10	Capt A. S. Wills's	KINGSWITCH
Jun 14	Mr J. A. Dewar's	FAUX TIRAGE
Jun 17	Lt Col Giles Loder's	THE COBBLER
Jun 17	Maj R. Macdonald-Buchanan's	ABERNANT
Jun 24	Mr G. R. H. Smith's	RIDGE WOOD
Jun 27	Mr J. A. Dewar's	POPLAR
Jun 28	Maj R. Macdonald-Buchanan's	KINLOCHEWE
Jun 29	Maj R. Macdonald-Buchanan's	ABERNANT
Jul 1	Lord Feversham's	KRAKATAO
Jul 5	Lt Col Giles Loder's	BRIDGENORTH
Jul 7	Capt A. S. Wills's	KINGSWITCH
Jul 8	Col B. Hornung's	LORD MAYOR
Jul 16	Mr G. R. H. Smith's	RIDGE WOOD
Jul 26	Maj R. Macdonald-Buchanan's	ABERNANT
Jul 27	Lord Feversham's	KRAKATAO
Jul 29	Maj R. Macdonald-Buchanan's	ROYAL FOREST
Jul 30	Capt A. S. Wills's	KINGSWITCH
Aug 2	Mr J. A. Dewar's	PERSIAN MAID
Aug 2	Mr J. A. Dewar's	ARC-EN-CIEL
Aug 6	Maj R. Macdonald-Buchanan's	BRECON BEACONS
Aug 8	Mr G. R. H. Smith's	RIDGE WOOD
Aug 10	Sir Percy Loraine's	SUSA
Aug 10	Mr F. Darling's	BOIS DES ISLES
Aug 10	Mr J. A. Dewar's	PERSIAN MAID
Aug 20	Mr G. R. H. Smith's	RIDGE WOOD
Aug 23	Maj R. Macdonald-Buchanan's	ABERNANT
Aug 24	Lord Feversham's	KRAKATAO

Appendix

COURSE	JOCKEY	PRIZE
Newmarket Stakes	G. Richards	2160
Badminston Stakes, Bath	J. Sword	244
Empire Handicap, Bath	G. Richards	345
Weston Plate, Bath	G. Richards	138
Druid Stakes, Salisbury	G. Richards	416
Salisbury Foal Stakes	G. Richards	278
Redenham Maiden Stakes, Salisbury	G. Richards	304
Fullerton Stakes, Salisbury	G. Richards	226
Branksome Handicap, Salisbury	G. Richards	303
Apprentice Plate, Chepstow	J. Sword	138
Tintern Abbey Plate, Chepstow	G. Richards	138
Mountain Ash Plate, Chepstow	G. Richards	158
City of Birmingham Cup, Birmingham	G. Richards	1103
Nimble Plate, Windsor	G. Richards	276
June Maiden Stakes, Lingfield Park	G. Richards	421
St James's Palace Stakes, Ascot	G. Richards	3926
Wokingham Stakes, Ascot	G. Richards	1905
King's Stand Stakes, Ascot	G. Richards	1535
Sandringham Stakes, Sandown	G. Richards	1081
Mabon Plate, Chepstow	G. Richards	138
Chepstow Stakes	J. Sword	599
July Cup, Newmarket	G. Richards	1586
Milton Handicap, Newmarket	G. Richards	950
Southampton Maiden Stakes, Salisbury	G. Richards	330
Quidhampton Maiden Stakes, Salisbury	G. Richards	317
Granville Stakes, Ascot	G. Richards	929
Commonwealth Stakes, Sandown	W. Carr	1001
King George Stakes, Goodwood	G. Richards	1205
Sussex Stakes, Goodwood	G. Richards	1101
Gordon Stakes, Goodwood	G. Richards	753
Chepstow Stakes, Chepstow	G. Richards	272
Channel Plate, Brighton	G. Richards	276
Brighton Handicap	G. Richards	1061
August Stakes, Warwick	J. Sword	223
Midland St Leger Trial, Birmingham	G. Richards	1263
Bridge Maiden Plate, Bath	G. Richards	138
Fernley Maiden Plate, Bath	G. Richards	138
Bathampton Plate, Bath	G. Richards	138
Oxfordshire Stakes, Newbury	G. Richards	1315
Nunthorpe Sweepstakes, York	G. Richards	1306
Duke of York Stakes, York	G. Richards	1153

	OWNER	HORSE
Aug 29	Mr J. A. Dewar's	ARC–EN–CIEL
Aug 31	Mr F. Darling's	BOIS DES ISLES
Sep 6	Mr J. A. Dewar's	ARC–EN–CIEL
Sep 8	Sir Percy Loraine's	WAT TYLER
Sep 10	Mr G. R. H. Smith's	RIDGE WOOD
Sep 24	Sir Percy Loraine's	WAT TYLER
Sep 27	Mr J. A. Dewar's	ARC–EN–CIEL
Sep 28	Mr J. A. Dewar's	PERSIAN MAID
Sep 29	Mr R. White's	BYLAND
Sep 30	Lady Bury's	RAMIFLORA
Oct 7	Sir Percy Loraine's	THE GOLDEN ROAD
Oct 14	Sir Percy Loraine's	WAT TYLER
Oct 22	Capt A. S. Wills's	GOLD MIST

1950

	OWNER	HORSE
Apr 1	Mr J. A. Dewar's	SEROCCO
Apr 5	Lt Col Giles Loder's	SERAPHIN
Apr 10	Sir Percy Loraine's	THE GOLDEN ROAD
Apr 12	Mr J. A. Dewar's	SUN VALLEY
Apr 22	Mr F. Darling's	CALSTONE
May 3	Capt A. S. Wills's	GOLD MIST
May 4	Maj R. Macdonald-Buchanan's	ABERNANT
May 10	Lt Col Giles Loder's	SERAPHIN
May 10	Mr J. A. Dewar's	SUN VALLEY
May 11	Capt A. S. Wills's	PARTICULAR
May 17	Sir Percy Loraine's	WAT TYLER
May 18	Mr J. A. Dewar's	MINARET
May 30	Lt Col Giles Loder's	CRAWLEY BEAUTY
Jun 12	Maj H. P. Holt's	AXEL MUNTHE
Jun 12	Mr J. A. Dewar's	THE TRAPPER
Jun 16	Mr D. E. Hely-Hutchinson's	KRAKATAO
Jun 19	Capt A. S. Wills's	PARTICULAR
Jun 20	Col B. Hornung's	ALKEN
Jun 21	Lt Col Giles Loder's	SERAPHIN
Jun 27	Lt Col Giles Loder's	FLIRTING
Jun 27	Mr D. E. Hely-Hutchinson's	KRAKATAO
Jun 28	Maj R. Macdonald-Buchanan's	ABERNANT
Jul 4	Sir Percy Loraine's	NAXOS

COURSE	JOCKEY	PRIZE
City of Coventry Stakes, Birmingham	G. *Richards*	502
Grenville Maiden Stakes, Bath	G. *Richards*	417
Beaufort Plate, Chepstow	G. *Richards*	138
Cleveland Handicap, Doncaster	G. *Richards*	885
St Leger Stakes, Doncaster	M. *Beary*	14,996
Knights' Royal Stakes, Ascot	D. *Smith*	2391
Great Foal Stakes, Newmarket	G. *Richards*	1389
Boscawen Stakes, Newmarket	G. *Richards*	534
Newmarket Autumn Foal Stakes	G. *Richards*	673
Maiden Stakes, Newmarket	J. *Sword*	618
Sandwich Maiden Stakes, Ascot	G. *Richards*	746
Select Stakes, Newmarket	G. *Richards*	627
Round Oak Handicap, Newbury	G. *Richards*	345

Races Won 66   Winning Stakes £62,523

COURSE	JOCKEY	PRIZE
Lambourn Stakes, Newbury	G. *Richards*	646
Stockbridge Maiden Stakes, Salisbury	G. *Richards*	288
Coventry Foal Stakes, Kempton	G. *Richards*	2072
Downs Maiden Plate, Bath	G. *Richards*	138
Cobham Stakes, Sandown	G. *Richards*	626
Primsore Sprint, Sandown	G. *Richards*	345
Lubbock Sprint Stakes, Sandown	G. *Richards*	480
Badminton Plate, Bath	G. *Richards*	138
Dyrham Park Maiden Stakes, Bath	G. *Richards*	300
County Maiden Stakes, Bath	J. *Sword*	244
Wiltshire Handicap, Salisbury	G. *Richards*	207
Redenham Maiden Stakes, Salisbury	G. *Richards*	325
Catherine of Aragon St Hurt Park	G. *Richards*	455
Lady Atking Plate, Worcester	G. *Richards*	207
Pershore Maiden Plate, Worcester	G. *Richards*	207
Rous Memorial Stakes, Ascot	G. *Richards*	1289
Westenhanger Maiden Plate, Folkestone	G. *Richards*	138
Marsh Stakes, Folkestone	G. *Richards*	290
Berkshire Foal Stakes, Newbury	G. *Richards*	1342
Barnwell Maiden Stakes, Newmarket	G. *Richards*	366
Bottisham Stakes, Newmarket	G. *Richards*	504
July Cup, Newmarket	G. *Richards*	1232
Hurstbourne Stakes, Salisbury	G. *Richards*	537

	OWNER	HORSE
Jul 13	Sir Percy Loraine's	WAT TYLER
Jul 21	Col B. Hornung's	ULUNDI
Jul 25	Maj R. Macdonald-Buchanan's	ABERNANT
Jul 26	Lt Col Giles Loder's	CRAWLEY BEAUTY
Jul 28	Mr D. E. Hely-Hutchinson's	KRAKATAO
Aug 1	Mrs R. Macdonald-Buchanan's	BRIMSTONE
Aug 2	Mr F. Darling's	CAPSIZE
Aug 3	Mr J. A. Dewar's	CONCUBINE
Aug 11	Lt Col Giles Loder's	FLIRTING
Aug 16	Maj H. P. Holt's	AXEL MUNTHE
Aug 17	Lt Col Giles Loder's	SERAPHIN
Aug 22	Maj R. Macdonald-Buchanan's	ABERNANT
Aug 23	Lord Feversham's	THE MAGISTRATE
Aug 29	Lt Col Giles Loder's	ABADAN
Aug 29	Maj H. P. Holt's	AXEL MUNTHE
Aug 30	Col B. Hornung's	POPE'S OAK
Aug 31	Mr J. A. Dewar's	RAY
Sep 12	Sir Percy Loraine's	QUARTERDECK
Sep 14	Mr J. A. Dewar's	MINARET
Sep 21	Maj R. Macdonald-Buchanan's	HAMPDEN FOREST
Sep 28	Col B. Hornung's	POPE'S OAK
Oct 7	Lt Col Giles Loder's	ABADAN
Oct 21	Capt A. S. Wills's	GOLD MIST
Oct 24	Mrs R. Macdonald-Buchanan's	CASTING VOTE

1951

May 3	Mr G. R. H. Smith's	CAVOUR II
May 17	Sir Percy Loraine's	HILARION
May 24	Capt A. S. Wills's	ADAGE
May 24	Sir Percy Loraine's	HILARION
May 26	His Majesty's	DEUCE
Jun 16	Mr J. A. Dewar's	MINARET
Jun 18	Maj R. Macdonald-Buchanan's	MOUNTAIN ASH
Jun 21	Capt A. S. Wills's	MONARCH MORE
Jul 10	Capt A. S. Wills's	GOLD MIST
Jul 10	Mr J. A. Dewar's	ARISTOPHANES
Jul 12	Maj R. Macdonald-Buchanan's	TUSCANY
Jul 12	Lt Col Giles Loder's	BEFORE THE MAST

COURSE	JOCKEY	PRIZE
Midsummer Stakes, Newmarket	G. *Richards*	574
Claremont Maiden Plate, Hurst Pk.	G. *Richards*	207
King George Stakes, Goodwood	G. *Richards*	879
Molecomb Stakes, Goodwood	G. *Richards*	2072
Chesterfield Cup, Goodwood	G. *Richards*	1503
Lord Leycester Maiden Plate, Birmingham	G. *Richards*	207
Bathampton Plate, Bath	G. *Richards*	138
Fillies' Maiden Plate, Bath	G. *Richards*	138
Budbrook Plate, Warwick	G. *Richards*	198
Taplow Plate, Windsor	G. *Richards*	138
Fulmer Plate, Windsor	G. *Richards*	207
Nunthorpe Sweepstakes, York	G. *Richards*	1350
Rous Sweepstakes, York	G. *Richards*	1,530
Union Stakes, Birmingham	G. *Richards*	853
Compton Wynyates Plate, Birmingham	G. *Richards*	207
Berwick Maiden Plate, Brighton	G. *Richards*	207
Kemp Town Plate, Brighton	G. *Richards*	207
Oldbury All-Aged Maiden P. Wolverh.	G. *Richards*	207
York House Plate, Bath	G. *Richards*	138
Clarence House Stakes, Ascot	G. *Richards*	695
Newmarket Autumn Produce Stakes	G. *Richards*	644
Diadem Stakes, Ascot	G. *Richards*	1,164
Round Oak Handicap, Newbury	G. *Richards*	345
Quy Maiden Stakes, Newmarket	G. *Richards*	548

Races Won 47   Winning Stakes £26,732

Culford Maiden Stakes, Newmarket	G. *Richards*	451
Wincanton Maiden Stakes, Salisbury	G. *Richards*	363
May Maiden Plate, Bath	G. *Richards*	138
County Maiden Stakes, Bath	G. *Richards*	301
Mayflower Stakes, Hurst Park	G. *Richards*	457
Fern Hill Stakes, Ascot	G. *Richards*	1235
Warwicks Breeders' Foal Stakes, Birmingham	G. *Richards*	1305
Kennett Maiden Stakes, Newbury	G. *Richards*	792
Wilton Handicap, Salisbury	G. *Richards*	207
Pembroke Maiden Plate, Salisbury	G. *Richards*	207
Quidhampton Maiden Stakes, Salisbury	G. *Richards*	360
Champagne Stakes, Salisbury	G. *Richards*	901

	OWNER	HORSE
Jul 12	Mr J. A. Dewar's	MINARET
Jul 17	Capt A. S. Wills's	SAFEHOLD
Aug 1	Mr J. A. Dewar's	AGITATOR
Aug 3	Lt Col Giles Loder's	ABADAN
Aug 3	Lt Col Giles Loder's	SEA PARROT
Aug 7	Mrs R. Macdonald-Buchanan's	SEPTIME
Aug 7	Sir Percy Loraine's	NAXOS
Aug 7	Mr G. R. H. Smith's	TABAJO
Aug 7	Lt Col Giles Loder's	MUCKLE HART
Aug 8	Mr T. Lilley's	ARMADA
Aug 13	Sir Percy Loraine's	NELLA
Aug 15	Lt Col Giles Loder's	MUCKLE HART
Aug 16	Mr T. Lilley's	NEW ROSE
Aug 21	Lt Col Giles Loder's	SEA PARROT
Aug 21	Lt Col Giles Loder's	ABADAN
Aug 31	His Majesty's	DEUCE
Sep 4	Lt Col Giles Loder's	MUCKLE HART
Sep 5	Mr J. A. Dewar's	LAVENDER WALK
Sep 5	Mrs Macdonald-Buchanan's	SEPTIME
Sep 5	Lord Feversham's	POINT d'ORGUE
Sep 6	His Majesty's	GOOD SHOT
Sep 6	Maj R. Macdonald-Buchanan's	LLEWELLYN
Sep 26	Mr J. A. Dewar's	REFRESHED
Sep 26	Sir Percy Loraine's	HILARION
Oct 1	His Majesty's	FAIR AND GAME
Oct 3	Mr J. A. Dewar's	AGITATOR
Oct 4	His Majesty's	DEUCE
Oct 5	Capt A. S. Wills's	MONARCH MORE
Oct 9	Mrs Noel Murless'	CRAYKE
Oct 13	His Majesty's	GOOD SHOT
Oct 17	Lt Col Giles Loder's	MUCKLE HART
Oct 19	Lt Col Giles Loder's	ABADAN
Nov 6	Lt Col Giles Loder's	WINGED FOOT

1952

Apr 12	Mr J. A. Dewar's	AGITATOR
Apr 14	Maj R. Macdonald-Buchanan's	FREQUENCY
Apr 16	Col B. Hornung's	BUCKHOUND

Appendix

COURSE	JOCKEY	PRIZE
Fleet Stakes, Salisbury	G. Richards	342
Spring Hall Stakes, Newmarket	G. Richards	342
Selsey Maiden Stakes, Goodwood	G. Richards	753
Chichester Stakes, Goodwood	G. Richards	589
Nassau Stakes, Goodwood	G. Richards	1258
Gloucester Stakes, Chepstow	C. Richards	329
Regency Handicap, Brighton	G. Richards	985
August Maiden Plate, Brighton	G. Richards	207
Beach Maiden Plate, Brighton	G. Richards	207
Hassocks Maiden Plate, Brighton	G. Richards	207
Hythe Maiden Plate, Folkestone	G. Richards	207
Fernley Maiden Plate, Bath	G. Richards	138
Fillies' Maiden Plate, Bath	G. Richards	138
Yorkshire Oaks, York	G. Richards	1795
Rose of York Sweepstakes, York	G. Richards	1625
Taplow Plate, Windsor	G. Richards	207
Compton Wynyates Plate, Birmingham	G. Richards	207
Grenville Nursery Handicap Stakes, Bath	G. Richards	322
Monument Maiden Plate, Bath	G. Richards	207
Didcot Maiden Plate, Bath	G. Richards	138
York House Plate, Bath	G. Richards	138
September Maiden Plate, Bath	G. Richards	138
Dorchester Maiden Stakes, Salisbury	G. Richards	467
Stonehenge Handicap, Salisbury	G. Richards	271
Ann Hathaway Maiden Plate, Birmingham	G. Richards	207
Hopeful Stakes, Newmarket	G. Richards	687
Newmarket Foal Stakes, Newmarket	G. Richards	738
Rous Memorial Stakes, Newmarket	G. Richards	845
Fillies' Maiden Plate, Nottingham	G. Richards	207
Tankerville Nursery Stakes, Ascot	G. Richards	712
Prendergast Stakes, Newmarket	G. Richards	635
Select Stakes, Newmarket	G. Richards	627
Queen Bess Maiden Plate, Birmingham	G. Richards	207

Races Won 45   Winning Stakes £22,799

2000gs. Trial Stakes, Kempton Park	G. Richards	1442
Coventry Foal Stakes, Kempton Park	G. Richards	1966
Column Produce Stakes, Newmarket	G. Richards	1650

173

	OWNER	HORSE
Apr 19	Mr J. A. Dewar's	REFRESHED
Apr 25	Mr T. Lilley's	TITANIUM
May 8	Mr G. R. H. Smith's	CAVOUR II
May 10	Mr J. A. Dewar's	ARISTOPHANES
May 14	Mr J. A. Dewar's	BLACKWOOD
May 14	Mr J. A. Dewar's	POETICUS
May 15	Maj R. Macdonald-Buchanan's	WESTER ROSS
May 21	Mr J. A. Dewar's	TURBULENCE
May 21	Mr J. A. Dewar's	CYRUS THE GREAT
May 22	Sir Percy Loraine's	HYMEN
May 22	Mr J. A. Dewar's	NEW FOREST
Jun 2	Duke of Norfolk's	ARDENT
Jun 4	Mr J. A. Dewar's	NEW FOREST
Jun 11	Mr J. A. Dewar's	TELYN
Jun 11	Mr J. A. Dewar's	NEW FOREST
Jun 12	The Queen's	INFERNAL MACHINE
Jun 13	Mr D. E. Hely-Hutchinson's	GOLD BUCKLE
Jun 14	Mr J. A. Dewar's	POETICUS
Jun 27	The Queen's	ARDENT
Jul 1	Maj R. Macdonald-Buchanan's	TORRID ZONE
Jul 8	Sir Percy Loraine's	HYMEN
Jul 9	Capt A. S. Wills's	KING KELPIE
Jul 10	Maj R. Macdonald-Buchanan's	DOUBLE BLUE
Jul 16	Mr J. A. Dewar's	BLACKWOOD
Jul 22	Mr J. A. Dewar's	POETICUS
Jul 24	Col B. Hornung's	SOPHIA
Jul 30	Mr J. A. Dewar's	AGITATOR
Aug 1	Lt Col Giles Loder's	BLOOD TEST
Aug 5	The Queen's	INFERNAL MACHINE
Aug 5	Capt A. S. Wills's	MONARCH MORE
Aug 5	Maj R. Macdonald-Buchanan's	DOUBLE BLUE
Aug 6	Mrs T. Lilley's	POLYKEM
Aug 6	Maj R. Macdonald-Buchanan's	CANDELABRA
Aug 21	Maj R. Macdonald-Buchanan's	WESTER ROSS
Aug 21	The Queen's	BLACK BEE
Aug 27	Capt A. S. Wills's	MONARCH MORE
Aug 28	Maj R. Macdonald-Buchanan's	CANDELABRA
Aug 29	The Queen's	INFERNAL MACHINE
Sep 3	Senator Euvaldo Lodi's	KAMERAN
Sep 6	Mr G. R. H. Smith's	CAVOUR II
Sep 30	Col B. Hornung's	SOPHIA

COURSE	JOCKEY	PRIZE
Lambourn Stakes, Newbury	G. Richards	584
Tudor Maiden Stakes, Sandown	G. Richards	882
Gillyflower Handicap, Sandown	G. Richards	474
Newnham Handicap, Chepstow	G. Richards	207
Badminton Plate, Bath	G. Richards	138
Hodcott Maiden Plate, Bath	G. Richards	138
May Maiden Plate, Bath	G. Richards	138
Warminster Stakes, Salisbury	G. Richards	388
Salisbury Foal Stakes	G. Richards	484
Redenham Stakes, Salisbury	G. Richards	394
Wincanton Stakes, Salisbury	G. Richards	378
Ross Plate, Chepstow	G. Richards	138
Bardolph Plate, Windsor	G. Richards	207
Shoreham Plate, Brighton	G. Richards	276
Portslade Plate, Brighton	G. Richards	207
Whitehawk Plate, Brighton	G. Richards	276
June Stakes, Lingfield Park	G. Richards	436
Southern Stakes, Lingfield	G. Richards	312
June Plate, Windsor	G. Richards	207
Herringswell Stakes, Newmarket	G. Richards	540
Hurstbourne Stakes, Salisbury	G. Richards	616
Weyhill Stakes, Salisbury	G. Richards	304
Bridgewater Stakes, Salisbury	G. Richards	235
Downs Plate, Bath	G. Richards	138
Faversham Plate, Folkestone	G. Richards	207
Two Year Old Stakes, Kempton	G. Richards	458
Sussex Stakes, Goodwood	G. Richards	957
Findon Maiden Stakes, Goodwood	G. Richards	625
Channel Plate, Brighton	G. Richards	276
Brighton Handicap	G. Richards	1004
August Maiden Plate, Brighton	G. Richards	207
South Coast Handicap, Brighton	G. Richards	207
Hassocks Plate, Brighton	G. Richards	207
Brockham Handicap, Bath	G. Richards	207
Fillies' Plate, Bath	G. Richards	138
Preston Park Handicap, Brighton	G. Richards	690
Saddlescombe Plate, Brighton	G. Richards	237
Taplow Plate, Windsor	G. Richards	276
Didcott Plate, Bath	G. Richards	138
Stayers' Handicap, Folkestone	G. Richards	242
Abingdon Mile Nursery, Newmarket	G. Richards	694

OWNER	HORSE

Oct 2	Col B. Hornung's	OLGA
Oct 15	Lt Col Giles Loder's	BLOOD TEST
Nov 4	The Queen's	HIGH SERVICE

1953

Apr 30	The Queen's	GAY TIME
May 21	Sir Victor Sassoon's	PRINCELY GIFT
May 28	Sir Victor Sassoon's	DEUCE
May 29	Col B. Hornung's	BUCKHOUND
Jun 2	Mrs T. Lilley's	WOOD CLARION
Jun 18	Lt Col Giles Loder's	BLOOD TEST
Jun 27	Sir Victor Sassoon's	DEUCE
Jul 1	Mr T. Lilley's	BLUE FIRE
Jul 2	Col B. Hornung's	OLGA
Jul 3	The Queen's	LANDAU
Jul 8	Mrs R. Macdonald-Buchanan's	LOVELY POLLY
Jul 14	Mr T. Lilley's	SUN FESTIVAL
Jul 30	Col B. Hornung's	BUCKHOUND
Aug 5	H.H. Aga Khan's	BARA BIBI
Aug 5	Maj R. Macdonald-Buchanan's	MOUNTAIN ASH
Aug 6	Mr Noel Murless'	PYRETHRUM
Aug 6	Sir Victor Sassoon's	MEERSCHAUM
Aug 7	Mr D. E. Hely-Hutchinson's	JAMIE
Aug 8	Sir Victor Sassoon's	HANS SACHS
Aug 10	Sir Victor Sassoon's	FLIGHT FORMATION
Aug 10	Sir Victor Sassoon's	DEUCE
Aug 14	Col B. Hornung's	OLGA
Aug 26	Sir Victor Sassoon's	DEUCE
Aug 27	Mr T. Lilley's	LINDA BELLE
Aug 27	Sir Victor Sassoon's	FLIGHT FORMATION
Sep 2	Col B. Hornung's	SOPHIA
Sep 2	Mr F. F. Tuthill's	PICTURE GALLERY
Sep 9	Col B. Hornung's	BUCKHOUND
Sep 12	The Queen's	LANDAU
Sep 16	Lady Cayzer's	BIG THRILL
Sep 17	Sir Percy Loraine's	TRIAL RUN
Sep 17	Lt Col Giles Loder's	BEDTIME STORY
Sep 22	Mr C. Steuart's	RASHLEIGH

COURSE	JOCKEY	PRIZE
Newmarket Foal Stakes	G. Richards	887
Prendergast Stakes, Newmarket	G. Richards	716
Queen Bess Plate, Birmingham	G. Richards	207

Races Won 47 Winning Stakes £21,735

March Stakes, Newmarket	A. Breasley	1013
Fullerton Stakes, Salisbury	G. Richards	327
Spital Handicap, Windsor	G. Richards	276
Claremont Handicap, Sandown	G. Richards	1019
Golden Coach Stakes, Kempton	G. Richards	595
Cork & Orrey Stakes, Ascot	G. Richards	1328
Forest Handicap, Windsor	G. Richards	276
Haughley Plate, Newmarket	G. Richards	193
Girton Handicap, Newmarket	G. Richards	550
Fulbourne Stakes, Newmarket	G. Richards	765
Tisbury Plate, Salisbury	G. Richards	207
Saxham Stakes, Newmarket	G. Richards	467
Trundle Stakes, Goodwood	G. Richards	1226
Hassocks Plate, Brighton	G. Richards	276
Black Rock Handicap, Brighton	P. Evans	276
Falmer Plate, Brighton	G. Richards	276
Town Hall Handicap, Brighton	G. Richards	276
De Warrenne Plate, Lewes	G. Richards	138
Ringmer Plate, Lewes	G. Richards	138
Hythe Plate, Folkestone	G. Richards	207
Romney Handicap, Folkestone	G. Richards	297
Hungerford Stakes, Newbury	G. Richards	526
Hollingbury Handicap, Brighton	G. Richards	389
Race Hill Plate, Brighton	G. Richards	276
Saddlescombe Plate, Brighton	G. Richards	276
Greystone Handicap, Bath	G. Richards	173
Monument Plate, Bath	G. Richards	207
Great Yorkshire Handicap, Doncaster	G. Richards	1264
Produce Stakes, Doncaster	G. Richards	1715
Herring Fisheries Stakes, Yarmouth	P. Evans	235
Pycombe Handicap, Brighton	G. Richards	276
Seven Dials Maiden Plate, Brighton	G. Richards	276
Dorchester Stakes, Salisbury	G. Richards	358

M

	OWNER	HORSE
Sep 22	Mr F. F. Tuthill's	PICTURE GALLERY
Oct 1	Col B. Hornung's	BUCKHOUND
Oct 2	The Queen's	LANDAU
Oct 2	Sir Victor Sassoon's	KEY
Oct 9	Sir Victor Sassoon's	ELOPEMENT
Oct 13	Sir Victor Sassoon's	PRINCELY GIFT
Oct 15	H.H. Aga Khan's	BARA BEGUM
Oct 15	H.H. Aga Khan's	BARA BIBI
Oct 23	Mrs T. Lilley's	COURT SPLENDOUR
Oct 30	Mrs Noel Murless'	NANDI
Oct 30	Sir Victor Sassoon's	PRINCELY GIFT

1954

Apr 3	H.H. Aga Khan's	NECHAO
Apr 8	Mr T. Lilley's	SUN FESTIVAL
Apr 19	Mrs T. Lilley's	COURT SPLENDOUR
Apr 19	Mrs D. M. FitzPatrick's	KEY
Apr 20	Sir Victor Sassoon's	NEAR DAWN
Apr 22	H.H. Aga Khan's	BARA BIBI
Apr 27	Sir Percy Loraine's	BABA ALI
Apr 29	Mr T. Lilley's	PETER REX
Apr 29	H.H. Aga Khan's	BOIS LE ROI
May 12	Sir Victor Sassoon's	ELOPEMENT
May 12	H.H. Aga Khan's	BOIS LE ROI
May 13	Mr C. Steuart's	RASHLEIGH
May 18	The Queen's	REJOICING
Jun 10	Col B. Hornung's	AGRIPPA
Jun 17	Mrs D. M. FitzPatrick's	KEY
Jun 17	Mr C. Steuart's	RASHLEIGH
Jun 18	The Queen's	LANDAU
Jun 26	Mrs R. N. Ryan's	FRISEUR
Jul 2	The Queen's	LANDAU
Jul 6	Mr C. Steuart's	FIVE ACES
Jul 9	Sir Victor Sassoon's	PRINCELY GIFT
Jul 13	Mrs Noel Murless'	SEPH
Jul 14	Sir Victor Sassoon's	LITTLE CLOUD
Jul 20	H.H. Aga Khan's	CHAKA
Jul 23	Mr C. Steuart's	FIVE ACES

COURSE	JOCKEY	PRIZE
Stockbridge Stakes, Salisbury	G. Richards	349
Jockey Club Stakes, Newmarket	G. Richards	5213
Boscawen Stakes, Newmarket	G. Richards	507
Chevington Maiden Stakes, Newmarket	G. Richards	489
Duke of Edinburgh Stakes, Ascot	G. Richards	1493
Clearwell Stakes, Newmarket	G. Richards	476
Alington Stakes, Newmarket	G. Richards	502
Histon Stakes, Newmarket	G. Richards	485
Horris Hill Stakes, Newbury	G. Richards	1202
Durham Maiden Handicap, Newmarket	G. Richards	399
Moulton Stakes, Newmarket	G. Richards	970

Races Won 44   Winning Stakes £28,182

COURSE	JOCKEY	PRIZE
Copper Horse Handicap, Windsor	G. Richards	276
Free Handicap Newmarket	G. Richards	1135
Coventry Stakes, Kempton Park	G. Richards	907
1000gs. Trial Stakes, Kempton	G. Richards	1395
Tamworth Plate, Birmingham	A. Richardson	207
Princess Elizabeth Stakes, Epsom	G. Richards	4022
Hastings Stakes, Newmarket	G. Richards	754
Botesdale Handicap, Newmarket	G. Richards	779
Culford Stakes, Newmarket	G. Richards	475
Newmarket Stakes	G. Richards	1897
Fen Sitton Stakes, Newmarket	G. Richards	433
Payne Stakes, Newmarket	G. Richards	954
Glasgow Stakes, York	G. Richards	417
June Plate, Windsor	W. Snaith	207
Cork & Orrey Stakes, Ascot	G. Richards	1264
King Edward VII Stakes, Ascot	G. Richards	4634
Rous Memorial Stakes, Ascot	G. Richards	1340
Northumberland Plate, Newcastle	G. Richards	2025
Ellesmere Stakes, Newmarket	G. Richards	742
Hurstbourne Stakes, Salisbury	G. Richards	628
Ditton Sprint Handicap, Sandown	G. Richards	423
Soltykoff Stakes, Newmarket	W. Snaith	1025
Zetland Stakes, Newmarket	W. Snaith	393
Whitstable Plate, Folkestone	W. Snaith	138
Red House Stakes, Doncaster	W. Snaith	882

	OWNER	HORSE
Jul 27	Sir Percy Loraine's	BABA ALI
Jul 28	The Queen's	LANDAU
Jul 30	Mrs D. M. FitzPatrick's	KEY
Aug 3	Mrs. T. Lilley's	WOOD ALARM
Aug 5	H.H. Aga Khan's	ROKHSA
Aug 12	H.H. Aga Khan's	QUEEN OF HIND
Aug 20	Prince Aly Khan's	FREPILLON
Aug 26	H.H. Aga Khan's	ROKHSA
Aug 31	Lt Col Giles Loder's	MISTRESS GRACE
Aug 31	Lt Col Giles Loder's	PREAMBLE
Sep 1	Mrs T. Lilley's	WOOD ALARM
Sep 1	Sir Victor Sassoon's	EVENING TRIAL
Sep 9	H.H. Aga Khan's	BARA BIBI
Sep 15	Sir Victor Sassoon's	MEERSCHAUM
Oct 6	Sir Victor Sassoon's	EVENING TRIAL
Oct 9	Sir Victor Sassoon's	ELOPEMENT
Oct 12	Sir Victor Sassoon's	PRINCELY GIFT
Oct 13	Mrs R. Macdonald-Buchanan's	SEPH
Oct 16	Mr C. Steuart's	RASHLEIGH

1955

	OWNER	HORSE
Apr 30	Sir Victor Sassoon's	LITTLE CLOUD
May 10	Mr C. Steuart's	FIVE ACES
May 19	Sir Victor Sassoon's	MOLTEN LAVA
May 30	Sir Victor Sassoon's	JUDICIAL
May 30	Sir Percy Loraine's	POKE BONNET
Jun 8	Lt Col R. Taylor's	BOIS LE ROI
Jun 10	Sir Victor Sassoon's	SCOLLATA
Jun 25	Sir Victor Sassoon's	LITTLE CLOUD
Jun 27	Sir Victor Sassoon's	A.A.
Jun 28	Sir Victor Sassoon's	PRINCELY GIFT
Jun 29	Prince Aly Khan's	KNIGHT VALIANT
Jul 1	Mrs R. Macdonald-Buchanan's	SEPH
Jul 2	Mr T. Lilley's	LADY SUPREME
Jul 7	Sir Victor Sassoon's	ABERVALE
Jul 12	Sir Victor Sassoon's	ELOPEMENT
Jul 13	The Queen's	JARDINIERE

COURSE	JOCKEY .	PRIZE
Craven Stakes, Goodwood	E. Mercer	684
Sussex Stakes, Goodwood	W. Snaith	1035
Nassau Stakes, Goodwood	W. Snaith	1629
August Stakes, Brighton	D. Smith	299
Alfriston Stakes, Brighton	C. Smirke	326
Upavon Stakes, Salisbury	C. Smirke	158*
Shipley Bridge Stakes, Lingfield	C. Smirke	405
Race Hill Stakes, Brighton	C. Smirke	330
Meriden Plate, Birmingham	W. Rickaby	276
Compton Wynyates Plate, Birmingham	W. Snaith	207
Monument Plate, Bath	C. Smirke	276
Greystones Handicap, Bath	C. Smirke	207
Park Hill Stakes, Doncaster	C. Smirke	3085
Dome Handicap Stakes, Brighton	W. Snaith	334
Askham Stakes, York	L. Piggott	362
Cumberland Lodge Stakes, Ascot	C. Smirke	2291
Challenge Stakes, Newmarket	L. Piggott	472
Prendergast Stakes, Newmarket	W. Snaith	696
Wheatsheaf Stakes, Sandown Park	L. Piggott	816

Races Won 44   Winning Stakes £41,240

* deadheat

Shefford Handicap, Newbury	L. Piggott	420
Wilburton Handicap, Newmarket	L. Piggott	717
Redenham Stakes, Salisbury	L. Piggott	420
Rose Hill Plate, Doncaster	L. Piggott	345
Vyner Maiden Stakes, Doncaster	L. Piggott	365
Pavilion Handicap Stakes, Brighton	L. Piggott	593
Elmire Plate, Thirsk	L. Piggott	207
Northumberland Plate, Newcastle	L. Piggott	2025
Montpelier Stakes, Brighton	L. Piggott	373
Waterbeach Handicap, Newmarket	L. Piggott	302
Stud Produce Stakes, Newmarket	L. Piggott	849
Soham Stakes Handicap, Newmarket	L. Piggott	340
Wood Green Plate, Alexandra Park	L. Piggott	207
Quidhampton Stakes, Salisbury	L. Piggott	365
Hardwicke Stakes, Ascot	L. Piggott	3995
King George V Stakes, Ascot	D. Smith	1625

	OWNER	HORSE
Jul 25	Mr N. S. C. Collin's	THE BEADLE
Jul 29	Sir Victor Sassoon's	PRINCELY GIFT
Aug 2	Sir Victor Sassoon's	GREENHEART
Aug 2	Sir Victor Sassoon's	BAND PRACTICE
Aug 3	Mrs R. Macdonald-Buchanan's	PERUKE
Aug 4	Sir Victor Sassoon's	PRAIRIES
Aug 4	Mr T. Lilley's	SUN SPARKLE
Aug 11	Sir Victor Sassoon's	RACKETEER
Aug 12	Sir Victor Sassoon's	PRINCELY GIFT
Aug 18	Lt Col Giles Loder's	PREAMBLE
Aug 24	Mrs R. Macdonald-Buchanan's	SEPH
Aug 24	Mrs D. M. FitzPatrick's	EXTASE
Aug 25	Sir Victor Sassoon's	FUNNY BUSINESS
Aug 29	Mr T. Lilley's	SUN SPARKLE
Sep 1	Prince Aly Khan's	RAIN CLOUD
Sep 8	Sir Victor Sassoon's	PRINCELY GIFT
Sept 29	The Queen's	ANNIE OAKLEY
Oct 5	The Queen's	ANNIE OAKLEY
Oct 15	Sir Percy Loraine's	POKE BONNET
Nov 1	Sir Victor Sassoon's	KANDY SAUCE

1956

Apr 25	Lady Ursula Vernon's	HUGH LUPUS
May 3	Lady Ursula Vernon's	HUGH LUPUS
May 19	The Queen's	CARROZZA
May 30	Sir Victor Sassoon's	SUNNY PASTURE
May 30	Sir Victor Sassoon's	ANTE UP
Jun 2	Sir Victor Sassoon's	ROCKLET
Jun 5	Col B. Hornung's	MANSBRIDGE
Jun 7	Prince Aly Khan's	KNIGHT VALIANT
Jun 9	Mr T. Lilley's	TARSUS
Jun 15	Sir Victor Sassoon's	OGWEN
Jun 15	Sir Victor Sassoon's	HUNTER'S HORN
Jun 19	Sir Victor Sassoon's	KANDY SAUCE
Jun 21	Mrs T. Lilley's	COURT COMMAND
Jun 22	Lady Ursula Vernon's	HUGH LUPUS
Jun 23	Mr H. M. Warner's	GROUNDED
Jun 27	Mr F. F. Tuthill's	PREAMBLE

Appendix

COURSE	JOCKEY	PRIZE
Islington S. Plate, Alexandra Park	*L. Piggott*	188
Chichester Stakes, Goodwood	*L. Piggott*	594
August Stakes, Brighton	*L. Piggott*	326
Beach Maiden Stakes, Brighton	*L. Piggott*	343
South Coast Handicap, Brighton	*L. Piggott*	369
Frank Pease Plate, Pontefract	*C. Lines*	207
Alfriston Stakes Brighton	*L. Piggott*	344
Bulford Stakes, Salisbury	*L. Piggott*	297
Hungerford Stakes, Newbury	*L. Piggott*	533
Rainbow Stakes, Sandown Park	*L. Piggott*	330
Wykeham Handicap, York	*L. Piggott*	1395
Berwick Stakes, Brighton	*F. Barlow*	293
Race Hill Stakes, Brighton	*L. Piggott*	299
Allies Two-Year-Old Plate, Lewes	*L. Piggott*	207
York House Plate, Bath. W.O.	*L. Piggott*	248
Portland Handicap, Doncaster	*L. Piggott*	2575
Wicken Maiden Stakes, Newmarket	*L. Piggott*	237
Askham Stakes, York	*L. Piggott*	385
Heather Nursery Handicap, Sandown	*L. Piggott*	540
Queen Bess Plate, Birmingham	*L. Piggott*	207

Races Won 36   Winning Stakes £23,065

Fryston Stakes, Pontefract	*W. Johnstone*	318
March Stakes, Newmarket	*W. Johnstone*	1047
Rosemary Plate, Hurst Park	*L. Piggott*	390
Fairfield Stakes, York	*L. Piggott*	410
Scarbrough Stakes, York	*L. Piggott*	292
Ladys Well Stakes, Thirsk	*D. Smith*	309
Woodcote Stakes, Epsom	*L. Piggott*	2053
Royal Stakes Handicap, Epsom	*L. Piggott*	626
Rivermead Stakes, Kempton Park	*L. Piggott*	688
Grimthorpe Plate, Doncaster	*L. Piggott*	207
Corporation Maiden Stakes, Doncaster	*L. Piggott*	436
Queen Anne Stakes, Ascot	*D. Smith*	1616
King Edward VII Stakes, Ascot	*L. Piggott*	4481
Hardwicke Stakes, Ascot	*W. Johnstone*	3623
Fenwolfe Stakes, Ascot	*L. Piggott*	861
Netheravon Handicap, Newbury	*L. Piggott*	276

	OWNER	HORSE
Jun 29	The Queen's	DECK TENNIS
Jun 29	Sir Victor Sassoon's	HUNTER'S HORN
Jun 30	Mr T. Lilley's	JARDINIERE
Jul 2	The Queen's	TENERETTA
Jul 6	Sir Victor Sassoon's	HUNTER'S HORN
Jul 9	Mrs D. M. FitzPatrick's	GUINEA
Jul 10	Sir Victor Sassoon's	HUNTER'S HORN
Jul 11	Mr T. Lilley's	SYLPHIDE
Jul 16	Mr F. F. Tuthill's	PREAMBLE
Jul 17	Sir Victor Sassoon's	OGWEN
Jul 21	Sir Victor Sassoon's	SPACE SHIP
Jul 21	Sir Victor Sassoon's	ADVENTURESS
Jul 27	Sir Victor Sassoon's	SPACE SHIP
Jul 27	The Queen's	ANTHRACITE
Aug 7	Prince Aly Khan's	STARLIT MOONLIGHT
Aug 8	Sir Victor Sassoon's	RISEBOROUGH
Aug 9	Col B. Hornung's	ABERCORN
Aug 13	Sir Victor Sassoon's	SPACE SHIP
Aug 14	Mrs D. M. FitzPatrick's	GUINEA
Aug 18	Mrs T. Lilley's	COURT COMMAND
Aug 29	Sir Victor Sassoon's	SPACE SHIP
Aug 30	Col B. Hornung's	ABERCORN
Sept 13	Lady Ursula Vernon's	HUGH LUPUS
Sep 15	Sir Victor Sassoon's	KANDY SAUCE
Sep 19	Sir Victor Sassoon's	MEERSCHAUM
Sep 20	Sir Victor Sassoon's	SIJUI
Oct 2	Sir Victor Sassoon's	KANDY SAUCE
Oct 11	The Queen's	TEN BELLS
Oct 18	Lady Ursula Vernon's	HUGH LUPUS
Oct 30	Sir Victor Sassoon's	KANDY SAUCE
Nov 1	Sir Victor Sassoon's	CREPELLO

1957

Apr 11	Lt Col Giles Loder's	SHEARWATER
Apr 13	Sir Victor Sassoon's	SIJUI
Apr 25	The Queen's	CARROZZA
Apr 27	Col B. Hornung's	SUN CHARGER
Apr 27	Col B. Hornung's	KINGS BARN

COURSE	JOCKEY	PRIZE
Fawdon Stakes, Newcastle	*L. Piggott*	501
St Oswald Stakes, Newcastle	*L. Piggott*	417
Northumberland Plate, Newcastle	*D. Smith*	2025
Hove Stakes, Brighton	*L. Piggott*	372
Stokesley Stakes, Stockton	*L. Piggott*	308
Crouch End Fillies' Plate, Alexandra Park	*L. Piggott*	207
Newark Plate, Nottingham	*L. Piggott*	207
Weyhill Stakes, Salisbury	*L. Piggott*	345
Shipston Stakes, Birmingham	*L. Piggott*	323
Soltykoff Stakes, Newmarket	*L. Piggott*	551
Clayton Plate, Doncaster	*L. Piggott*	276
Huddersfield Plate, Doncaster	*L. Piggott*	207
Claremont Plate, Hurst Park	*L. Piggott*	306
Coxwold Maiden Stakes, Thirsk	*C. Lines*	486
Beach Two Years Old Stakes, Brighton	*L. Piggott*	324
Southdown Stakes, Brighton	*L. Piggott*	275
Falmer Stakes, Brighton	*L. Piggott*	299
Hemlock Stone Plate, Nottingham	*L. Piggott*	207
Oxton Plate, Nottingham	*L. Piggott*	207
Oxfordshire Stakes, Newbury	*L. Piggott*	1073
Goldstone Stakes, Brighton	*L. Piggott*	317
Kemp Town Stakes, Brighton	*L. Piggott*	328
Scarbrough Stakes, Doncaster	*W. Johnstone*	1401
Atalanta Stakes, Sandown Park	*L. Piggott*	506
Dome Handicap Stakes, Brighton	*L. Piggott*	316
Hastings Stakes, Yarmouth	*P. Tulk*	282
Old Rowley Stakes, Newmarket	*L. Piggott*	780
York Apprentice Stakes	*J. Gifford*	441
Champion Stakes, Newmarket	*W. Johnstone*	4030
Limekiln Stakes, Newmarket	*L. Piggott*	979
Dewhurst Stakes, Newmarket	*L. Piggott*	1943

Races Won 47   Winning Stakes £37,872

Craven Stakes, Newmarket	*L. Piggott*	735
Fred Darling Stakes, Newbury	*L. Piggott*	1207
Princess Elizabeth Stakes, Epsom	*L. Piggott*	6461
Royal Stakes, Sandown Park	*L. Piggott*	1727
Marcus Beresford Stakes, Sandown	*L. Piggott*	595

	OWNER	HORSE
Apr 30	Lt Col Giles Loder's	ARCTIC EXPLORER
May 1	Sir Victor Sassoon's	CREPELLO
May 15	Lt Col Giles Loder's	ARCTIC EXPLORER
May 15	Col B. Hornung's	SUN CHARGER
Jun 5	Sir Victor Sassoon's	CREPELLO
Jun 7	The Queen's	CARROZZA
Jun 14	Col B. Hornung's	MANSBRIDGE
Jun 19	Col B. Hornung's	ABELIA
Jun 20	Lt Col Giles Loder's	ARCTIC EXPLORER
Jun 22	The Queen's	FLAKE WHITE
Jun 26	Sir Victor Sassoon's	BABY FLINDERS
Jun 28	Sir Victor Sassoon's	SATAN'S SLIDE
Jun 28	The Queen's	IMPALA
Jun 29	Sir Victor Sassoon's	PINCHED
Jul 3	Col B. Hornung's	ABELIA
Jul 4	Sir Victor Sassoon's	BABY FLINDERS
Jul 4	Mr T. Lilley's	SYLPHIDE
Jul 6	Sir Victor Sassoon's	SWEET ANGEL
Jul 13	Lt Col Giles Loder's	ARCTIC EXPLORER
Jul 17	Mr T. Lilley's	SYLPHIDE
Jul 30	Col B. Hornung's	ABELIA
Aug 6	Sir Victor Sassoon's	BOCCACIO
Aug 8	The Queen's	CANDY TUFT
Aug 9	Sir Victor Sassoon's	STONEBORER
Aug 15	Mrs T. Lilley's	COURT COMMAND
Aug 17	Sir Victor Sassoon's	ROMAN NOSE
Aug 23	Sir Victor Sassoon's	RISEBOROUGH
Aug 28	Mrs. T. Lilley's	ANGEL BABY
Aug 29	Mr C. Steuart's	MADAM RECORDER
Aug 29	Sir Victor Sassoon's	PRINCE MOON
Sep 3	The Queen's	CANDY TUFT
Sep 6	Sir Victor Sassoon's	STONEBORER
Sep 7	Sir Victor Sassoon's	SATAN'S SLIDE
Sep 18	Sir Victor Sassoon's	STRUNG UP
Sep 18	Miss Julia Murless'	MEERSCHAUM
Sep 21	Sir Victor Sassoon's	PIN-SHEEL
Sep 26	Col B. Hornung's	BARLEYCROFT
Sep 27	Sir Victor Sassoon's	PINCHED
Sep 28	Lt Col R. Taylor's	BRILLIANT STONE
Oct 5	Sir Victor Sassoon's	BOCCACCIO
Oct 12	Col B. Hornung's	ABELIA

COURSE	JOCKEY	PRIZE
Hastings Stakes, Newmarket	L. Piggott	547
2000 Guineas Stakes, Newmarket	L. Piggott	13598
Fen Ditton Stakes, Newmarket	L. Piggott	372
Newmarket Stakes	L. Piggott	1786
The Derby, Epsom	L. Piggott	18,659
The Oaks, Epsom	L. Piggott	16,101
Red Rose Stakes, Manchester	L. Piggott	1326
Queen Mary Stakes, Ascot	L. Piggott	3559
King Edward VII Stakes, Ascot	L. Piggott	5101
Fenwolf Stakes, Ascot	L. Piggott	725
Berkshire Foal Stakes, Newbury	L. Piggott	1535
Fawdon Fillies' Stakes, Newcastle	L. Piggott	504
St Oswald Stakes, Newcastle	L. Piggott	384
Seaton Delaval Stakes, Newcastle	L. Piggott	2361
July Stakes, Newmarket	L. Piggott	2086
Plantation Stakes, Newmarket	L. Piggott	599
Girton Handicap, Newcastle	L. Piggott	429
Stud Produce Stakes, Newmarket	L. Piggott	800
Eclipse Stakes, Sandown Park	L. Piggott	7673
Falmouth Stakes, Newmark	L. Piggott	1358
Molecomb Stakes, Goodwood	L. Piggott	2975
Channel Stakes, Brighton	L. Piggott	407
Alfriston Stakes, Brighton	I. Piggott	470
Rubbing House Stakes, Newmarket	L. Piggott	477
Poulsen Stakes, Sandown Park	L. Piggott	511
Lambton Stakes, Stockton	L. Piggott	297
Freckenham Stakes, Newmarket	L. Piggott	290
Berwick Stakes, Brighton	L. Piggott	464
Race Hill Stakes, Brighton	L. Piggott	440
August Handicap, Brighton	L. Piggott	943
Meriden Fillies' Plate, Birmingham	L. Piggott	276
Straitlace Stakes, Manchester	L. Piggott	534
Rivermead Stakes, Kempton Park	L. Piggott	677
Herring Fisheries Stakes, Yarmouth	L. Piggott	197
Dome Handicap Stakes, Brighton	G. Starkey	447
Imperial Produce Stakes, Kempton	L. Piggott	6931
Clarence House Stakes, Ascot	L. Piggott	679
Royal Lodge Stakes, Ascot	L. Piggott	3840
Blue Seal Stakes, Ascot	L. Piggott	1565
Autumn Foal Stakes, Newbury	L. Piggott	1998
Cornwallis Stakes, Ascot	L. Piggott	1578

OWNER	HORSE

	OWNER	HORSE
Oct 15	Mr Noel Murless'	CHEETAH
Oct 30	The Queen's	SNOW CAT

1958

	OWNER	HORSE
Apr 16	Mr C. H. Dracoulis's	PRIMERA
Apr 26	Lt Col Giles Loders's	ARTIC EXPLORER
Apr 26	The Queen's	SNOW CAT
May 6	Sir Victor Sassoon's	PRINCE MOON
May 8	Mr C. H. Dracoulis's	PRIMERA
May 24	Col B. Hornung's	ABELIA
Jun 4	Sir Victor Sassoon's	PINCHED
Jun 20	The Queen's	SNOW CAT
Jun 20	Lt Col Giles Loder's	CARNOUSTIE
Jun 21	Mr C. H. Dracoulis's	PRIMERA
Jul 12	Prince Aly Khan's	PETITE ETOILE
Jul 15	The Queen's	COURT ONE
Jul 15	Mr T. Lilley's	DAME MELBA
Jul 19	Lt Col Giles Loder's	PARROTIA
Jul 31	Lt Col Giles Loder's	CARNOUSTIE
Aug 2	Prince Aly Khan's	ROSE PALE
Aug 4	Sir Victor Sassoon's	PRINCE MOON
Aug 7	Col B. Hornung's	SOLIPTIC
Aug 7	The Queen's	PERSIAN WHEEL
Aug 12	Mrs D. M. FitzPatrick's	FILCO
Aug 13	Prince Aly Khan's	PETITE ETOILE
Aug 15	The Queen's	SHORT SENTENCE
Aug 23	Mrs T. Lilley's	ANGEL BABY
Sep 13	The Queen's	PINDARA
Sep 23	Sir Victor Sassoon's	PINE TREE

1959

	OWNER	HORSE
Apr 14	The Queen's	PINDARA
Apr 15	Prince Aly Khan's	PETITE ETOILE
Apr 16	Mr C. Steuart's	PINICOLA
Apr 18	Lt Col Giles Loder's	CARNOUSTIE

COURSE	JOCKEY	PRIZE
Hundon Maiden Handicap, Newmarket	*L. Piggott*	346
Dalham Stakes, Newmarket	*L. Piggott*	328

Races Won 48   Winning Stakes £116,908

COURSE	JOCKEY	PRIZE
April Stakes, Newmarket	*L. Piggott*	285
Coronation Stakes, Sandown Park	*L. Piggott*	984
The Royal Stakes, Sandown Park	*L. Piggott*	1744
Great Cheshire Handicap, Chester	*L. Piggott*	977
Eaton Handicap Stakes, Chester	*L. Piggott*	757
Alington Stakes, Sandown Park	*L. Piggott*	1184
St James's Stakes, Epsom	*L. Piggott*	2431
Rous Memorial Stakes, Ascot	*E. Smith*	1561
Windsor Castle Stakes, Ascot	*L. Piggott*	2071
Churchill Stakes, Ascot	*L. Piggott*	1370
Star Stakes, Sandown Park	*L. Piggott*	631
Falmouth Stakes, Newmarket	*D. Smith*	1309
Saxham Stakes, Newmarket	*L. Piggott*	340
Princess Margaret Stakes, Ascot	*L. Piggott*	993
Rous Memorial Stakes, Goodwood	*L. Piggott*	1207
Box Hill Plate, Epsom	*L. Piggott*	336
Earle Dorling Memorial Stakes, Epsom	*L. Piggott*	525
Cliftonville Handicap, Brighton	*L. Piggott*	552
Falmer Stakes, Brighton	*L. Piggott*	503
Midland Plate, Nottingham	*D. Smith*	207
Rose Stakes, Sandown Park	*L. Piggott*	523
St Hugh's Stakes, Newbury	*L. Piggott*	1222
New Chapel Handicap, Lingfield Park	*A. Breasley*	390
Solario Two Year Old Stakes, Sandown	*L. Piggott*	1953
Farnham Royal Plate, Windsor	*L. Piggott*	276

Races Won 25   Winning Stakes £24,331

COURSE	JOCKEY	PRIZE
Craven Stakes, Newmarket	*L. Piggott*	758
Free Handicap Stakes, Newmarket	*G. Moore*	893
Rowley Maiden Stakes, Newmarket	*L. Piggott*	342
Classic Trial Stakes, Thirsk	*L. Piggott*	1164

	OWNER	HORSE
Apr 23	Mr J. R. Hindley's	ROSE OF MEDINA
May 1	Prince Aly Khan's	PETITE ETOILE
May 5	Sir Victor Sassoon's	BOCCACCIO
May 7	Mr C. H. Dracoulis's	PRIMERA
May 8	Sir Victor Sassoon's	BLACKBEARD
May 14	Sir Victor Sassoon's	COLLYRIA
May 18	Prince Aly Khan's	DANCE TIME
May 19	Col B. Hornung's	DONA ANA
May 21	The Queen's	WHITE HOUSE
May 23	Mr T. Lilley's	OPEN SKY
May 26	Sir Victor Sassoon's	BLEEP
May 30	Mr T. Lilley's	DAME MELBA
Jun 5	Prince Aly Khan's	PETITE ETOILE
Jun 5	Mr J. A. Sutton's	WHIPSNADE
Jun 6	Mr T. Lilley's	BEAU COURT
Jun 8	Mr T. Lilley's	COURT PRINCE
Jun 16	Lord Feversham's	MACQUARIO
Jun 18	The Queen's	PINDARI
Jun 19	Mr C. Steuart's	PINICOLA
Jun 26	Mrs Noel Murless'	INGA
Jul 3	Mr C. H. Dracoulis's	PRIMERA
Jul 15	Mrs Noel Murless'	INGA
Jul 16	Mr J. R. Hindley's	LUCKY STREAM
Jul 25	Mr J. R. Hindley's	LUCKY STREAM
Jul 28	Mr Stanhope Joel's	PRIMERA
Jul 28	Mr T. Lilley's	COURT PRINCE
Jul 29	Prince Aly Khan's	PETITE ETOILE
Aug 5	Mrs T. Lilley's	ASTRADOR
Aug 6	Sir Victor Sassoon's	PURE PITCH
Aug 7	Sir Victor Sassoon's	SAUCY QUEEN
Aug 10	Sir Victor Sassoon's	LAMINATE
Aug 14	Sir Victor Sassoon's	SLEIPNER
Aug 15	Mrs T. Lilley's	ASTRADOR
Aug 18	Prince Aly Khan's	PETITE ETOILE
Aug 19	Mr Stanhope Joel's	PRIMERA
Aug 19	The Queen's	PINDARA
Aug 22	Sir Victor Sassoon's	RED PINS
Aug 26	The Queen's	SHORT SENTENCE
Aug 26	Sir Victor Sassoon's	RED PINS
Aug 26	Mr T. Lilley's	MANDOLINA
Aug 28	Sir Victor Sassoon's	SAUCY QUEEN

COURSE	JOCKEY	PRIZE
Princess Elizabeth Stakes, Epsom	L. *Piggott*	5807
1000 Guineas, Newmarket	D. *Smith*	13,254
Great Cheshire Handicap, Chester	L. *Piggott*	1024
Ormonde Stakes, Chester	L. *Piggott*	2347
Royal George Stakes, Kempton Park	L. *Piggott*	553
Haverhill Stakes, Newmarket	L. *Piggott*	632
Jane Seymour Stakes, Hurst Park	L. *Piggott*	598
Anne of Cleeve's Stakes, Hurst Park	L. *Piggott*	699
Wolverton Maiden Plate, Manchester	L. *Piggott*	207
Mark Price Handicap, Manchester	L. *Piggott*	579
Glasgow Mn. Three Years Old Stakes, York	L. *Piggott*	559
Sandleford Priory Stakes, Newbury	L. *Piggott*	1133
Oaks Stakes, Epsom	L. *Piggott*	21,155
Ebbisham Stakes, Epsom	D. *Smith*	3443
Rivermead Stakes, Kempton Park	L. *Piggott*	779
Long Eaton Stakes, Nottingham	P. *Robinson*	298
Britannia Stakes, Ascot	E. *Smith*	1659
King Edward VII Stakes, Ascot	L. *Piggott*	5237
Rous Memorial Stakes, Ascot	E. *Smith*	1515
Grimthorpe Plate, Doncaster	L. *Piggott*	207
Princess of Wale's Stakes, Newmarket	L. *Piggott*	2588
Red House Stakes, Doncaster	L. *Piggott*	864
Clayton Plate, Doncaster	L. *Piggott*	291
Virginia Stakes, Hurst Park	L. *Piggott*	549
Bentinck Stakes, Goodwood	L. *Piggott*	1103
Charlton Stakes, Goodwood	L. *Piggott*	1122
Sussex Stakes, Goodwood	L. *Piggott*	2730
Hassocks Stakes, Brighton	L. *Piggott*	559
Falmer Stakes, Brighton	L. *Piggott*	520
Rubbing House Stakes, Newmarket	L. *Piggott*	473
Nottinghamshire Breeders Yearling Stakes	E. *Hide*	1034
Newton Stakes, Newbury	L. *Piggott*	361
Washington Singer Stakes, Newbury	L. *Piggott*	1103
Yorkshire Oaks, York	L. *Piggott*	7049
Ebor Handicap, York	L. *Piggott*	10,093
Great Voltigeur Sweepstakes, York	L. *Piggott*	10,508
Ramsey Maiden Stakes, Newmarket	L. *Piggott*	353
Preston Park Handicap, Brighton	L. *Piggott*	910
Telscombe Handicap, Brighton	L. *Piggott*	497
Berwick Stakes, Brighton	L. *Piggott*	542
August Plate, Windsor	L. *Piggott*	345

	OWNER	HORSE
Aug 29	Mrs T. Lilley's	ASTRADOR
Sep 7	Mr T. Lilley's	OPEN SKY
Sep 10	Sir Victor Sassoon's	COLLYRIA
Sep 17	Mr. T. Lilley's	COURT PRINCE
Sep 18	Sir Victor Sassoon's	RED PINS
Sep 18	Mrs T. Lilley's	ASTRADOR
Sep 24	Mr J. A. Sutton's	WHIPSNADE
Sep 25	Mr J. R. Hindley's	ROSE OF MEDINA
Sep 25	Sir Victor Sassoon's	ST PADDY
Sep 26	Lt Col Giles Loder's	HIGH PITCH
Oct 1	Mr T. Lilley's	COURT PRINCE
Oct 2	Sir Victor Sassoon's	BOCCACCIO
Oct 7	Sir Victor Sassoon's	LAMINATE
Oct 9	Mr Charles Carlow's	SLEIPNER
Oct 16	Sir Victor Sassoon's	SAUCY QUEEN
Oct 17	Prince Aly Khan's ·	PETITE ETOILE
Oct 24	Sir Victor Sassoon's	RED PINS
Nov 3	Sir Victor Sassoon's	PIN TABLE

1960

	OWNER	HORSE
Apr 21	Sir Victor Sassoon's	PLUMP
May 7	Prince Aly Khan's	PETITE ETOILE
May 11	Sir Victor Sassoon's	OFF KEY
May 12	Mrs V. Lilley's	PINZORA
May 18	Sir Victor Sassoon's	ST PADDY
May 27	Sir Victor Sassoon's	SUNNY WAY
May 28	Lt Col Giles Loder's	GREEN OPAL
May 28	Mrs V. Lilley's	FAVORITA
Jun 1	Sir Victor Sassoon's	ST PADDY
Jun 2	The late Prince Aly Khan's	PETITE ETOILE
Jun 3	Mrs V. Lilley's	BEAU COURT
Jun 9	Mrs V. Lilley's	FAVORITA
Jun 9	Sir Victor Sassoon's	OFF KEY
Jun 11	Col B. Hornung's	DOLGELLEY
Jun 16	Sir Victor Sassoon's	SUNNY WAY
Jun 30	Mrs V. Lilley's	FAVORITA
Jul 1	Mr Stanhope Joel's	PRIMERA

COURSE	JOCKEY	PRIZE
Star & Garter Plate, Windsor	*L. Piggott*	690
Harcourt Handicap, Windsor	*L. Piggott*	345
Park Hill Stakes, Doncaster	*E. Smith*	5203
Tote Investors Cup, Ayr	*L. Piggott*	2254
Arion Handicap, Kempton Park	*L. Piggott*	557
Sirenia Nursery Handicap, Kempton	*L. Piggott*	525
Marlborough House Stakes, Ascot	*L. Piggott*	1069
Princess Royal Stakes, Ascot	*L. Piggott*	2398
Royal Lodge Stakes, Ascot	*L. Piggott*	3083
Blue Seal Stakes, Ascot	*L. Piggott*	2356
Jockey Club Stakes, Newmarket	*L. Piggott*	4431
Falkland Handicap, Newbury	*L. Piggott*	699
Malton Stakes, York	*L. Piggott*	646
Cardigan Stakes, Ascot	*L. Piggott*	524
Southfield Handicap, Newmarket	*L. Piggott*	601
Champion Stakes, Newmarket	*L. Piggott*	10,406
Irwin Handicap, Doncaster	*L. Piggott*	1226
Queen Bess Plate, Birmingham	*L. Piggott*	276

Races Won 63   Winning Stakes £145,725

Princess Elizabeth Stakes, Epsom	*L. Piggott*	6410
Victor Wild Stakes, Kempton Park	*L. Piggott*	574
Fen Ditton Maiden Stakes, Newmarket	*E. Smith*	311
Haverhill Stakes, Newmarket	*E. Smith*	633
Dante Sweepstakes, York	*L. Piggott*	1875
Shaw Maiden Plate, Newbury	*L. Piggott*	420
Sandleford Priory Stakes, Newbury	*E. Smith*	1311
Elcot Maiden Plate, Newbury	*L. Piggott*	465*
The Derby, Epsom	*L. Piggott*	33,052
Coronation Cup, Epsom	*L. Piggott*	2966
Headley Handicap, Epsom	*L. Piggott*	994
Patcham Stakes, Brighton	*L. Piggott*	421
Royal Standard Stakes, Manchester	*E. Smith*	1726
Kingston Plate, Sandown Park	*L. Piggott*	345
King George V Stakes, Ascot	*L. Piggott*	1770
July Stakes, Newmarket	*L. Piggott*	1549
Princess of Wales' Stakes, Newmarket	*L. Piggott*	2775

* deadheat

	OWNER	HORSE
Jul 8	Dr Carlo Vittadini's	EXAR
Jul 11	Mr Stanhope Joel's	FAUST
Jul 12	Lt Col Giles Loder's	GREEN OPAL
Jul 12	Mrs V. Lilley's	KING'S SON
Jul 15	Sir Victor Sassoon's	SUNNY WAY
Jul 28	Dr Carlo Vittadini's	EXAR
Jul 30	Sir Percy Loraine's	ALCAZAR
Aug 2	Mr Andrew Johnstone's	EDDY
Aug 6	Sir Victor Sassoon's	TUDOR LOVE
Aug 8	Mrs V. Lilley's	FAVORITA
Aug 9	Mrs V. Lilley's	ADONIUS
Aug 11	Dr Carlo Vittadini's	EXAR
Aug 11	Lt Col Giles Loder's	PRINCELY FOLLY
Aug 12	Mrs V. Lilley's	SWEET LOLA
Aug 12	Mr L. H. H. Moody's	EBLOUISSANTE
Aug 17	Sir Victor Sassoon's	ST PADDY
Aug 19	Mrs Noel Murless'	KELD
Aug 24	Lady Ursula Vernon's	PRINCESS LIDI
Aug 29	Mrs V. Lilley's	ADONIUS
Sep 3	Mrs V. Lilley's	FAVORITA
Sep 8	Dr Carlo Vittadini's	EXAR
Sep 10	Sir Victor Sassoon's	ST PADDY
Sep 14	Lord Feversham's	MACQUARIO
Sep 23	Lt Col Giles Loder's	GREEN OPAL
Oct 8	Mrs V. Lilley's	FAVORITA

1961

Apr 11	Mrs V. Lilley's	AURELIUS
Apr 13	Sir Victor Sassoon's	PINTURISCHIO
Apr 22	H.H. Aga Khan's	PETITE ETOILE
May 16	The Queen's	AIMING HIGH
May 20	Mrs V. Lilley's	FAVORITA
May 20	Sir Victor Sassoon's	ST PADDY
May 22	Mrs V. Lilley's	MAGIC COURT
Jun 1	H.H. Aga Khan's	PETITE ETOILE
Jun 7	The Queen's	PERDIX
Jun 9	Sir Victor Sassoon's	SUNNY WAY
Jun 14	Mrs V. Lilley's	FAVORITA

COURSE	JOCKEY	PRIZE
July Stayers' Stakes, Sandown	*L. Piggott*	487
Crazy Gang Stakes, Kempton Park	*L. Piggott*	1788
Falmouth Stakes, Newmarket	*L. Piggott*	1354
Soltykoff Stakes, Newmarket	*L. Piggott*	588
Balmoral Stakes, Ascot	*L. Piggott*	569
Goodwood Cup, Goodwood	*L. Piggott*	3137
Chipstead Maiden Stakes, Epsom	*L. Piggott*	365
Beach Two Year Old Stakes, Brighton	*L. Piggott*	488
Bunbury Maiden Stakes, Newmarket	*L. Piggott*	292
Nottinghamshire Breeders' Yearling Stakes	*L. Piggott*	1128
Robin Hood Plate, Nottingham	*L. Piggott*	207
Poulsen Stakes, Sandown Park	*L. Piggott*	485
Pax Stakes, Sandown Park	*L. Piggott*	454
Sparsholt Plate, Newbury	*L. Piggott*	420
St Hugh's Stakes, Newbury	*L. Piggott*	1332
Great Voltigeur Sweepstakes, York	*L. Piggott*	5951
Grantchester Two Yr Old Stks, Newmarket	*L. Piggott*	323
Berwick Stakes, Brighton	*L. Piggott*	550
Compton Wynyate Plate, Birmingham	*L. Piggott*	276
Autumn Breeders' Foal Stakes, Manchester	*L. Piggott*	1758
Doncaster Cup, Doncaster	*L. Piggott*	3390
St Leger Stakes, Doncaster	*L. Piggott*	30,379
Dome Handicap Stakes, Brighton	*L. Piggott*	428
Princess Royal Stakes, Ascot, (Newbury)	*L. Piggott*	2369
Cornwallis Stakes, Ascot (Kempton)	*L. Piggott*	2182

Races Won 42   Winning Stakes £118,297

Craven Stakes, Newmarket	*L. Piggott*	724
Wood Ditton Stakes, Newmarket	*L. Piggott*	559
Coronation Stakes, Sandown Park	*L. Piggott*	986
Glasgow Maiden Stakes, York	*L. Piggott*	951
Alington Stakes, Sandown Park	*L. Piggott*	1061
Coombe Stakes, Sandown Park	*L. Piggott*	1011
Christopher Wren Stakes, Hurst Park	*L. Piggott*	581
Coronation Cup, Epsom	*L. Piggott*	3894
Shoreham Stakes, Brighton	*L. Piggott*	461
Hwfa Williams Handicap, Sandown Park	*L. Piggott*	1089
Jersey Stakes, Ascot	*L. Piggott*	1910

	OWNER	HORSE
Jun 14	The Queen's	AIMING HIGH
Jun 15	Mrs. V. Lilley's	AURELIUS
Jun 16	H.H. Aga Khan's	PETITE ETOILE
Jun 16	Sir Victor Sassoon's	ST PADDY
Jul 7	Sir Victor Sassoon's	SUNNY WAY
Jul 8	Sir Victor Sassoon's	OFF KEY
Jul 8	Sir Victor Sassoon's	ST PADDY
Jul 12	Mrs Noel Murless'	CAERPHILLY
Jul 13	Sir Victor Sassoon's	YOUNG LOCHINVAR
Jul 20	Mr C. Steuart's	PINICOLA
Jul 27	Mrs Noel Murless'	CAERPHILLY
Aug 1	Sir Victor Sassoon's	OFF KEY
Aug 10	The Queen's	WIMBLEDON
Aug 12	Mrs V. Lilley's	SECRET SESSION
Aug 12	Mr J. R. Hindley's	MELODIUS CHARM
Aug 14	Mrs Noel Murless'	CAERPHILLY
Aug 19	Mrs E. B. Holmes's	MEREWORTH
Sep 1	Mrs V. Lilley's	SECRET SESSION
Sep 8	Lt Col Giles Loder's	AZNIP
Sep 8	H.H. Aga Khan's	PETITE ETOILE
Sep 9	Mrs V. Lilley's	AURELIUS
Sep 30	Lady Sassoon's	ST PADDY
Oct 6	Col B. Hornung's	PELLEGRINO
Oct 21	Lady Sassoon's	GOLDEN VOICE
Oct 30	Mrs V. Lilley's	PANTHERA

1962

Apr 28	Lt Col Giles Loder's	FERNELEY
May 15	Lt Col Giles Loder's	ROMANTIC
May 19	Mrs V. Lilley's	AURELIUS
May 30	Lady Sassoon's	CYCLONE AUDREY
Jun 1	The Queen's	ICARUS
Jun 11	Lady Sassoon's	SUNNY WAY
Jun 11	Lady Sassoon's	DER RING
Jun 11	Col B. Hornung's	ABADDON
Jun 14	Lady Sassoon's	LUCKY GWEN
Jun 22	Mrs V. Lilley's	AURELIUS
Jun 28	Lt Col Giles Loder's	PRINCESS CECILIA

COURSE	JOCKEY	PRIZE
Coronation Stakes, Ascot	*L. Piggott*	3563
King Edward VII Stakes, Ascot	*L. Piggott*	3499
Rous Memorial Stakes, Ascot	*L. Piggott*	1528
Hardwicke Stakes, Ascot	*L. Piggott*	2504
July Stayers' Stakes, Sandown Park	*L. Piggott*	492
Victoria Handicap, Sandown Park	*L. Piggott*	508
Eclipse Stakes, Sandown Park	*L. Piggott*	17,056
Chesterfield Maiden Stakes, Newmarket	*L. Piggott*	484
Upend Stakes, Newmarket	*L. Piggott*	474
Blackbird Handicap	*L. Piggott*	474
Lavant Stakes, Goodwood	*L. Piggott*	647
Vaux Gold Tankard, Redcar	*L. Piggott*	10,460
Alfriston Stakes, Brighton	*L. Piggott*	513
Rubbing House Stakes, Newmarket	*L. Piggott*	412
Duxford Maiden Stakes, Newmarket	*L. Piggott*	521
Nottinghamshire Breeders Yearling Stakes	*L. Piggott*	886
Washington Singer Stakes, Newbury	*L. Piggott*	1473
Straightlace Stakes, Manchester	*L. Piggott*	468
September Maiden Stakes, Doncaster	*L. Piggott*	1681
Scarbrough Stakes, Doncaster	*L. Piggott*	1196
St Leger Stakes, Doncaster	*L. Piggott*	29,818
Jockey Club Stakes, Newmarket	*L. Piggott*	2282
Sandwich Stakes, Ascot	*L. Piggott*	1323
Feversham Plate, Doncaster	*L. Piggott*	207
Queen Bess Plate, Birmingham	*L. Piggott*	276

Races Won 36   Winning Stakes £95,972

COURSE	JOCKEY	PRIZE
Royal Stakes, Sandown Park	*L. Piggott*	1825
Zetland Stakes, York	*L. Piggott*	836
Coombe Stakes, Sandown Park	*L. Piggott*	1025
Burton Plate, Lincoln	*S. Smith*	207
Shaw Maiden Plate, Newbury	*L. Piggott*	420
Harewood Handicap, Doncaster	*D. Smith*	1552
Rossington Stakes, Doncaster	*D. Smith*	364
Jane Seymour Stakes, Hurst Park	*A. Breasley*	603
Whitsuntide Stakes, Manchester	*E. Smith*	1300
Hardwicke Stakes, Ascot	*A. Breasley*	3761
Kingsclere Stakes, Newbury	*A. Breasley*	553

	OWNER	HORSE
Jun 30	Mrs J. R. Hindley's	CREPT IN
Jun 30	Mrs V. Lilley's	BLEU AZUR
Jul 4	Lt Col Giles Loder's	RAMANTIC
Jul 6	Lady Sassoon's	DER RING
Jul 9	H.H. Aga Khan's	KOSHKA
Jul 11	Lady Sassoon's	RIBOTLIGHT
Jul 13	Col B. Hornung's	ABADDON
Jul 14	Mrs V. Lilley's	BLEU AZUR
Jul 20	Lady Sassoon's	TWILIGHT ALLEY
Aug 1	Lt Col Giles Loder's	ROMANTIC
Aug 2	Lt Col Giles Loder's	PRINCESS CECILIA
Aug 6	Mr M. W. Wickham-Boynton's	UHURU
Aug 6	Lady Sassoon's	RIBOTLIGHT
Aug 6	H.H. Aga Khan's	KOSHKA
Aug 10	Mr M. W. Wickham-Boynton's	ANKOLE
Sep 4	Mr M. W. Wickham-Boynton's	MBARARA
Sep 7	Mrs V. Lilley's	AURELIUS
Sep 11	Lt Col Giles Loder's	ALBATROS
Sep 21	Lt Col Giles Loder's	CHARMER
Oct 6	Lt Col Giles Loder's	FOLLOW SUIT
Oct 6	Lady Sassoon's	CANDY GIFT
Oct 11	Lady Sassoon's	ANGEL'S HEAD
Oct 11	Mr C. A. B. St George's	EL GALLO
Oct 18	Lady Sassoon's	YOUNG LOCHINVAR

1963

Apr 25	Lady Sassoon's	AMORELLA
May 8	Lady Sassoon's	THE CREDITOR
May 22	Lady Sassoon's	CREPES D'ENFER
Jun 1	Mr C. A. B. St George's	EL GALLO
Jun 8	Mr J. Hindley's	RED CHORUS
Jun 10	Mrs V. Hue-Williams's	BALLY ROYAL
Jun 10	Lady Sassoon's	FIDEVE
Jun 19	Lady Sassoon's	THE CREDITOR
Jun 20	Mr C. A. B. St George's	EL GALLO
Jun 20	Lady Sassoon's	TWILIGHT ALLEY
Jun 24	Lady Sassoon's	FIDEVE

COURSE	JOCKEY	PRIZE
Lonsdale Stakes, Doncaster	A. J. Russell	514
George Payne Stakes, Newmarket	D. Smith	301
July Stakes, Newmarket	A. Breasley	2526
Surbiton Handicap Sandown Park	A. Breasley	534
Fillies' Maiden Plate, Nottingham	A. Breasley	276
Wakefield Stakes, Doncaster	D. Smith	308
Horne Stakes, Lingfield Park	A. Breasley	694
Butlin Stakes, Lingfield Park	A. Breasley	1627
Cranborne Chase Stakes, Ascot	W. Rickaby	1150
Richmond Stakes, Goodwood	L. Piggott	3215
Lavant Stakes, Goodwood	L. Piggott	613
Nell Gwyn Stakes, Epsom	A. Breasley	547
Dove Plate, Newcastle	L. Piggott	415
Langlee Plate, Newcastle	L. Piggott	355
Derwent Plate, Redcar	F. Durr	207
Meriden Fillies' Plate, Birmingham	L. Piggott	276
Atlanta Stakes, Sandown Park	L. Piggott	822
Clumber Maiden Stakes, Doncaster	L. Piggott	1243
Avington Stakes, Kempton Park	L. Piggott	659
Dewhurst Stakes, Newmarket	L. Piggott	4501
Newholme Stakes, Windsor	D. W. Morris	374
Leyburn Stakes, York	L. Piggott	516
Ainsty Sweepstakes, York	L. Piggott	510
Severals Stakes, Newmarket	L. Piggott	434

Races Won 35   Winning Stakes £35,063

COURSE	JOCKEY	PRIZE
Princess Elizabeth Stakes, Epsom	L. Piggott	4436
Stewards' Stakes, Chester	L. Piggott	1024
Wheatsheaf Stakes, Sandown Park	L. Piggott	513
Falmouth Handicap, Doncaster	L. Piggott	383
Lancashire Oaks, Manchester	L. Piggott	2223
Caves Handicap Plate, Nottingham	L. Piggott	401
Cropwell Bishop Plate, Nottingham	L. Piggott	402
Jersey Stakes, Ascot	L. Piggott	1817
Cork & Orrery Stakes, Ascot	L. Piggott	1643
Gold Cup, Ascot	L. Piggott	10,398
Warwicks. Breeders' Two Year Old Stakes, Birmingham	L. Piggott	1866

	OWNER	HORSE
Jun 26	H.H. Aga Khan's	MORNING CALM
Jun 29	Lady Sassoon's	DER RING
Jul 11	Mrs J. R. Hindley's	CREPT IN
Jul 12	Mr M. W. Wickham-Boynton's	LOIDIEN
Jul 24	Col B. Hornung's	CASABIANCA
Jul 24	Mr M. W. Wickham-Boynton's	LOIDIEN
Jul 25	Mrs V. Hue-Williams's	BALLY ROYAL
Jul 26	Mrs V. Hue-Williams's	DIEU SOLEIL
Jul 27	Lady Sassoon's	SWEET MOSS
Jul 27	Mr F. R. Hue-Williams's	ZINGALINE
Aug 3	Mrs V. Hue-Williams's	CREATION
Aug 3	Mrs V. Hue-Williams's	BALLY ROYAL
Aug 6	Mr F. R. Hue-Williams's	ZINGALINE
Aug 9	Lady Sassoon's	CREPES BRAVES
Aug 10	Mrs V. Hue-Williams's	KEY WESI
Aug 13	The Queen's	CANDIA
Aug 17	Mr F. R. Hue-Williams's	PETER LE GRAND
Aug 24	Lady Sassoon's	THE CREDITOR
Aug 29	Lady Sassoon's	DER RING
Aug 31	Mr C. A. B. St George's	EL GALLO
Sep 7	Lady Sassoon's	CREPES D'ENFER
Sep 19	The Queen's	ARBUTUS
Sep 19	Lt Col Giles Loder's	CHARMER
Sep 20	Lady Sassoon's	CREPES D'ENFER
Sep 23	Mrs Dare Wigan's	CLOUDBREAK
Sep 27	Col B. Hornung's	CASABIANCA
Sep 28	Mrs V. Hue-Williams's	IMPACT
Sep 28	Lady Sassoon's	THE CREDITOR
Oct 16	Mr C. A. B. St George's	ROYAL AVENUE
Oct 18	Mrs M. E. Whitney-Tippett's	ROYAL DESIRE
Nov 7	Mr C. A. B. St George's	ROYAL AVENUE

1964

Apr 18	Mr C. A. B. St George's	ROYAL AVENUE
May 6	Lt Col Giles Loder's	PERSIAN GARDEN
May 7	Lady Sassoon's	SWEET MOSS
May 9	Lady Sassoon's	CREPES BRAVES
May 16	Mr C. A. B. St George's	ROYAL AVENUE

COURSE	JOCKEY	PRIZE
Twyford Stakes, Newbury	*L. Piggott*	512
Wideopen Handicap, Newcastle	*L. Piggott*	401
Doncaster Handicap, Doncaster	*L. Piggott*	520
Twilight Maiden Plate, Manchester	*W. Snaith*	403
Battersea Park Stakes, Sandown	*L. Piggott*	703
Cromwell Road Handicap, Sandown	*L. Piggott*	488
Foxwarren Handicap, Sandown	*L. Piggott*	641
Ecchinswell Maiden Plate, Newbury	*L. Piggott*	504
Donnington Castle Stakes, Newbury	*L. Piggott*	1625
Chattis Hill Stakes, Newbury	*L. Piggott*	640
Links Maiden Stakes, Newmarket	*L. Piggott*	381
Clare Handicap, Newmarket	*L. Piggott*	898
Channel Stakes, Brighton	*L. Piggott*	800
Holderness Plate, Redcar	*W. Snaith*	403
Bunbury Maiden Stakes, Newmarket	*A. Breasley*	358
Moland Maiden Fillies' Plate, Nottingham	*W. Snaith*	403
Washington Singer Stakes, Newbury	*L. Piggott*	1438
Invicta Stakes, Newmarket	*L. Piggott*	1247
Newhaven Handicap, Brighton	*L. Piggott*	418
Daily Mirror Handicap, Sandown Park	*L. Piggott*	1763
Redhill Stakes, Epsom	*L. Piggott*	917
Seven Dials Stakes, Brighton	*L. Piggott*	394
Ovingdean Stakes, Brighton	*E. Smith*	370
Tangiers Stakes Kempton Park	*L. Piggott*	944
Kirby Plate, Leicester	*L. Piggott*	402
Royal Lodge Stakes, Ascot (Newbury)	*L. Piggott*	3852
Clarence House Stakes, Ascot (Newbury)	*L. Piggott*	569
Queen Elizabeth Stakes, Ascot (Newbury)	*L. Piggott*	5186
Mentmore Stakes, Kempton Park	*L. Piggott*	993
Houghton Stakes, Newmarket	*L. Piggott*	1787
Farewell Handicap, Manchester	*L. Piggott*	401

Races Won 42 Winning Stakes £55,468

John Porter Stakes, Newbury	*L. Piggott*	1966
Grosvenor Stakes, Chester	*L. Piggott*	1179
Dee Stakes, Chester	*L. Piggott*	2420
Grand Stand Handicap Stakes, Haydock Pk.	*L. Piggott*	398
Grand Prix de Printemps, Saint Cloud	*L. Piggott*	15,560

	OWNER	HORSE
May 26	Lady Sassoon's	SWEET MOSS
May 30	Lady Sassoon's	THE CREDITOR
Jun 2	Mrs B. Hornung's	GOLDENDALE
Jun 10	Mr J. R. Hindley's	MWANZA
Jun 16	Mrs V. Hue-Williams's	I, TITAN
Jun 24	Mrs V. Hue-Williams's	VERSAILLES
Jun 25	Lady Sassoon's	CREPES D'ENFER
Jun 29	Lady Sassoon's	CREPES BRAVES
Jul 3	The Queen's	ARBUTUS
Jul 3	Mrs L. McVey's	ASTRELLITA
Jul 4	Lt Col Giles Loder's	JOYFUL
Jul 6	Mr J. R. Hindley's	MWANZA
Jul 11	Mrs V. Hue-Williams's	DIEU SOLEIL
Jul 11	Mr M. W. Wickham-Boynton's	AMFISSA
Jul 16	Mr C. A. B. St George's	LEONARDO
Jul 16	Mr Arpad Plesch's	PALM
Jul 21	The Queen's	ARBUTUS
Jul 23	Mr Arpad Plesch's	PALM
Jul 25	Lt Col Giles Loder's	PERSIAN GARDEN
Jul 29	Mrs V. Hue-Williams's	I, TITAN
Jul 30	Lady Sassoon's	SWEET MOSS
Aug 1	Miss Julia Murless'	CROSSET
Aug 1	Mrs V. Hue-Williams's	DIEU SOLEIL
Aug 1	Mr C. A. B. St George's	LEONARDO
Aug 1	Mr Arpad Plesch's	PALM
Aug 4	Mrs M. E. Whitney-Tippett's	ROYAL DESIRE
Aug 4	Mrs L. McVey's	ASTRELLITA
Aug 6	H.H. Aga Khan's	RUANDA
Aug 7	Mr J. R. Hindley's	ALLEY CAT
Aug 11	Mr J. A. Sutton's	ATONEMENT
Aug 22	Mr C. A. B. St George's	LEONARDO
Aug 27	Lady Sassoon's	DER RING
Aug 27	Lt Col J. Hornung's	CASABIANCA
Aug 31	Mr J. A. Sutton's	FEDERAL
Sep 4	Mrs L McVey's	ASTRELLITA
Sep 5	Mr C. A. B. St George's	LEONARDO
Sep 11	Lady Sassoon's	CREPES D'ENFER
Sep 16	Mr C. A. B. St George's	ARTHUR DUFFY
Sep 16	Mrs V. Hue-Williams's	IMPACT
Sep 17	Lady Sassoon's	DER RING
Sep 17	Lt Col Giles Loder's	PERSIAN GARDEN

Appendix

COURSE	JOCKEY	PRIZE
Dante Sweepstakes, York	L. Piggott	2790
Lockinge Stakes, Newbury	L. Piggott	2316
Ladbroke Gold Cup, Epsom	L. Piggott	2825
Portslade Stakes, Brighton	L. Piggott	447
Queen's Vase, Ascot	L. Piggott	3753
Twyford Stakes, Newbury	L. Piggott	536
Newbury Summer Cup	L. Piggott	1592
Palace Handicap, Brighton	L. Piggott	422
Stewards' Stakes Handicap, Haydock Park	W. Snaith	453
July Plate, Haydock Park	W. Snaith	414
Star Maiden Fillies' Plate, Sandown	L. Piggott	414
Newark Plate, Nottingham	L. Piggott	414
Town & County Cup Handicap, Lingfield	L. Piggott	2400
Equestrian Stakes, Lingfield Park	L. Piggott	1518
Dereham Plate, Great Yarmouth	L. Piggott	345
Doncaster Handicap, Doncaster	L. Piggott	482
Burton Stakes, Leicester	L. Piggott	347
Bow Street Handicap Stakes, Sandown Park	L. Piggott	469
Morland Brewery Stakes, Newbury	L. Piggott	1535
Vaux Gold Tankard, Redcar	S. Clayton	10,450
Gordon Stakes, Goodwood	L. Piggott	4963
Golden Fleece Plate, Thirsk	J. Sime	414
Earle Dorlimg Mem. Handicap Stks, Epsom	L. Piggott	836
Box Hill Stakes, Epsom	L. Piggott	873
Diomed Handicap Stakes, Epsom	L. Piggott	824
Brighton Handicap, Brighton	L. Piggott	1839
Channel Stakes, Brighton	L. Piggott	761
Falmer Apprentice Stakes, Brighton	D. Sheffield	381
South Durham Plate, Redcar	L. Piggott	414
Oxton Fillies' Plate, Nottingham	L. Piggott	414
Dynatron Stakes, Newmarket	L. Piggott	1245
Newhaven Handicap, Brighton	L. Piggott	798
Kemp Town Stakes, Brighton	L. Piggott	407
Meriden Fillies' Plate, Birmingham	S. Clayton	414
Bridget Stakes, Epsom	L. Piggott	796
Stanley Stakes, Epsom	L. Piggott	1893
Falkland Stakes, Newbury	L. Piggott	426
Dyke Stakes, Brighton	L. Piggott	468
Bramber Handicap, Brighton	L. Piggott	392
Pyecombe Handicap, Brighton	L. Piggott	421
Brighton Autumn Cup	L. Piggott	1832

OWNER	HORSE

Sep 24	Mr F. R. Hue-Williams's	VEROUSSIA
Sep 28	Lady Sassoon's	SWEET MOSS
Oct 16	Lt Col Giles Loder's	ALAN ADARE
Oct 17	Lady Sassoon's	MONACO PRINCESS
Oct 22	Mrs V. Hue-Williams's	IMPACT

1965

May 21	Mr F. R. Hue-Williams's	BALLY RUSSE
May 21	Mrs Noel Murless'	ANGELLO
Jun 16	Lt Col J. Hornung's	CASABIANCA
Jun 16	Mr M. W. Wickham-Boynton's	BRACEY BRIDGE
Jun 18	Lady Sassoon's	SWEET MOSS
Jun 25	Mr J. R. Hindley's	STOCK BECK
Jun 26	Lord Dulverton's	CLARITY
Jul 9	The Queen's	DARFUR
Jul 10	H.H. Aga Khan's	ZAHEDAN
Jul 10	Lord Dulverton's	CLARITY
Jul 17	Lady Sassoon's	SOFT ANGELS
Jul 17	The Queen's	BATTLE-WAGGON
Jul 21	H.H. Aga Khan	ZAHEDAN
Jul 30	Lt Col J. Hornung's	AUNT EDITH
Jul 31	Mr J. R. Hindley's	STOCK BECK
Aug 3	Mrs Dare Wigan's	CORNFLOWER
Aug 3	Hon Mrs S. Beatty's	MISS ROSA
Aug 11	Mr M. W. Wickham-Boynton's	EVERY BLESSING
Aug 12	Mr J. R. Hindley's	STOCK BECK
Aug 12	Mr C. A. B. St George's	EL COMMANDANTE
Sep 2	Duke of Westminster's	MINERA
Sep 2	Lady Sassoon's	BALBI
Sep 10	Lt Col Giles Loder's	ALAN ADARE
Sep 10	Mr M. W. Wickham-Boynton's	BRACEY BRIDGE
Sep 14	Mr J. R. Hindley's	LINDOSA
Sep 15	Lt Col Giles Loder's	REED WARBLER
Sep 17	Lady Sassoon's	MISS LANE
Sep 18	Mr M. W. Wickham-Boynton's	EVERY BLESSING
Sep 19	Lt Col J. Hornung's	AUNT EDITH
Sep 23	Mr M. W. Wickham-Boynton's	BRACEY BRIDGE
Sep 25	Lady Sassoon's	SOFT ANGELS

COURSE	JOCKEY	PRIZE
Chertsey Stakes, Ascot	*L. Piggott*	552
Midland Breeders' Three Yr Old Stks, B'ham	*W. Snaith*	2039
Houghton Stakes, Newmarket	*L. Piggott*	1939
Fillies' Final Maiden Stakes, Newmarket	*L. Piggott*	405
Ormonde Stakes, Newbury	*L. Piggott*	398

Races Won 51   Winning Stakes £81589

Goldstone Stakes, Lingfield	*L. Piggott*	525
Elmire Plate, Thirsk	*W. Rickaby*	414
Royal Hunt Cup, Ascot	*L. Piggott*	5332
Ribblesdale Stakes, Ascot	*L. Piggott*	9147
Rous Memorial Stakes, Ascot	*L. Piggott*	1375
Corporation Maiden Stakes, Doncaster	*W. Snaith*	412
Clayton Maiden Stakes, Newmarket	*W. Snaith*	401
Henry Gee Maiden Stakes, Chester	*L. Piggott*	420
Gold Star Stakes, Chester	*L. Piggott*	813
Red Rose Stakes, Chester	*L. Piggott*	827
Princess Margaret Stakes, Ascot	*L. Piggott*	2231
Fountains Maiden Stakes, York	*W. Rickaby*	411
National Stakes, Sandown Park	*L. Piggott*	8058
Nassau Stakes, Goodwood	*L. Piggott*	2948
Earle Dorling Memorial Handicap, Epsom	*L. Piggott*	798
Beach Two Year Old Stakes, Brighton	*L. Piggott*	459
Channel Stakes, Brighton	*L. Piggott*	742
Tyldesley Plate, Haydock Park	*L. Piggott*	414
Colonel Ashton Stakes, Haydock Park	*L. Piggott*	824
Alexander Rigby Plate, Haydock Park	*L. Piggott*	414
Linenhall Stakes, Chester	*L. Piggott*	393
Rouge Rose Stakes, Chester	*L. Piggott*	538
Arlington Stakes, Newbury	*A. Breasley*	395
Park Hill Stakes, Doncaster	*L. Piggott*	3929
Chisledown Stakes, Goodwood	*L. Piggott*	1102
Dyke Stakes, Brighton	*A. Breasley*	469
Standish Handicap, Haydock Park	*L. Piggott*	414
Firth of Clyde Stakes, Ayr	*L. Piggott*	827
Prix Vermeille, Lonchamp	*L. Piggott*	30,485
Princess Royal Stakes, Ascot	*L. Piggott*	1949
Royal Lodge Stakes, Ascot	*L. Piggott*	5688

	OWNER	HORSE
Oct 2	Mr J. R. Hindley's	LINDOSA
Oct 6	Mr M. W. Wickham-Boynton's	EVERY BLESSING
Oct 7	Mr Arpad Plesch's	POMATO
Oct 14	Mrs Dare Wigan's	BOLTING
Oct 15	Lady Sassoon's	EDOLO

1966

Apr 21	Mr M. W. Wickham-Boynton's	EVERY BLESSING
May 4	Duke of Westminster's	WATERGATE
May 5	Lady Sassoon's	BIOMYDRIN
May 12	Lt Col J. Hornung's	AUNT EDITH
May 14	Mr M. W. Wickham-Boynton's	VARINIA
May 28	Lady Sassoon's	PADDY'S LIGHT
Jun 14	Mr F. R. Hue-Williams's	BALLY RUSSE
Jun 17	Mr G. A. Pope's	HILL RISE
Jun 22	Mr H. J. Joel's	GOLDEN REWARD
Jun 22	Hon Mrs S. Beatty's	TEESDALE
Jun 23	Mr F. R. Hue-Williams's	TATARIN
Jul 2	Mrs V. Hue-Williams's	MAGICOTE
Jul 13	Mr H. J. Joel's	PINK GEM
Jul 15	Mr F. R. Hue-Williams's	TATARIN
Jul 16	Lt Col J. Hornung's	AUNT EDITH
Jul 16	Mr R. C. Boucher's	FLEET
Jul 16	Mr F. R. Hue-Williams's	BALLY RUSSE
Jul 23	Mr F. R. Hue-Williams's	SPEED OF SOUND
Jul 23	Hon Mrs S. Beatty's	ABBEYFIELD
Jul 30	Lady Sassoon's	GEORGINKA
Aug 6	Mrs Noel Murless'	HERBACEOUS
Aug 11	Lady Sassoon's	EDOLO
Aug 16	Mr H. J. Joel's	ROYAL PALACE
Aug 19	Mr J. A. Sutton's	FULL STRETCH
Aug 19	Lady Sassoon's	ASTRAL GREEN
Aug 24	Mrs V. Hue-Williams's	ROYAL SAINT
Aug 29	Mr E. Loder's	GREEN HALO
Aug 30	Lady Sassoon's	ASTRAL GREEN
Sep 2	Mr F. R. Hue-Williams's	SPEED OF SOUND
Sep 12	Mr J. A. Sutton's	FULL STRETCH
Sep 14	Mrs Dare Wigan's	BOLTING

COURSE	JOCKEY	PRIZE
Haverhill Stakes, Newmarket	*L. Piggott*	524
Apprentice Stakes, York	*D. Sheffield*	432
Leyburn Stakes, York	*L. Piggott*	547
Snailwell Stakes, Newmarket	*L. Piggott*	418
Fillies' Final Stakes, Newmarket	*L. Piggott*	389

Races Won 36   Winning Stakes £85,464

COURSE	JOCKEY	PRIZE
Princess Elizabeth Stakes, Epsom	*L. Piggott*	2724
Grosvenor Stakes, Chester	*L. Piggott*	897
Ormonde Stakes, Chester	*L. Piggott*	1426
Yorkshire Cup, York	*L. Piggott*	3043
Carreras Piccadilly Oaks Trial, Lingfield	*S. Clayton*	2644
Halliford Stakes, Kempton Park	*A. Breasley*	615
Queen's Vase, Ascot	*A. Breasley*	3416
Rous Memorial Stakes, Ascot	*W. Rickaby*	1426
Ilsley Stakes, Newbury	*A. Breasley*	506
Twyford Stakes, Newbury	*S. Clayton*	453
Childrey Stakes, Newbury	*A. Breasley*	455
Chiddingstone Stakes, Lingfield	*S. Clayton*	426
Princess Maiden Stakes, Newmarket	*L. Piggott*	495
Cranbourne Chase Stakes, Ascot	*L. Piggott*	845
King George & Queen Elizabeth Stks, Ascot	*L. Piggott*	29,167
Princess Maiden Stakes, Ascot	*L. Piggott*	1996
Sunninghill Park Stakes, Ascot	*L. Piggott*	752
Donnington Castle Stakes, Newbury	*L. Piggott*	890
Chattis Hill Stakes, Newbury	*L. Piggott*	477
Links Maiden Stakes, Newmarket	*W. Rickaby*	367
Bunbury Maiden Stakes, Newmarket	*L. Piggott*	354
Restoration Stakes, Haydock Park	*L. Piggott*	400
Acomb Stakes, York	*L. Piggott*	1408
Sevenoaks Plate, Lingfield Park	*L. Piggott*	414
Shipley Bridge Stakes, Lingfield	*L. Piggott*	456
Saddlescombe Stakes, Brighton	*L. Piggott*	475
Fifinella Fillies' Stakes, Epsom	*L. Piggott*	1421
Redhill Stakes, Epsom	*L. Piggott*	393
Solario Stakes, Sandown Park	*L. Piggott*	1802
Bexley Stakes, Goodwood	*L. Piggott*	463
Southwick Handicap, Brighton	*L. Piggott*	624

	OWNER	HORSE
Sep 15	Major S. Vernon's	PLOTINA
Sep 15	Mrs Noel Murless'	ST. CHAD
Sep 15	Mr M. W. Wickham-Boynton's	NELION
Sep 15	Lady Sassoon's	SUCARYL
Sep 15	Duke of Wesminster's	MINERA
Sep 22	Mrs V. Hue-Williams's	ROYAL SAINT
Sep 23	Mr H. J. Joel's	ROYAL PALACE
Sep 24	Hon Mrs. Beatty's	FAB
Sep 24	Mr G. A. Pope's	HILL RISE
Sep 28	Mr R. C. Boucher's	FLEET
Sep 28	Hon Mrs S. Beatty's	ABBEYFIELD
Oct 3	Hon Mrs S. Beatty's	TEESDALE
Oct 5	Major S. Vernon	PLOTINA
Oct 6	Mr M. W. Wickham-Boynton's	VARINIA
Oct 10	Mr M. W. Wickham-Boynton's	NELION
Oct 15	Lady Sassoon's	LOVE FOR SALE
Oct 24	Lady Sassoon's	COMIC OPERA
Oct 26	Major S. Vernon's	PLOTINA

1967

Apr 19	H.M. The Queen's	HOPEFUL VENTURE
Apr 20	Lt Col J. Hornung's	CRANBERRY SAUCE
Apr 21	Mrs V. Hue-Williams's	ROYAL SAINT
Apr 28	Lt Col J. Hornung's	ST. PADARN
Apr 28	Lady Sassoon's	CATHEY 111
Apr 29	Mrs V. Hue-Williams's	SUN ROCK
Apr 29	Mr Stanhope Joel's	BUSTED
May 3	Mr H. J. Joel's	ROYAL PALACE
May 4	Mr R. C. Boucher's	FLEET
May 9	Mr H. J. Joel's	PINK GEM
May 10	H.M. The Queen's	HOPEFUL VENTURE
May 11	H.M. The Queen's	RIGHT WHEEL
May 20	Lt Col J. Hornung's	CRANBERRY SAUCE
May 24	Mr H. J. Joel's	ROYAL FALCON
Jun 1	Mrs Noel Murless'	ST. CHAD
Jun 7	Mr H. J. Joel's	ROYAL PALACE
Jun 15	Mrs V. Hue-Williams's	SUN ROCK
Jun 16	Hon Mrs S. Beatty's	ABBEYFIELD

COURSE	JOCKEY	PRIZE
Troon Stakes, Ayr	*L. Piggott*	454
Ladykirk Stakes, Ayr	*L. Piggott*	806
Royal Nursery Handicap Plate, Yarmouth	*J. Gorton*	414
Linenhall Stakes, Chester	*W. Rickaby*	435
Black Friars Stakes, Chester	*W. Rickaby*	638
Chertsey Stakes, Ascot	*L. Piggott*	922
Royal Lodge Stakes, Ascot	*L. Piggott*	5500
Blue Seal Stakes, Ascot	*L. Piggott*	1996
Queen Elizabeth II Stakes, Ascot	*L. Piggott*	5203
Cheveley Park Stakes, Newmarket	*L. Piggott*	9467
Bentick Nursery Handicap, Newmarket	*J. Gorton*	467
Westonbirt Stakes, Newbury	*L. Piggott*	426
Middleham Nursery Handicap Stakes, York	*L. Piggott*	595
Mornington Stakes, Ascot	*L. Piggott*	792
Kirkewhite Nursery H'cap Plate, Nottingham	*L. Piggott*	414
Houghton Stakes, Newmarket	*L. Piggott*	1693
Carlton Maiden Fillies' Plate, Nottingham	*R. Street*	414
Primrose Stakes, Ascot	*L. Piggott*	416

Races won 49   Winning Stakes £92,282

Wood Ditton Stakes, Newmarket	*G. Moore*	795
Nell Gwyn Stakes, Newmarket	*G. Moore*	1205
Fred Darling Stakes, Newbury	*L. Piggott*	2316
Tudor Stakes, Sandown Park	*G. Moore*	494
April Maiden Fillies Stakes, Sandown Park	*G. Moore*	530
Royal Stakes, Sandown Park	*L. Piggott*	1264
Coronation Stakes, Sandown Park	*G. Moore*	2276
2000 gns. Stakes, Newmarket	*G. Moore*	31,080
1000 gns. Stakes, Newmarket	*G. Moore*	24,848
Cheshire Oaks, Chester	*G. Moore*	1192
Grosvenor Stakes, Chester	*G. Moore*	837
Burghclere Stakes, Newbury	*A. Barclay*	496
Pretty Polly Stakes, Newmarket	*G. Moore*	1192
Jack Hylton Memorial Stks, Kempton Park	*G. Moore*	939
Brighthelmstone Handicap, Brighton	*G. Moore*	1167
Derby Stakes, Epsom	*G. Moore*	61,918
Newbury Summer Cup Handicap, Newbury	*A. Barclay*	1197
Alington Stakes, Sandown Park	*G. Moore*	764

	OWNER	HORSE
Jun 17	Lt Col J. Hornung's	CRANBERRY SAUCE
Jun 21	Mrs Noel Murless'	ST. CHAD
Jun 21	Mr R. C. Boucher's	FLEET
Jul 1	Lady Sassoon's	PILOCARPINE
Jul 6	Mr H. J. Joel's	ROYAL FALCON
Jul 7	Mrs Noel Murless'	LOWNA
Jul 8	Major S. Vernon's	PLOTINA
Jul 8	Mr H. F. Oppenheimer's	ATTALUS
Jul 8	Mr Stanhope Joel's	BUSTED
Jul 11	HM The Queen's	HOPEFUL VENTURE
Jul 12	Mrs Noel Murless'	HERBACEOUS
Jul 12	Mr C. A. B. St George's	LORENZACCIO
Jul 12	Lady Sassoon's	BALLY'S MIL
Jul 12	Mr C. A. B. St George's	RAFAELLO
Jul 15	Mr Stanhope Joel's	BUSTED
Jul 25	Mrs Noel Murless'	LOWNA
Jul 7	Mrs V. Hue-Williams's	SUN ROCK
Jul 28	Lady Sassoon's	SUCARYL
Jul 29	Mrs V. Hue-Williams's	REX BRITANNICUS
Aug 5	Mr J. R. Hindley's	MOSSALINA
Aug 5	Mr C. A. B. St George's	RIVA
Aug 10	Mrs Noel Murless'	HERBACEOUS
Aug 11	Mrs Noel Murless'	ST. CHAD
Aug 12	Mr H. F. Oppenheimer's	ATTALUS
Aug 12	H.M. The Queen's	HOPEFUL VENTURE
Aug 16	Mrs V. Hue-Williams's	REX BRITANNICUS
Aug 18	Lt Col J. Hornung's	MONTANA GIRL
Aug 26	Mrs Noel Murless'	ST. CHAD
Aug 28	Mr H. F. Oppenheimer's	HARDIESSE
Aug 30	Lt Col J. Hornung's	ST. PADARN
Sep 1	Mrs Noel Murless'	CAERGWRLE
Sep 2	Mr H. J. Joel's	MINERA
Sep 2	Lady Sassoon's	BALLY'S MIL
Sep 3	Mr Stanhope Joel's	BUSTED
Sep 6	Mrs V. Hue-Williams's	ROYAL SAINT
Sep 12	Mr H. J. Joel's	BUNKER
Sep 15	Mr H. J. Joel's	PINK GEM
Sep 16	Mr H. J. Joel's	HURRY HURRY
Sep 16	Mrs V. Hue-Williams's	SUN ROCK
Sep 28	Mrs J. R. Hindley's	AUTUMN MELODY

Appendix

COURSE	JOCKEY	PRIZE
Prix Fille de l'Air, Saint-Cloud	A. Barclay	7547
Jersey Stakes, Royal Ascot	G. Moore	1437
Coronation Stakes, Royal Ascot	G. Moore	4285
Wills Two Year Old Goblet Stks, Newcastle	A. Barclay	1157
Nightingale Stakes, Kempton Park	G. Moore	441
Alice Hawthorn Stakes, Chester	G. Moore	414
Red Rose Stakes, Chester	R. Maddock	873
Battersea Park Stakes, Sandown Park	G. Moore	830
Eclipse Stakes, Sandown Park	W. Rickaby	22,697
Hardwick Stakes, Newmarket	G. Moore	2452
Seaview Handicap, Brighton	A. Barclay	1151
July Stakes, Newmarket	G. Moore	1201
Kennett Maiden Stakes, Newmarket	G. Moore	454
Plantation Maiden Stakes, Newmarket	G. Moore	413
King George VI and The Queen Elizabeth Stakes, Ascot Heath	G. Moore	24,389
Molecomb Stakes, Goodwood	G. Moore	1628
Gordon Stakes, Goodwood	G. Moore	4704
News of the World Stakes, Goodwood	G. Moore	7993
Clare Handicap, Newmarket	A. Barclay	859
Bunbury Maiden Stakes, Newmarket	G. Moore	356
Egerton Apprentice Stakes, Newmarket	R. Street	383
Restoration Stakes, Haydock Park	G. Moore	411
Hungerford Stakes, Newbury	G. Moore	1524
Washingofrd Singer Stakes, Newbury	G. Moore	781
Oxfordshire Stakes, Newbury	G. Moore	3347
Frank Stone Handicap, Yarmouth	A. Barclay	552
Sevenoaks Plate, Lingfield Park	G. Moore	414
Wills Mile, Goodwood	G. Moore	6893
Wills Two Year Old Goblet Stks, Newcastle	A. Barclay	1831
Prix Quincey, Deauville	G. Moore	7762
Combermere Stakes, Chester	A. Barclay	409
Tote Investors Trophy, Chester	A. Barclay	1666
Rouge Rose Stakes, Chester	A. Barclay	389
Prix Henri Foy, Longchamp	G. Moore	7570
Strensall Sweepstakes, York	G. Moore	1201
Great Yorkshire Handicap, York	G. Moore	1761
Park Hill Stakes, Doncaster	G. Moore	2383
Crookham Two Year Old Stks, Newbury	G. Moore	1698
Peter Hastings Stakes, Newbury	G. Moore	3387
Wetwang Fillies' Plate, Beverley	A. Barclay	414

	OWNER	HORSE
Sep 29	Lady Sassoon's	SUCARYL
Sep 29	Mr R. C. Boucher's	FLEET
Oct 7	Lt Col J. Hornung's	CRANBERRY SAUCE
Oct 13	Mrs J. R. Hindley's	AUTUMN MELODY
Oct 18	Lady Sassoon's	ABBIE WEST

1968

	OWNER	HORSE
Apr 15	Lady Sassoon's	THE MOORINGS
Apr 15	Mrs Noel Murless'	CAERGWRLE
Apr 17	Lady Sassoon's	SUGAR APPLE
Apr 18	Lady Sassoon's	ABBIE WEST
Apr 26	Lord Howard de Walden's	LOTUS BLUE
Apr 27	Mr H. J. Joel's	ROYAL PALACE
May 2	Mrs Noel Murless'	CAERGWRLE
May 7	Mr H. F. Oppenheimer's	HARDIESSE
May 8	Lt Col J. Hornung's	PADELLA
May 9	H.M. The Queen's	HOPEFUL VENTURE
May 18	Mrs J. R. Hindley's	CELINA
May 30	Mr H. J. Joel's	ROYAL PALACE
Jun 5	Mr H. J. Joel's	ROYAL FALCON
Jun 5	Mr H. J. Joel's	ASH LAWN
Jun 9	Mr C. A. B. St George's	LORENZACCIO
Jun 12	Mr H. J. Joel's	ANGLO-AMERICAN
Jun 14	Hon Mrs S. Beatty's	TOP LINE
Jun 15	Lt Col J. Hornung's	MONTANA GIRL
Jun 18	Mr H. J. Joel's	ROYAL PALACE
Jun 20	Mr H. J. Joel's	CONNAUGHT
Jun 21	H.M. The Queen's	HOPEFUL VENTURE
Jun 26	Mr E. J. Loder's	MY ADVANTAGE
Jun 29	Lady Sassoon's	YOU ALL
Jun 30	Mr H. F. Oppenheimer's	HARDIESSE
Jul 6	Mr H. J. Joel's	ROYAL PALACE
Jul 7	H.M. The Queen's	HOPEFUL VENTURE
Jul 13	Mrs H. Cecil's	READY WIT
Jul 20	Mrs J. R. Hindley's	CELINA
Jul 20	Lady Sassoon's	PADDY'S COURT
Jul 24	Lt Col J. Hornung's	MONTANA GIRL
Jul 26	Mr George A. Pope Jr's	HILL RUN

COURSE	JOCKEY	PRIZE
David Robinson Stakes, Ascot Heath	*G. Moore*	8258
Michael Sobell Stakes, Ascot Heath	*G. Moore*	3829
Sun Chariot Stakes, Newmarket	*G. Moore*	2284
Askham Sweepstakes, York	*A. Barclay*	423
Heather Maiden Plate, Sandown Park	*G. Moore*	414

Races Won 63   Winning Stakes £279,775

COURSE	JOCKEY	PRIZE
Coventry Stakes, Kempton Park	*A. Barclay*	1237
1000 gns. Trial Stakes, Kempton Park	*A. Barclay*	1237
Wood Ditton Stakes, Newmarket	*A. Barclay*	851
Nell Gwyn Stakes, Newmarket	*A. Barclay*	1182
April Maiden Fillies' Stakes, Sandown Park	*A. Barclay*	504
Coronation Stakes, Sandown Park	*A. Barclay*	2220
1000 gns. Stakes, Newmarket	*A. Barclay*	19,682
Cheshire Oaks, Chester	*A. Barclay*	1178
Stewards' Stakes, Chester	*A. Barclay*	833
Ormonde Stakes, Chester	*A. Barclay*	1109
Pretty Polly Stakes, Newmarket	*A. Barclay*	1312
Coronation Cup, Epsom	*A. Barclay*	11,096
Pavilion Handicap, Brighton	*A. Barclay*	791
Portslade Stakes, Brighton	*A. Barclay*	487
Prix Jean Prat, Chantilly	*A. Barclay*	13,282
Threadneedle Street Stakes, Kempton Park	*A. Barclay*	942
Rosemary Maiden Plate, Sandown Park	*A. Barclay*	414
Raynes Fillies' Stakes, Sandown Park	*A. Barclay*	757
Prince of Wales Stakes, Royal Ascot	*A. Barclay*	4630
King Edward VII Stakes, Royal Ascot	*A. Barclay*	4452
Hardwicke Stakes, Royal Ascot	*A. Barclay*	8007
Ilsley Plate, Newbury	*A. Barclay*	414
Clayton Maiden Stakes, Newmarket	*A. Barclay*	389
Prix de Malleret, Longchamp	*A. Barclay*	8628
Eclipse Stakes, Sandown Park	*A. Barclay*	22,077
Grand Prix de Saint-Cloud, Saint-Cloud	*A. Barclay*	54,451
Donnington Castle Stakes, Newbury	*A. Barclay*	855
Irish Guineas Stakes, The Curragh	*A. Barclay*	20,461
Zetland Maiden Stakes, Newmarket	*R. Street*	425
St. James' Fillies Stakes, Sandown Park	*A. Barclay*	774
Hyperion Stakes, Ascot Heath	*A. Barclay*	2562

	OWNER	HORSE
Jul 27	Mr H. J. Joel's	ROYAL PALACE
Jul 30	Mr H. J. Joel's	WELSH PAGEANT
Jul 31	Lt Col J. Hornung's	SEA LAVENDER
Aug 2	Mr George A. Pope Jr's	HILL SHADE
Aug 10	Lt Col J. Hornung's	PERUVIAN SAINT
Aug 13	Mr H. J. Joel's	WELSH PAGEANT
Aug 21	Mr M. W. Wickham-Boynton's	GO ON
Aug 21	Mr H. J. Joel's	CONNAUGHT
Aug 21	Lady Sassoon's	ABBIE WEST
Aug 22	Hon Mrs S. Beatty's	TOP LINE
Sep 5	Lt Col J. Hornung's	MONTANA GIRL
Sep 6	Lady Sassoon's	PADDY'S COURT
Sep 12	Mr H. F. Oppenheimer's	ATTALUS
Sep 18	Mr H. F. Oppenheimer's	ATTALUS
Sep 19	Mr H. F. Oppenheimer's	TWENTY CARATS
Sep 21	Mr George A. Pope Jr's	HILL SHADE
Sep 26	Mr Stanhope Joel's	CALIBAN
Sep 27	Mr H. F. Oppenheimer's	HARDIESSE
Oct 3	Mr George A. Pope Jr's	HILLITA
Oct 5	Mr George A. Pope's Jr's	HILL SHADE

1969

Apr 15	Mr H. J. Joel's	PADDY'S PROGRESS
Apr 16	Mr H. J. Joel's	WELSH PAGEANT
Apr 18	Lt Col J. Hornung's	SEA LAVENDER
Apr 22	Mr Stanhope Joel's	CALIBAN
Apr 26	Mr H. J. Joel's	CONNAUGHT
May 14	Mr M. W. Wickham-Boynton's	LOVERS LANE
May 17	Mr Stanhope Joel's	SAINTLY SONG
May 17	Mr M. W. Wickham-Boynton's	BORANA
May 17	Mrs Dare Wigan's	THIKA
May 30	Lady Sassoon's	RANGONG
Jun 4	Mr H. J. Joel's	WELSH PAGEANT
Jun 8	Mr George A. Pope Jr's	HILL RUN
Jun 13	Lady Sassoon's	ROYAL PANCAKE
Jun 14	Mr George A. Pope Jr's	DOMINEERING
Jun 17	Mr H. J. Joel's	CONNAUGHT

COURSE	JOCKEY	PRIZE
King George VI and The Queen Elizabeth Stakes, Ascot Heath	*A. Barclay*	24,021
New Ham Stakes, Goodwood	*A. Barclay*	866
Selsey Stakes, Goodwood	*A. Barclay*	879
Nassau Stakes, Goodwood	*A. Barclay*	1656
Rectory Stakes, Lingfield Park	*W. Rickaby*	480
Home Ales Stakes, Nottingham	*A. Barclay*	1491
Hall Quay Stakes, Great Yarmouth	*R. Street*	383
Great Voltigeur Sweepstakes, York	*A. Barclay*	3263
Wykeham Handicap, York	*A. Barclay*	1142
Galtres Stakes, York	*A. Barclay*	1044
Crathorne Stakes, York	*A. Barclay*	601
St George's Stakes, Chester	*A. Barclay*	498
Scarbrough Stakes, Doncaster	*A. Barclay*	850
Doonside Cup, Ayr	*A. Barclay*	1612
Ladykirk Stakes, Ayr	*A. Barclay*	810
Soflons Stakes Handicap, Kempton Park	*A. Barclay*	5796
Clarence House Stakes, Ascot Heath	*A. Barclay*	884
Rosemary Stakes, Ascot Heath	*A. Barclay*	1704
Severals Stakes, Newmarket	*A. Barclay*	782
Sun Chariot Stakes, Newmarket	*A. Barclay*	2330

Races won 51   Winning Stakes £238,331

COURSE	JOCKEY	PRIZE
Craven Stakes, Newmarket	*A. Barclay*	1643
Totalisator Free Handicap, Newmarket	*A. Barclay*	4007
Fred Darling Stakes, Newbury	*A. Barclay*	2295
Blue Riband Trial Stakes, Epsom	*A. Barclay*	3511
Coronation Stakes, Sandown Park	*A. Barclay*	2817
Musidora Stakes, York	*A. Barclay*	2403
Blue Peter Stakes, Newmarket	*A. Barclay*	494
Pretty Polly Stakes, Newmarket	*A. Barclay*	1713
Fen Ditton Maiden Stakes, Newmarket	*A. Barclay*	650
Aston Park Stakes, Newbury	*A. Barclay*	808
St James Stakes, Epsom	*A. Barclay*	3193
Prix Jean Prat, Chantilly	*A. Barclay*	13,011
June Fillies' Plate, Sandown Park	*A. Barclay*	694
Soltykoff Stakes, Newmarket	*A. Barclay*	618
Prince of Wales Stakes, Royal Ascot	*A. Barclay*	4171

	OWNER	HORSE
Jun 27	Hon Mrs S. Beatty's	BRILLY
Jun 28	Mr M. W. Wickham-Boynton	BORANA
Jun 30	Mrs J. R. Hindley's	PADDLE BOAT
Jul 2	Mr J. R. Hindley's	ST. PADINA
Jul 4	Mr George A. Pope Jr's	DOMINEERING
Aug 8	Mrs Ogden Phipps'	POLITICO
Aug 11	Mr H. J. Joel's	PRINCE CONSORT
Aug 16	Lady Sassoon's	RANGONG
Aug 19	Mrs C. Wetherill's	TIMMY MY BOY
Aug 21	Lady Sassoon's	A-BYE
Aug 21	Mr George A. Pope Jr's	WARREN HILL
Aug 22	Mrs V. Hue-Williams's	ROYAL HOUSE
Aug 28	Mr M. W. Wickham-Boynton's	KARATINA
Aug 30	Mr H. J. Joel's	WELSH PAGEANT
Aug 30	Mrs C. Wetherill's	TIMMY MY BOY
Sep 4	Mr E. J. Loder's	GREEN CHIFFON
Sep 5	Lady Sassoon's	CREOLE KELLY
Sep 9	Mr Stanhope Joel's	SAINTLY SONG
Sep 9	Lt Col J. Hornung's	QUEENBOROUGH 11
Sep 10	Mrs Ogden Phipps's	POLITICO
Sep 11	Mrs Stanhope Joel's	LUPE
Sep 11	Lady Sassoon's	A-BYE
Sep 17	Lady Sassoon's	SABBATHICAL
Sep 18	Mr Garfield Weston's	PADDY'S HONEY
Sep 20	Lady Sassoon's	ROYAL PANCAKE
Sep 20	Lt Col J. Hornung's	QUEENBOROUGH 11
Sep 20	Lord Howard de Walden's	QUEEN'S KEYS
Sep 24	Mr F. R. Hue-Williams's	OBELISK
Sep 25	Mr E. J. Loder's	GREEN CHIFFON
Sep 27	Mr George A. Pope Jr's	DOMINEERING
Oct 8	Mrs Ogden Phipps's	KHADINE
Oct 9	Mr H. J. Joel's	CALSHOT LIGHT
Oct 25	Lady Sassoon's	RANGONG

1970

Apr 16	Mr F. R. Hue-Williams'	OBELISK
Apr 25	Lady Sassoon's	CRY BABY

Appendix

COURSE	JOCKEY	PRIZE
Skylark Maiden Stakes, Kempton Park	*A. Barclay*	514
Pretty Polly Stakes, The Curragh	*A. Barclay*	1975
Hove Stakes, Brighton	*L. Piggott*	546
Oulton Maiden Stakes, Great Yarmouth	*A. Barclay*	472
Battersea Park Plate, Sandown Park	*A. Barclay*	690
Beacon Maiden Plate, Newmarket	*A. Barclay*	690
Greenhead Maiden Stakes, Newcastle	*A. Barclay*	728
Geoffrey Freer Stakes, Newbury	*A. Barclay*	4151
Prix de Hastings, Deauville	*F. Head*	1592
Limoklin Stakes, Goodwood	*A. Barclay*	640
Seven Points Stakes, Goodwood	*A. Barclay*	637
Mapleton Stakes, Lingfield Park	*A. Barclay*	484
Race Hill Stakes, Brighton	*A. Barclay*	516
Northern Goldsmith's Handicap, Newcastle	*A. Barclay*	3256
Prix de Saint-Crespin, Deauville	*F. Head*	3092
Ovingdean Stakes, Brighton	*A. Barclay*	524
Autumn Maiden Plate, Sandown Park	*G. Lewis*	690
Champagne Stakes, Doncaster	*A. Barclay*	5152
September Stakes, Doncaster	*A. Barclay*	855
Prince of Wales's Nursery Handicap Stakes Doncaster	*A. Barclay*	2027
Devonshire Maiden Stakes, Doncaster	*A. Barclay*	1062
Princess Mary Nursery Handicap Stakes, Doncaster	*A. Barclay*	883
Monument Plate, Great Yarmouth	*G. Lewis*	552
Troon Plate, Ayr	*A. Barclay*	690
Firth of Clyde Stakes, Ayr	*A. Barclay*	872
Brodick Stakes, Ayr	*A. Barclay*	654
Wavertree Stakes, Newmarket	*B. Taylor*	620
Nutfield Plate, Lingfield Park	*J. Gorton*	552
South Lancashire Stakes, Haydock Park	*G. Lewis*	527
Royal Lodge Stakes, Ascot	*A. Barclay*	5628
Malton Stakes, York	*A. Barclay*	1101
Leyburn Stakes, York	*A. Barclay*	789
St Simon Stakes, Newbury	*G. Lewis*	3683

Races won 48   Winning Stakes £88,876

Nell Gwyn Stakes, Newmarket	*A. Barclay*	1651
Royal Stakes, Sandown Park	*A. Barclay*	1572

	OWNER	HORSE
May 2	Mr H. J. Joel's	WELSH PAGEANT
May 5	Mrs Ogden Phipps'	POLITICO
May 5	Mr J. R. Mullion's	CUMBERNAULD
May 6	Mrs Stanhope Joel's	LUPE
May 12	Mr H. J. Joel's	PEMBROKE CASTLE
May 14	Lady Sassoon's	RANGONG
May 16	Lady Sassoon's	ROYAL PANCAKE
May 18	Mr C. A. B. St George's	LORENZACCIO
May 25	Mr C. A. B. St George's	LORENZACCIO
May 25	Lt Col J. Hornung's	FIELD-OFFICER
May 26	Mr H. J. Joel's	CONNAUGHT
May 26	Mr J. R. Hindley's	CHARLOTINA
May 30	Mr H. J. Joel's	WELSH PAGEANT
Jun 3	Mr Stanhope Joel's	SAINTLY SONG
Jun 4	Mr Stanhope Joel's	CALIBAN
Jun 6	Mrs Stanhope Joel's	LUPE
Jun 16	Mr H. J. Joel's	WELSH PAGEANT
Jun 16	Mr H. J. Joel's	CONNAUGHT
Jun 16	Mr Stanhope Joel's	SAINTLY SONG
Jun 17	Mr H. J. Joel's	PRINCE CONSORT
Jun 17	Lord Howard de Walden's	PARMELIA
Jun 24	Mr H. J. Joel's	CALSHOT LIGHT
Jun 24	Mr F. R. Hue-Williams'	OBELISK
Jul 4	Mr H. J. Joel's	CONNAUGHT
Jul 7	Mr H. J. Joel's	PRINCE CONSORT
Jul 22	Mrs Noel Murless'	FAIRYFIELD
Jul 31	Lord Howard de Waldon's	DULCET
Aug 6	Mr H. J. Joel's	WATERFORD GLASS
Aug 10	Mrs J. R. Hindley's	MELODINA
Aug 14	Lord Howard de Walden's	MAGIC FLUTE
Aug 18	Mrs Stanhope Joel's	LUPE
Aug 21	Mr M. W. Wickham-Boynton's	KARENINA
Aug 23	Mr C. A. B. St George's	LORENZACCIO
Aug 31	Mrs G. A. Turner's	YELDA
Aug 31	Mr H. J. Joel's	PLYMOUTH SOUND
Sep 5	Mr H. J. Joel's	WATERFORD GLASS
Sep 6	Mr C. A. B. St George's	LORENZACCIO
Sep 10	Lord Howard de Walden's	PARMELIA
Sep 11	Mr George A. Pope Jr's	HILL CIRCUS
Sep 11	Mr H. J. Joel's	CALSHOT LIGHT
Sep 16	Mr George A. Pope Jr's	HILL COMMAND

COURSE	JOCKEY	PRIZE
Victoria Cup (Handicap), Newmarket	*A. Barclay*	3289
Chester Vase, Chester	*A. Barclay*	3400
Grosvenor Stakes, Chester	*A. Barclay*	698
Cheshire Oaks, Chester	*A. Barclay*	1643
Glasgow Stakes, York	*A. Barclay*	918
Yorkshire Cup, York *	*A. Barclay*	3829
Pretty Polly Stakes, Newmarket	*A. Murray*	1677
Prix Prince Chevalier, Saint-Cloud	*L. Piggott*	2379
Prix de la Fouillouse, Saint-Cloud	*W. Pyers*	3152
Cardinal Wolsey Stakes, Sandown Park	*A. Barclay*	693
Westbury Stakes, Sandown Park	*A. Barclay*	1537
Chequers Fillies' Stakes, Sandown Park	*A. Barclay*	602
Lockinge Stakes, Newbury	*A. Barclay*	7632
St James Stakes, Epsom	*A. Barclay*	3374
Coronation Cup, Epsom	*A. Barclay*	11,430
Oaks Stakes, Epsom	*A. Barclay*	31,320
Queen Anne Stakes, Royal Ascot	*A. Barclay*	2220
Prince of Wales Stakes, Royal Ascot	*A. Barclay*	3983
St James's Palace Stakes, Royal Ascot	*A. Barclay*	4952
Bessborough Stakes (H'cap), Royal Ascot	*A. Barclay*	2196
Ribblesdale Stakes, Royal Ascot	*A. Barclay*	4767
Hermitage Stakes, Newbury	*A. Barclay*	596
Empire Stakes (Handicap), Newbury	*A. Barclay*	1036
Eclipse Stakes, Sandown Park	*A. Barclay*	27,220
Princess of Wales' Stakes, Newmarket	*A. Barclay*	2360
St James' Fillies Stakes, Sandown Park	*A. Barclay*	770
Finden Stakes, Goodwood	*A. Barclay*	906
City of Norwich Stakes, Yarmouth	*A. Barclay*	454
Seaton Delaval Stakes, Newcastle	*A. Barclay*	2065
St Hugh's Stakes, Newbury	*A. Barclay*	851
Yorkshire Oaks, York	*A. Barclay*	6040
Lady Hill Stakes, Haydock Park	*A. Barclay*	492
Prix Quincey, Deauville	*L. Piggott*	7857
Wills Two Year Old Goblet Stks, Newcastle	*A. Barclay*	1892
Virginia Stakes, Newcastle	*A. Barclay*	1562
Rouge Rose Stakes, Chester	*A. Barclay*	532
Prix Foy, Longchamp	*L. Piggott*	7562
Park Hill Stakes, Doncaster	*A. Barclay*	4472
Devonshire Maiden Stakes, Doncaster	*A. Barclay*	1125
Arlington Stakes, Newbury	*A. Murray*	799
Monument Plate, Yarmouth	*G. Lewis*	518

OWNER	HORSE

Sep 16	Mr H. J. Joel's	PEMBROKE CASTLE
Sep 19	Mr M. W. Wickham-Boynton's	KARENINA
Sep 26	Mr H. J. Joel's	WELSH PAGEANT
Sep 30	Lord Howard de Walden's	MAGIC FLUTE
Sep 30	Mr H. J. Joel's	HOLLY BLUE
Oct 6	Mr F. R. Hue-Williams'	ALTESSE ROYALE
Oct 6	Mrs V. Hue-Williams'	RELATE
Oct 12	Lt Col J. Hornung's	QUEENBOROUGH 11
Oct 15	Mr H. J. Joel's	FRASCATI
Oct 17	Mr C. A. B. St George's	LORENZACCIO
Oct 24	Mrs Ogden Phipps'	POLITICO
Oct 26	Mr George A. Pope Jr's	HILL DAISY
Oct 29	Mr George A. Pope Jr's	HILL RUN
Oct 29	Mrs V. Hue-Williams'	RELATE

1971

Apr 12	Mrs G. A. Turner's	YELDA
Apr 14	Mr H. J. Joel's	PEMBROKE CASTLE
Apr 24	Mr H. J. Joel's	PEMBROKE CASTLE
Apr 29	Mr F. R. Hue-Williams'	ALTESSE ROYALE
May 4	Sir R. Macdonald-Buchanan's	PARTHIAN PLAIN
May 5	Mrs G. A. Turner's	YELDA
May 6	Mr M. W. Wickham-Boynton's	HABBARI
May 14	Mr H. J. Joel's	MAINA
May 18	Mr H. J. Joel's	PADD'S PROGRESS
May 22	Mr H. J. Joel's	WELSH PAGEANT
Jun 3	Mrs Stanhope Joel's	LUPE
Jun 3	Mr George A. Pole Jr's	SHINING HILL
Jun 5	Mr F. R. Hue-Williams'	ALTESSE ROYALE
Jun 16	Lord Howard de Walden's	MAGIC FLUTE
Jun 17	Sir R. Macdonald-Buchanan's	PHILIP OF SPAIN
Jun 28	Lt Col J. Hornung's	MOCKBRIDGE
Jul 2	Mr H. J. Joel's	MAINA
Jul 6	Mrs Stanhope Joel's	LUPE
Jul 13	Mrs Ogden Phipps'	POLITICO
Jul 10	Lady Sassoon's	EXECUTIVE
Jul 10	Sir R. Macdonald-Buchanan's	PARTHIAN PLAIN
Jul 17	Mr F. R. Hue-Williams'	ALTESSE ROYALE

COURSE	JOCKEY	PRIZE
Doonside Cup, Ayr	A. *Barclay*	2467
Firth of Clyde Stakes, Ayr	A. *Barclay*	866
Queen Elizabeth II Stakes, Ascot	A. *Barclay*	5511
Cheveley Park Stakes, Newmarket	A. *Barclay*	10,851
Lowther Maiden Fillies' Stakes, Newmarket	A. *Barclay*	607
Founders' Plate, Lingfield Park	A. *Barclay*	552
Burr Plate, Lingfield Park	A. *Barclay*	552
Arden Stakes, Warwick	G. *Lewis*	415
Chesterton Maiden Plate, Newmarket	A. *Barclay*	690
Champion Stakes, Newmarket	G. *Lewis*	25,079
St Simon Stakes, Newbury	G. *Lewis*	3596
Flawborough Mdn Fillies' Stks, Nottingham	G. *Lewis*	402
Mildenhall Stakes, Newmarket	G. *Lewis*	450
Zetland Plate, Newmarket	G. *Lewis*	414

Races Won 57   Winning Stakes £220,475

COURSE	JOCKEY	PRIZE
Masaka Stakes, Kempton Park	G. *Lewis*	1654
Rubbing House Stakes, Newmarket	G. *Lewis*	2256
Coronation Stakes, Sandown Park	G. *Lewis*	2755
1000 gns. Stakes, Newmarket	Y. *Saint-Martin*	22704
Grosvenor Stakes, Chester	G. *Starkey*	690
Cheshire Oaks, Chester	A. *Murray*	2341
Wynn Handicap, Chester	J. *Lindley*	714
Oaks Trial Stakes, Lingfield Park	L. *Piggott*	2315
Madeira Stakes, Brighton	G. *Lewis*	563
Lockinge Stakes, Newbury	G. *Lewis*	7635
Coronation Cup, Epsom	G. *Lewis*	11,343
Chipstead Stakes, Epsom	G. *Lewis*	852
Oaks Stakes, Epsom	G. *Lewis*	30,215
Coronation Stakes, Royal Ascot	G. *Lewis*	4452
New Stakes, Royal Ascot	G. *Lewis*	4730
Bevendean Stakes, Brighton	G. *Lewis*	587
Lancashire Oaks, Haydock Park	L. *Piggott*	2418
Princess of Wales's Stakes, Newmarket	G. *Lewis*	2355
Ash Stakes, Kempton Park	G. *Lewis*	810
Overton Maiden Stakes, Newbury	G. *Lewis*	625
Morland Brewery Trophy H'cap, Newbury	G. *Lewis*	2971
Irish Guinness Oaks, The Curragh	G. *Lewis*	22,766

	OWNER	HORSE
Jul 23	Mr George A. Pope Jr's	SHADY FELLOW
Jul 27	Lady Sassoon's	EXECUTIVE
Jul 31	Mr Stanhope Joel's	NO SURTAX
Aug 13	Mr H. J. Joel's	CALSHOT LIGHT
Aug 13	Mr H. J. Joel's	WELSH PAGEANT
Aug 14	Mrs V. Hue-Williams'	YAROSLAV
Aug 14	Mr F. R. Hue-Williams'	HOLY PRINCE
Aug 19	Mr Stanhope Joel's	NO SURTAX
Aug 27	Lt Col J. Hornung's	LAZY GREY
Aug 30	Mrs G. A. Turner's	YELDA
Aug 30	Lord Howard de Walden's	DULCET
Aug 28	Mr C. A. B. St George's	CHARLADOUCE
Sep 1	Lord Howard de Walden's	MAGIC FLUTE
Sep 2	Mr H. J. Joel's	RED SIGNAL
Sep 2	Mr George A. Pope Jr's	CALIFORNIA HILL
Sep 4	Mrs Noel Murless'	SARKLESS KITTY
Sep 4	Mrs Reginald Hindley's	MELODINA
Sep 10	Mr John A. Sutton's	FRESH START
Sep 11	Mr Louis Freedman's	ABWAH
Sep 11	Mr Stanhope Joel's	ALONSO
Sep 13	Mr Louis Freedman's	MISS ROCKET
Sep 16	Sir R. Macdonald-Buchanan's	BECK
Sep 16	Mrs V. Hue-Williams'	RELATE
Sep 22	Lt Col J. Hornung's	MOCKBRIDGE
Sep 23	Mr Stanhope Joel's	REDUNDANT
Sep 23	Mr George A. Pope Jr's	HILL CIRCUS
Sep 24	Mr George A. Pope Jr's	SHADY FELLOW
Sep 25	Mrs V. Hue-Williams'	YAROSLAV
Sep 27	Mr Louis Freedman's	PILAMENON
Sep 29	Mr Louis Freedman's	CUPID'S DELIGHT
Oct 2	Mr George A. Pope Jr's	HILL CIRCUS
Oct 6	Mr Louis Freedman's	PILAMENON
Oct 6	Mr H. J. Joel's	SELHURST
Oct 6	Sir R. Macdonald-Buchanan's	BECK
Oct 8	Mr H. J. Joel's	PEMBROKE CASTLE
Oct 8	Lord Howard de Walden's	MAGIC FLUTE
Oct 9	Mr George A. Pope Jr's	HILL CIRCUS
Oct 11	Mr M. W. Wickham-Boynton's	NYERI
Oct 15	Mrs Noel Murless'	QUEENSFERRY
Oct 15	Mrs S. M. Castello's	ROYAL SHIRAZ
Oct 19	Mr H. J. Joel's	CALSHOT LIGHT

COURSE	JOCKEY	PRIZE
Granville Stakes, Ascot	G. Lewis	956
Craven Stakes Handicap, Goodwood	W. Carson	827
Links Stakes, Newmarket	R. Street	596
Russley Stakes Handicap, Newbury	G. Lewis	588
Hungerford Stakes, Newbury	G. Lewis	2268
Washington Singer Stakes, Newbury	G. Lewis	1194
Yattendon Stakes, Newbury	G. Lewis	680
Galtres Stakes, York	G. Lewis	1768
Cowdray Nursery Handicap, Goodwood	G. Lewis	658
Virginia Stakes, Newcastle	G. Lewis	1562
Bridget Handicap Stakes, Epsom	J. Lindley	1173
Prix Michel Houyvet, Deauville	Y. Saint-Martin	3622
Strensall Stakes, York	G. Lewis	1737
Tadcaster Stakes, York	L. Piggott	857
Rottingdean Stakes, Brighton	G. Lewis	510
Linenhall Stakes, Chester	G. Lewis	530
Rouge Rose Stakes, Chester	G. Lewis	530
Devonshire Maiden Stakes, Doncaster	G. Lewis	1032
Harwell Maiden Stakes, Newbury	G. Lewis	632
Crookham Two Year Old Stks, Newbury	G. Lewis	1890
Chisledown Stakes, Goodwood	G. Lewis	629
Troon Plate, Ayr	G. Lewis	690
Royal Caledonian Hunt Cup, Ayr	G. Lewis	690
Bilhurst Nursery Handicap, Lingfield Park	G. Lewis	552
Clarence House Stakes, Ascot	G. Lewis	938
Rosemary Stakes, Ascot	G. Lewis	804
Miss Selfridge Stakes, Ascot	G. Lewis	1022
Royal Lodge Stakes, Ascot	G. Lewis	5883
Fiskerton Maiden Fillies' Stks, Nottingham	G. Lewis	580
Lowther Maiden Fillies' Stakes, Newmarket	G. Lewis	608
Sun Chariot Stakes, Newmarket	G. Lewis	4281
Oxted Stakes, Lingfield Park	A. Murray	500
Middlethorpe Stakes, York	G. Lewis	719
Malton Stakes, York	G. Lewis	815
Mitre Stakes, Ascot	G. Lewis	600
Marlborough House Stakes, Ascot	G. Lewis	884
Princess Royal Stakes, Ascot	G. Lewis	2382
Honiley Maiden Plate, Warwick	G. Lewis	380
Boadicea Stakes, Newmarket	G. Lewis	595
Boscawen Nursery Handicap, Newmarket	A. Murray	690
Rookery Handicap, Sandown Park	G. Lewis	664

	OWNER	HORSE
Oct 23	Mr H. J. Joel's	FRASCATI
Oct 30	Mr Louis Freedman's	CUPID'S DELIGHT

1972

	OWNER	HORSE
Apr 11	Mr H. J. Joel's	LEICESTER
Apr 29	Mrs V. Hue-Williams's	RELATE
May 4	Mr H. J. Joel's	SELHURST
May 19	Mr H. J. Joel's	SELHURST
May 19	Mrs Noel Murless'	SARKLESS KITTY
May 27	Sir Reginald Macdonald-Buchanan's	PARTHIAN PLAIN
May 30	Mr George A. Pole Jr's	TICKING HILL (USA)
Jun 16	Lt Col J. Hornung's	WHORTLEBERRY
Jun 23	Mr H. J. Joel's	SELHURST
Jun 23	Mr Stanhope Joel's	REDUNDANT
Jun 30	Mrs Noel Murless'	CAERDEON
Jul 1	Mr H. J. Joel's	THE ADMIRAL
Jul 1	Mr M. W. Wickham-Boynton's	DANCING EMMA
Jul 4	Mr George A. Pope Jr's	MYSTERIOUS
Jul 7	Mr Louis Freedman's	ABWAH
Jul 7	Mr Louis Freedman's	ATTICA MELI
Jul 19	Mrs S. Castello's	ROYAL SHIRAZ
Jul 21	Mr H. J. Joel's	THE ADMIRAL
Jul 28	Mr Louis Freedman's	ATTICA MELI
Jul 29	Mr H. J. Joel's	COLOURFUL
Jul 31	Lt Col J. Hornung's	ST ANGELINA
Aug 1	Mr Stanhope Joel's	REDUNDANT
Aug 11	Mr John A. Sutton's	DAY OF RECKONING
Aug 15	Mr Louis Freedman's	ATTICA MELI
Aug 15	Mrs V. Hue-Williams's	RELATE
Aug 16	Mr Louis Freedman's	ABWAH
Aug 19	Mr H. J. Joel's	COLOURFUL
Aug 19	Mr Louis Freedman's	COTE D'AZUR
Aug 23	Mr E. J. Loder's	MELODRAMATIC
Aug 23	Mr George A. Pope Jr's	SHADY FELLOW (USA)
Aug 23	Mr H. J. Joel's	MONKEY TRICKS
Aug 28	Mr H. J. Joel's	JOLIE FLEUR
Aug 28	Lt Col J. Hornung's	ST ANGELINA
Aug 31	Mr George A. Pope Jr's	TWINKLING HILL (USA)

COURSE	JOCKEY	PRIZE
St Simon Stakes, Newbury	B. Taylor	3623
South Lancashire Stakes, Haydock Park	G. Lewis	606

Races Won 65   Winning Stakes £180,496

Craven Stakes, Newmarket	G. Lewis	2414
March Handicap, Newmarket	G. Lewis	1704
Ormonde Stakes, Chester	G. Lewis	2299
Aston Park Stakes, Newbury	G. Lewis	1527
Sandleford Priory Stakes, Newbury	G. Lewis	1628
Haydock Park Stakes, Haydock	G. Lewis	1068
Chequers Fillies Stakes, Sandown Park	G. Lewis	915
Raynes Maiden Plate, Sandown Park	G. Lewis	690
Hardwicke Stakes, Royal Ascot	G. Lewis	11,072
Britannia Stakes, Royal Ascot	G. Lewis	3624
Hackwood Stakes, Newbury	G. Lewis	1556
Hametus Maiden Stakes, Newmarket	J. Gorton	1082
Stockil Stakes, Doncaster	G. Lewis	561
Cherry Hinton Stakes, Newmarket	G. Lewis	4545
Southern Sprint Handicap, Sandown Park	G. Lewis	918
July Plate, Sandown Park	G. Lewis	690
Wellington Handicap, Sandown Park	G. Lewis	1079
Sunninghill Park Stakes, Ascot	G. Lewis	898
Danizette Handicap, Goodwood	G. Lewis	1052
Links Stakes, Newmarket	B. Taylor	926
Darlaston Maiden Plate, Wolverhampton	G. Lewis	276
Brighton Handicap, Brighton	G. Lewis	1114
Sparsholt Stakes, Newbury	A. Murray	787
Yorkshire Oaks, York	G. Lewis	8442
Prix de Roux, Deauville	J. Desaint	6095
Wykeham Stakes (Handicap), York	G. Lewis	1482
Chiddingstone Stakes, Lingfield Park	A. Murray	486
Hermitage Green Stakes, Haydock Park	G. Lewis	597
Saddlescomb Stakes, Brighton	G. Lewis	678
George Robey Chall. Trophy (H'p), Brighton	G. Lewis	1156
Cobholm Stakes, Great Yarmouth	F. Durr	569
Leaf Maiden Stakes, Newcastle	G. Lewis	566
Ferry Stakes, Chepstow	R. Street	413
Ovingdean Stakes, Brighton	A. Murray	734

Q

	OWNER	HORSE
Sep 1	Mr Stanhope Joel's	REDUNDANT
Sep 1	Mr Louis Freedman's	COTE D'AZUR
Sep 6	Mr H. J. Joel's	FRASCATI
Sep 7	Mr Louis Freedman's	ATTICA MELI
Sep 9	Mr M. W. Wickham-Boynton's	DANCING EMMA
Sep 13	Mr George A. Pope Jr's	SHADY FELLOW (USA)
Sep 14	Mr Louis Freedman's	ABWAH
Sep 15	Mr H. J. Joel's	GLASS SLIPPER
Sep 20	Mr H. J. Joel's	FATHER CHRISTMAS
Sep 23	Mr Garfield Weston's	ADIOS
Sep 29	Mr H. J. Joel's	THE ADMIRAL
Sep 29	Mr H. J. Joel's	FRASCATI
Oct 3	Lt Col J. Hornung's	GOLDEN THORN
Oct 4	Sir Reginald Macdonald-Buchanan's	GRILSE RUN
Oct 4	Mr H. J. Joel's	COLOURFUL
Oct 7	Mr Louis Freedman's	ATTICA MELI
Oct 7	Mr Garfield Weston's	GOSPILL HILL

1973

Apr 11	Mr Louis Freedman's	OWEN DUDLEY
Apr 13	Mr George A. Pope Jr's	MYSTERIOUS
Apr 24	Mr Garfield Weston's	GOSPILL HILL
Apr 26	Mr H. J. Joel's	FATHER CHRISTMAS
May 3	Mr George A. Pope Jr's	MYSTERIOUS
May 3	Mr George A. Pope Jr's	MONTMARTRE (USA)
May 9	Mr Louis Freedman's	MILLY MOSS
May 15	Mr Louis Freedman's	OWEN DUDLEY
May 17	Mr Louis Freedman's	ABWAH
May 29	Mr H. J. Joel's	THE ADMIRAL
May 29	Mr M. W. Wickham-Boynton's	BAMBURI
May 31	Mr H. J. Joel's	FATHER CHRISTMAS
Jun 2	Lt Col J. Hornung's	GOLDEN THORN
Jun 6	Mr M. W. Wickham-Boynton's	FISHERMANS BRIDGE
Jun 8	Mr Louis Freedman's	OWEN DUDLEY
Jun 9	Mr George A. Pope Jr's	MYSTERIOUS
Jun 9	Lord Porchester's	TOM
Jun 16	Mr M. W. Wickham-Boynton's	FISHERMANS BRIDGE
Jul 13	The Hon Mrs S. Beatty's	MAIDEN ERLEGH

COURSE	JOCKEY	PRIZE
September Handicap, Kempton Park	G. Lewis	1006
St George's Stakes, Chester	L. Piggott	747
Great Yorkshire Handicap Stakes, York	G. Lewis	1713
Park Hill Stakes, Doncaster	G. Lewis	4335
Duchess of York Stakes, Kempton Park	G. Lewis	1959
Royal Burgh of Ayr Handicap, Ayr	G. Lewis	2484
Bass Special Stakes (Handicap), Ayr	G. Lewis	1637
Beenham Stakes, Newbury	A. Murray	579
Malthouse Plate, Lingfield Park	G. Lewis	414
Royal Lodge Stakes, Ascot	G. Lewis	6083
Outland Stakes (Handicap), Haydock Park	A. Murray	1247
Seventh Contest Stakes, Haydock Park	G. Lewis	1096
Founders Plate, Lingfield Park	G. Lewis	552
Bramham Moor Stakes, York	G. Lewis	760
Middlethorpe Stakes, York	G. Lewis	1173
Princess Royal Stakes, Ascot	G. Lewis	2526
Sandwich Stakes, Ascot	G. Lewis	1260

Races Won 51   Winning Stakes £93,231

Wood Ditton Stakes, Newmarket	G. Lewis	947
Fred Darling Stakes, Newbury	G. Lewis	2334
Blue Riband Trial Stakes, Epsom	G. Lewis	4087
Evelyn Handicap Stakes, Epsom	G. Lewis	1041
1000 gns. Stakes, Newmarket	G. Lewis	25,229
Hastings Maiden Plate, Newmarket	G. Lewis	1035
Cheshire Oaks, Chester	G. Lewis	2435
Dante Stakes, York	G. Lewis	3051
Duke of York Stakes, York	G. Lewis	2989
Henry II Stakes, Kempton Park	G. Lewis	3514
Chequers Fillies Stakes, Kempton Park	G. Lewis	927
Brighton Festival Handicap, Brighton	G. Lewis	1160
Richard Marsh Handicap, Newmarket	G. Lewis	962
Ebbisham Handicap, Epsom	G. Lewis	3734
Diomed Stakes, Epsom	G. Lewis	7685
Oaks Stakes, Epsom	G. Lewis	35,417
Walter Nightingall Stakes, Epsom	G. Lewis	1545
Rosemary Fillies Stakes, Kempton Park	G. Lewis	942
Ridgeway Stakes (Handicap), Newbury	G. Lewis	992

	OWNER	HORSE
Jul 25	Sir Reginald Macdonald-Buchanan's	ESTAMINET
Jul 25	Mr E. J. Loder's	MELODRAMATIC
Jul 27	Mr M. W. Wickham-Boynton's	BAMBURI
Aug 4	Mrs Dare Wigan's	SPLASHING
Aug 4	Mr H. J. Joel's	ROSE PINK
Aug 18	Mr Louis Freedman's	ATTICA MELI
Aug 21	Mr George A. Pope Jr's	MYSTERIOUS
Aug 27	Mr H. J. Joel's	FATHER CHRISTMAS
Aug 27	Mr E. J. Loder's	MELODRAMATIC
Sep 4	Lt Col J. Hornung's	PARTRIDGE GREEN
Sep 8	Mr George A. Pope Jr's	MONTMARTRE (USA)
Sep 13	Mr Louis Freedman's	ATTICA MELI
Oct 3	Mrs Stanhope Joel's	MOUNT PLENTY
Oct 11	Mr H. J. Joel's	CHARTER DAY
Oct 13	Mrs Dare Wigan's	SPLASHING

1974

Apr 15	Mr Louis Freedman's	STAR COURT
Apr 17	Col F. R. Hue-Williams's	IMPERIAL PRINCE
Apr 17	Mr Louis Freedman's	OWEN DUDLEY
May 11	Mrs Dare Wigan's	TURNKEY
May 14	Mr H. J. Joel's	HONOURED GUEST
Jun 12	Sir Reginald Macdonald-Buchanan's	ESTAMINET
Jun 28	Lt Col J. Hornung's	PARTRIDGE GREEN
Jun 29	Mrs Noel Murless'	THE HOBMAN
Jun 29	Mr Louis Freedman's	ALL HALLOWS
Jul 3	Mr H. J. Joel's	FATHER CHRISTMAS
Jul 5	Mr Louis Freedman's	MIL'S BOMB
Jul 13	Sir Reginald Macdonald-Buchanan's	CAPTAIN'S ESCORT
Jul 18	Mrs Noel Murless'	AMIGO
Jul 19	Mr Louis Freedman's	WEST TWO
Jul 20	Sir Reginald Macdonald-Buchanan's	STIRLING CASTLE
Jul 20	Sir Reginald Macdonald-Buchanan's	ESTAMINET
Jul 31	Mr H. J. Joel's	MELODY HOUR
Aug 2	Lt Col J. Hornung's	SAUCEBOAT
Aug 3	Mr Louis Freedman's	MIL'S BOMB
Aug 10	Mrs Noel Murless'	OSWALDKIRK
Aug 13	Mr M. W. Wickham-Boynton's	ASTERINA
Aug 20	Mr H. J. Joel's	FATHER CHRISTMAS

COURSE	JOCKEY	PRIZE
Milburn Plate, Kempton Park	G. *Lewis*	690
St James' Fillies Stakes, Kempton Park	G. *Lewis*	1166
Red Oaks Stakes (Handicap), Ascot	G. *Lewis*	1104
Pegasus Maiden Stakes, Newmarket	G. *Moore*	756
Links Stakes, Newmarket	G. *Moore*	613
Geoffrey Freer Stakes, Newbury	G. *Lewis*	5551
Yorkshire Oaks, York	G. *Lewis*	11,350
Ranmore Handicap Stakes, Epsom	G. *Lewis*	1184
Bridget Handicap Stakes, Epsom	G. *Lewis*	1173
Coldean Stakes, Brighton	G. *Lewis*	635
Arlington Stakes, Newbury	G. *Lewis*	950
Doncaster Cup, Doncaster	G. *Lewis*	3996
Quy Maiden Fillies Plate, Newmarket	G. *Lewis*	690
Edenbridge Plate, Lingfield Park	G. *Lewis*	552
Cornwallis Stakes, Ascot	G. *Lewis*	2550

Races Won 34   Winning Stakes £132,994

COURSE	JOCKEY	PRIZE
Masaka Stakes, Kempton Park	G. *Lewis*	1690
Ladbroke Wood Ditton Stakes, Newmarket	G. *Lewis*	1738
Earl of Sefton Stakes, Newmarket	G. *Lewis*	3980
County Stakes, Ayr	A. *Barclay*	600
Dante Stakes, York	G. *Lewis*	2965
Hermitage Stakes, Newbury	G. *Lewis*	981
Wire Mill Handicap Plate, Lingfield Park	G. *Lewis*	759
Chester Stakes, Newcastle	A. *Barclay*	1924
Durham Stakes, Newcastle	A. *Barclay*	1028
Friend-James Memorial Handicap, Brighton	G. *Lewis*	1149
Lancashire Oaks, Haydock Park	G. *Lewis*	5477
Brambletye Stakes, Lingfield Park	G. *Lewis*	491
Bridal Suite Mdn Fillies Plate, Nottingham	A. *Barclay*	345
St Catherine's Stakes, Newbury	G. *Lewis*	1377
Donnington Castle Stakes, Newbury	A. *Barclay*	1280
Brightwalton Stakes (Handicap), Newbury	A. *Barclay*	1010
Findon Stakes, Goodwood	G. *Lewis*	985
Selsey Stakes, Goodwood	G. *Lewis*	1105
Nassau Stakes, Goodwood	G. *Lewis*	5594
Dalham Hall Stud Stakes, Newmarket	A. *Barclay*	843
Seaton Delayal Stakes, Newcastle	G. *Lewis*	5646
Rose of York Stakes (Handicap), York	G. *Lewis*	2584

OWNER	HORSE

Aug 24	Sir Reginald Macdonald-Buchanan's	ESTAMINET
Aug 26	Mrs Noel Murless'	OSWALDKIRK
Sep 11	Mrs Noel Murless'	CAER-GAI
Sep 12	Mr Louis Freedman's	MIL'S BOMB
Sep 13	Mr H. J. Joel's	MELODY HOUR
Sep 23	Mrs Dare Wigan's	TURNKEY
Oct 31	Col F. R. Hue-Williams's	GOLDEN SWAN
Nov 1	Mr H. J. Joel's	SHALLOW STREAM
Nov 2	Lt Col J. Hornung's	CHOLITA

1975

May 7	Mr H. J. Joel's	DAZZLING LIGHT
May 14	Mr H. J. Joel's	MOONLIGHT NIGHT (FR)
May 30	Mr H. J. Joel's	TIGER TRAIL
Jun 5	Mr Garfield Weston's	BARRETTSTOWN (USA)
Jun 6	Mr H. J. Joel's	DAZZLING LIGHT
Jun 11	Mr T. J. Smith's	BOLD AUSSIE (USA)
Jun 23	Mrs Dare Wigan's	GLIDING
Jul 10	Lt Col J. Hornung's	SAUCEBOAT
Jul 16	Mr H. J. Joel's	TIGER TRAIL
Jul 31	Mr H. J. Joel's	DAZZLING LIGHT
Aug 7	Mr George A. Pope Jr's	SUNNIEST DAY
Aug 7	Mrs Dare Wigan's	GLIDING
Aug 8	Mr Louis Freedman's	BALLY'S GIFT
Aug 15	Sir Reginald Macdonald-Buchanan's	STIRLING CASTLE
Aug 21	Sir Reginald Macdonald-Buchanan's	SPANISH AIR
Aug 25	Mr H. J. Joel's	DAZZLING LIGHT
Aug 26	Mrs Noel Murless'	OSWALDKIRK
Aug 29	Mrs Noel Murless'	MAY BECK
Sep 6	Sir Reginald Macdonald-Buchanan's	STIRLING CASTLE
Sep 11	Sir Reginald Macdonald-Buchanan's	CONNAUGHT SQUARE
Sep 12	Mr Louis Freedman's	GREY HOME
Sep 17	Mr Louis Freedman's	MIL'S BOMB
Sep 23	Lt Col J. Hornung's	BINES BRIDGE
Oct 9	Mr George A. Pope Jr's	JUMPING HILL (USA)
Oct 10	Lt Col J Hornung's	SAUCEBOAT
Oct 11	Mr Louis Freedman's	ILLUMINATION
Oct 25	Mr Louis Freedman's	ILLUMINATION

COURSE	JOCKEY	PRIZE
Northern Goldsmiths' H'p Stakes, Newcastle	G. Lewis	3909
Topcliffe Stakes, Ripon	A. Barclay	1106
Danum Stakes, Doncaster	A. Barclay	1375
Park Hill Stakes, Doncaster	G. Lewis	6351
Princess Mary Nursery H'p Stks, Doncaster	G. Lewis	1333
Barleythorpe Stud Stakes, Leicester	G. Lewis	2443
Isleham Maiden Plate, Newmarket	G. Lewis	690
Zetland Plate, Newmarket	G. Lewis	690
Duchess Maiden Stakes, Newmarket	G. Lewis	584

Races Won 31 Winning Stakes £62,043

COURSE	JOCKEY	PRIZE
Sefton Stakes, Chester	G. Lewis	1151
Musidora Stakes, York	G. Lewis	3045
Halliford Maiden Plate, Kempton Park	G. Lewis	414
Banner Panda Handicap Stakes, Epsom	G. Lewis	1628
Ebbisham Handicap Stakes, Epsom	G. Lewis	3742
Hermitage Stakes, Newbury	A. Murray	944
Sheepcote Handicap, Brighton	G. Lewis	850
Child Stakes, Newmarket	G. Lewis	4318
Charles Greenwood Plate (H'p), Kempton Pk.	G. Lewis	690
Tapestry Handicap, Goodwood	G. Lewis	1383
Cliftonville Stakes, Brighton	G. Lewis	712
Edburton Handicap, Brighton	G. Lewis	658
Mapleton Plate, Lingfield Park	G. Lewis	552
Stratton Stakes (Handicap), Newbury	G. Lewis	1101
City of York Nursery Stakes (H'cap), York	G. Lewis	1848
Bridget Handicap Stakes, Epsom	G. Lewis	1200
Harvest Cross Handicap Stakes, Ripon	A. Barclay	665
Combermere Stakes, Chester	A. Barclay	554
Geoffrey Hamlyn H'cap Stks, Sandown Park	G. Lewis	2393
Milton Stakes, Doncaster	G. Lewis	1746
Waterbeach Stakes, Goodwood	G. Lewis	709
Doonside Cup, Ayr	G. Lewis	2530
Malthouse Plate, Lingfield Park	G. Lewis	414
Little-Go Stakes (Handicap), York	A. Barclay	1618
Marlborough House Stakes, Ascot	A. Barclay	1396
Stamford Bridge Stakes (Maidens), York	A. Barclay	1270
Venus Stakes, Doncaster	E. Hide	665

Races Won 27 Winning Stakes £38,202

OWNER	HORSE

1976

	OWNER	HORSE
Apr 8	Mr H. J. Joel's	TIGER TRAIL
May 12	Mr George A. Pope Jr's	JUMPING HILL (USA)
Jun 16	Mr George A. Pope Jr's	JUMPING HILL (USA)
Jun 25	Mr Louis Freedman's	PADDINGTON
Jul 1	Mr H. J. Joel's	DANISH KING
Jul 2	Mr H. J. Joel's	MISS PINKIE
Jul 6	Mr Noel Murless'	MAY BECK
Jul 8	Mr George A. Pope Jr's	J. O. TOBIN (USA)
Jul 8	Mr Louis Freedman's	PADDINGTON
Jul 10	Mr H. J. Joel's	MISS PINKIE
Jul 14	Mr H. J. Joel's	TIGER TRAIL
Jul 21	Mr H. J. Joel's	MOSSBERRY
Jul 28	Mr George A. Pope Jr's	J. O. TOBIN (USA)
Jul 30	Mr H. J. Joel's	TIGER TRAIL
Jul 31	Mr Louis Freedman's	PADDINGTON
Aug 3	Mrs Noel Murless'	CAKE POPPER
Aug 7	Mr H. J. Joel's	TIGER TRAIL
Aug 10	Mr M. W. Wickham-Boynton's	OMNIA
Aug 18	Mr H. J. Joel's	EMPRESS OF RUSSIA
Aug 31	Mr H. J. Noel's	TIGER TRAIL
Sep 1	Mr H. J. Noel's	ROYAL PLUME
Sep 1	Lt Col Sir John Hornung's	SAUCEBOAT
Sep 8	Mr George A. Pope Jr's	J. O. TOBIN (USA)
Sep 10	Mr H. J. Joel's	ROYAL PLUME
Sep 13	Mrs Noel Murless'	CAKE POPPER
Sep 14	Mrs Noel Murless'	BLAKEY RIDGE
Sep 24	Mr H. J. Joel's	ROYAL PLUME
Sep 24	Mr H. J. Joel's	MISS PINKIE
Sep 27	Mr Louis Freedman's	ABODE
Oct 19	Mr H. J. Joel's	ELIZABETHAN
Oct 30	Mrs Noel Murless'	FERRYBRIDGE
Nov 2	Lt Col Sir John Hornung's	TINSLEY GREEN

COURSE	JOCKEY	PRIZE
Freddy Fox Handicap Stakes, Haydock Park	A. Barclay	816
Hambleton Handicap Stakes, York	L. Piggott	1991
Royal Hunt Cup (Handicap), Royal Ascot	L. Piggott	9623
Picnic Stakes, Lingfield Park	L. Piggott	798
Arundel Stakes, Brighton	B. Taylor	1213
Catnic Components Plate, Sandown Park	L. Piggott	1035
Hamilton Handicap Stakes, Newmarket	L. Piggott	1813
Fulbourn Maiden Stakes, Newmarket	L. Piggott	1973
Limekilns Stakes, Newmarket	L. Piggott	1590
Courage Stakes, York	L. Piggott	3251
Princess Stakes (Handicap), Kempton Park	G. Lewis	1506
Petticoat Lane H'p Stakes, Sandown Park	L. Piggott	1293
Richmond Stakes, Goodwood	L. Piggott	14,124
Pampisford Handicap Stakes, Newmarket	L. Piggott	1165
Rous Memorial Stakes, Goodwood	L. Piggott	3460
Alfriston Stakes, Brighton	L. Piggott	958
New England Handicap Stakes, Newmarket	F. Durr	1705
Tyne Maiden Stakes, Newcastle	P. Tulk	886
Rottingdean Stakes, Brighton	A. Bond	638
Playboy Handicap Stakes, Kempton Park	L. Piggott	1682
Sancton Stakes, York	L. Piggott	2400
Strensall Stakes, York	L. Piggott	2397
Laurent Perrier Champagne Stks, Doncaster	L. Piggott	10,194
Vernons Org. Two Yr. Old Plate, Doncaster	L. Piggott	1725
East Dean Nursery H'p Stks, Goodwood	L. Piggott	1444
Norfolk and Suffolk Stakes, Gt. Yarmouth	G. Lewis	627
S. G. B. Stakes, Ascot	L. Piggott	2863
Argos Star Fillies' Mile, Ascot	L. Piggott	5608
Staunton Maiden Stakes, Nottingham	W. Carson	636
Mitre Stakes, Sandown Park	L. Piggott	841
Salford Maiden Stakes, Haydock Park	B. Taylor	1144
Ticehurst Stakes, Lingfield Park	L. Piggott	657

Races Won 32   Winning Stakes £81,706

233

R

Summary

	Total for each year		*Grand Total*	
YEAR	RACES WON	VALUE	RACES WON	VALUE
		£		£
1935	1	103	1	103
1936	1	196	2	299
1937	4	568	6	867
1938	7	1,310	13	2,177
1939	10	2,417	23	4,594
1940	1	206	24	4,800
1941	–	–	24	4,800
1942	–	–	24	4,800
1943	2	511	26	5,311
1944	5	1,642	31	6,953
1945	9	3,429	40	10,382
1946	34	15,326	74	25,708
1947	32	22,636	106	48,344
1948	63	67,046	169	115,390
1949	66	62,523	235	177,913
1950	47	26,732	282	204,645
1951	45	22,799	327	227,444
1952	47	21,735	374	249,179
1953	44	28,182	418	277,361
1954	44	41,240	462	318,601
1955	36	23,065	498	341,666
1956	47	37,872	545	379,538
1957	48	116,908	593	496,446
1958	25	24,331	618	520,777
1959	63	145,725	681	666,502
1960	42	118,297	723	784,799
1961	36	95,972	759	880,771
1962	35	35,063	794	915,834
1963	42	55,468	836	971,302

	Total for each year		*Grand Total*	
YEAR	RACES WON	VALUE	RACES WON	VALUE
		£		£
1964	51	81,589	887	1,052,891
1965	36	85,464	923	1,138,355
1966	49	92,282	972	1,230,637
1967	63	279,775	1035	1,510,412
1968	51	238,331	1086	1,748,743
1969	48	88,876	1134	1,837,619
1970	57	220,475	1191	2,058,094
1971	65	180,496	1256	2,238,590
1972	51	93,231	1307	2,331,821
1973	34	132,994	1341	2,464,815
1974	31	62,043	1372	2,526,858
1975	27	38,202	1399	2,565,060
1976	32	81,706	1431	2,646,766

Index

Index